Chicken Soup for the Soul.

The Advice that Changed My Life

Chicken Soup for the Soul: The Advice that Changed My Life
101 Stories of Epiphanies and Wise Words
Amy Newmark

Published by Chicken Soup for the Soul, LLC www.chickensoup.com
Copyright ©2023 by Chicken Soup for the Soul, LLC. All Rights Reserved.

Front cover photo courtesy of iStockphoto.com (©tatyana_tomsickova)
Back cover and interior photo courtesy of iStockphoto.com (©RichVintage)
Photo of Amy Newmark courtesy of Susan Morrow at SwickPix

Cover and Interior by Daniel Zaccari

Publisher's Cataloging-in-Publication data

Title: Chicken soup for the soul : the advice that changed my life / Amy Newmark.
Description: Cos Cob, CT: Chicken Soup for the Soul, LLC, 2023.
Identifiers: LCCN: 2022951644 | ISBN: 978-1-61159-100-2 (paperback) |
    978-1-61159-337-2 (ebook)
Subjects: LCSH Self-actualization (Psychology) | Self-realization--Anecdotes. | Inspiration.
    | Conduct of life--Anecdotes. | Encouragement--Literary collections. | Self help. |
    BISAC SELF-HELP / Personal Growth / General
Classification: LCC BF637.S4 .C45 2023| DDC 158.1--dc23

Library of Congress Control Number: 2022951644

PRINTED IN THE UNITED STATES OF AMERICA
on acid∞free paper

30 29 28 27 26 25 24 23   01 02 03 04 05 06 07 08 09

The Advice
that Changed
My Life

101 Stories of Epiphanies
and Wise Words

Amy Newmark

Chicken Soup for the Soul, LLC
Cos Cob, CT

Changing your world one story at a time®
www.chickensoup.com

Table of Contents

❶

~Be Confident~

1. The High School Guidance Counselor, *Don Locke*...............1
2. A Teachable Moment, *Lila W. Guzman*...........................4
3. Sometimes, It's Just a Can of Beans, *Jeanette Hurt*................6
4. Words to Live Large By, *Janice Preston Horton*...................8
5. Just Ask, *Nancy Emmick Panko*...............................11
6. Keep It Simple, *Rosanne Trost*...............................14
7. Allow Yourself an Enemy or Two, *Maureen R. O'Donnell*......17
8. A Forever After Moment, *Robyn Gerland*....................20
9. Pretty Dark, *Zirrina Maxwell*................................22

❷

~Be Grateful~

10. Curbside Promises, *Jamie A. Richardson*.......................27
11. The Advice I Didn't Want to Hear, *Wendy Portfors*.............30
12. Three Good Things, *MaryBeth Wallace*.......................32
13. The Power of a Thank-You Note, *Connie K. Pombo*...........35
14. Coming Out of the Chains, *Ander Fernán*...................38
15. Love's Lens, *Gwen Cooper*...................................41
16. Just Like Us, *D.J. Sartell*...................................44
17. Living Life at 90-9, *Brenda Leppington*......................47

❸
~Face Your Fears~

18. Walk This Way, *Jennifer Kennedy* 51
19. The Next Right Thing, *Kelly A. Smith* 55
20. Two Roads Diverged, *Darlene Carpenter Herring* 57
21. You Can't Strike Out, *Darrell Horwitz* 59
22. Sometimes Laughter Isn't the Best Medicine,
    Ashleigh Russell 62
23. The Reluctant Traveler, *Glenda Ferguson* 65
24. I Could Never Do That, *Ava Pennington* 68
25. Do Something About It Every Day, *Jan Comfort* 71
26. The Long Way Around, *Jill Burns* 73

❹
~Get On with Life~

27. Choosing Joy over Grief, *Marvin Yanke* 77
28. The Power of Yes, *Kay L. Campbell* 80
29. Why Didn't I Realize That Sooner?
    Stephanie Schiano Wallace 84
30. See How Much Is Left, *Melissa Edmondson* 86
31. Falling Down, *Laura McKenzie* 90
32. Heeding Her Words, *Connie Kaseweter Pullen* 93
33. Do Something Small, *Emily Rusch* 95

❺
~Choose Your Battles~

34. Loving or Right? *Sarah Barnum* 99
35. But It's Only... *Elizabeth A. Atwater* 102
36. Be What's Missing, *Kitty Chappell* 105
37. Pick Your Battles, *Barbara LoMonaco* 108
38. Right or Nice, *Susan Traugh* 111

39. Control Your Second Thought, *Elton A. Dean* 114
40. Now I Get It, *Carolyn Barrett* 116

6

~Live Life to the Fullest~

41. One Radio Broadcast Changed My Life, *Jim Cathcart*......... 120
42. A Stranger in a Bookstore, *Cherry March*............................ 124
43. The Price of Every Decision, *James C. Magruder*................. 127
44. Let Yourself Fly, *Kiesa Kay* 130
45. Bookends of Wisdom, *Cate Bronson* 134
46. The Flying Train, *David Hull*... 138
47. Permission to Say No, *Adrienne Matthews* 140
48. Banned? Me? I Don't Think So, *Jody Lebel*........................ 143
49. The "Why Do It?" Guy, *Jon Peirce*..................................... 147
50. Courtside Decision, *Marie T. Palecek*................................. 150
51. Green Truck Moments, *Phyllis McKinley* 154

7

~Make the Effort~

52. Do Your Best, *David M. Williamson*.................................... 157
53. Three Little Words for Success… Every Day,
    Eve S. Rossmiller.. 161
54. Flying Solo, *Daryle Elizabeth Hunt* 163
55. Use Your Time Wisely, *Patricia Ruhaak*.............................. 166
56. Give It Two Weeks, *Courtney McKinney-Whitaker*.............. 168
57. A Misattributed Quote, *Billie Holladay Skelley* 171
58. The Method to a Method-Acting Director's Madness,
    Jon Peirce 174
59. Be All There, *RoChelle Crow* 178
60. A New Day, *Ree Pashley*.. 180
61. My Dad, My Heart, Our Sport, *Keith Manos* 183
62. Eat the Crust First, *Claudia Irene Scott* 186

8

~Pursue Your Passion~

63. The Contest that Changed My Life, *Gary Stein*...................189
64. I'm Going with You, *Stephen Rusiniak*.....................................194
65. Keep Showing Up, *Sophie Bolich*...198
66. A Lesson in Staying Where You Are, *Samantha Hawkins*.....201
67. The Words I Needed to Hear, *Tamara Bell*...........................205
68. A Woman Walks into a Pub, *Barbara Espinosa Occhino*.......208
69. You Are a Writer, *Monty Joynes*..212
70. Think of Everything as an Adventure, *Kathleen Gerard*......216
71. Breathing Belief into Those Who Doubt,
    Carole Brody Fleet...219

9

~Put Things in Perspective~

72. Reality, *Wendy Hobday Haugh*...223
73. A Hundred Years from Now, *Linda Sabourin*.........................225
74. Time Travel, *Chelsea Ohlemiller*...228
75. The Best of Me, *Devora Adams*...230
76. The Time Will Pass Anyway, *Charlie Morrow*.......................234
77. Roadblocks, *Thomas Brooks*..236
78. A Glimmer of Hope, *Judith Shapiro*.......................................239
79. Look at the Fish, *Laura Jane Bender*......................................242
80. Save Yourself, *Jesica Ryzynski*...246
81. The Blessing of Work, *Jennifer Priest Mitchell*....................249

10

~Reach Out and Connect~

82. The Longest Hug, *Debbie Jones Warren*................................253
83. Go with the Flow, *Jill Guerin*...256
84. Go Help Someone Else, *Sheryl Green*....................................259

85. To Hug or Not to Hug, *Chana Rubinstein*............................ 262
86. Elizabeth Versus Elizabeth,
      Elizabeth Rose Reardon Farella 264
87. One Final Lesson, *Laura Niebauer Palmer*........................... 267
88. A New World, *Donna Anderson* 271
89. Assertive vs. Aggressive, *Mary J. Staller*............................ 274
90. Always Be Nice to the Receptionist, *Lori Kempf Bosko*........ 278

⑪

~Take Care of Yourself~

91. Yes or No, *Monica A. Andermann*..................................... 282
92. Never Look Back, *Elizabeth A. Dreier*............................... 285
93. Attraversiamo, *Melissa Edmondson* 288
94. Through His Eyes, *B.J. Taylor*... 292
95. Winds of Change, *Mary T. Post* 295
96. Wise Granny, *Amy Mewborn*.. 299
97. I Whispered, "Yes..." *Lainie Belcastro* 301
98. Not Chopped Liver, *Risa Nye*... 304
99. Fast Wisdom, *Charlotte Louise Nystrom*........................... 307
100. Simplify! *D.E. Brigham* 311
101. It's Okay to Say No, *Jacquie McTaggart*............................ 314

Meet Our Contributors.. 317
Meet Amy Newmark... 331
Thank You 333
About Chicken Soup for the Soul.. 334

Be Confident

The High School Guidance Counselor

*No one can make you feel inferior
without your consent.*
~Eleanor Roosevelt

I was anxiously sitting in the hallway on one of those colorful fiberglass chairs they used to have in high schools back in the 1960s. My discomfort had less to do with the hard chair and more to do with the fact that I was waiting for a guidance counselor to discuss the electives I might choose in my approaching sophomore year.

I had been painfully shy all my life, and being introduced to adults was tough for me. I'm pretty sure my timidity had something to do with being born an introvert, but it was also the product of a good bit of criticism aimed in my direction. So, who was the perpetrator? It was the last person in the world you might suspect and the last person I'd want to blame because I loved her dearly: my mom.

I know that sounds horrible and more than a little unappreciative. And, honestly, I hate to fault her because she was in all other respects a wonderful mother. But for some reason, at least in my mind, she had this one little flaw: She was critical of my appearance.

There were three specific criticisms of my physical appearance that I was oblivious to until my mom pointed them out to me. The first was when I was five years old and wearing shorts in the summertime. My mom made the observation that my knees were too bony. *Too bony for what?* I wondered. *Too bony to live? Probably not. Too bony to be healthy? Maybe.* But then, of course, my mind went to the obvious inference: too bony to be shown in public.

Now, I hadn't heard this criticism from anyone else, so I thought maybe it was just an isolated, subjective opinion until… I was standing in line in my gym shorts, waiting to do some cartwheels in my first-grade gym class, when the little girl in front of me, whom I had never spoken to in my short life, turned around, looked down at my kneecaps and, with a sour expression, said, "Boy, you've got knobby knees." And so, there it was… My first physical oddity was confirmed: My legs were too skinny. As a response, I didn't wear shorts even on the hottest summer days — basically, for the next forty years — until I realized my legs had finally become relatively normal in size.

The second criticism came when I was about to enter junior high. I was at home doing something with my shirt off and my mom said, "Your ribs show too much." I spent the next few days alone and shirtless in front of the bathroom mirror analyzing my physique. I came to the realization that my ribs did stick out more than the average kid my age. And so, when tryouts for the junior-high basketball team arrived, I didn't show up. I loved basketball dearly and was pretty decent at it despite my short stature. But I knew that the uniforms had cut-off sleeves, which meant my ribs would show when I played, and so I was forced to make up all kinds of lame excuses to my friends as to why I didn't try out for the team. And so, for my two years of junior high, I sat up in the stands watching the games, wishing I were down on the court playing.

Number three. I was in junior high school when my mom informed both my older sister and me that if we wanted to get nose reductions, she would gladly pay for them. Up to that point in my life, I didn't even know I had a nose in need of reduction. But from then on, I took my mom's advice when she suggested that whenever I had my photo taken, I should tilt my head back a bit to avoid my nose looking quite so gigantic. My sister and I both turned down the nose-job offer, but the criticism just added to the ever-growing list of reasons to feel insecure about my appearance.

Obviously, I can't put this all on dear old mom. The truth is, if I hadn't been such a ridiculously sensitive kid, I wouldn't have taken all these criticisms to heart.

Suddenly, the office door swung open. A tall lady with frizzy, strawberry-colored hair held the door for a student as he walked out. She looked at me, and said in a welcoming tone, "Come on in."

I stood up and walked through the door into the classroom. "Here, have a seat," she said, directing me to a chair across from her desk. I was looking down at my shoes when, referring to some paperwork, she said, "So, you are Donald Locke, correct?"

"Yes," I said, my eyes aimlessly gazing around the room. Then this lady hesitated for a moment and said these simple words that I still remember more than fifty years later.

"Look at me, Donald." She spoke those words like she knew me. I looked up into her eyes. "You are a good-looking boy. There's no reason why you shouldn't look everyone you meet straight in the eye."

What? Me — a good-looking boy? Really? Since when? Could it be she was nearsighted? Or was there a possibility that I wasn't that ugly, skinny, big-nosed kid whom I saw every time I looked in the mirror? Someone thought I was actually good-looking. This lady was there to help me decide what my scholastic interests were and what classes I should take. But what she said to me concerning my looks was a hundred times more important than suggesting any electives. In fact, I remember nothing else from that meeting with the woman except those words of encouragement and good advice.

I've always found it interesting that, somewhere, a tall woman with frizzy strawberry hair spent her entire life unaware of how a few positive comments she made to an awkward fifteen-year-old kid with very low self-esteem changed how he saw himself for the rest of his life.

Ever since that day, I've made a point of making good eye contact with people — because it's what we all deserve.

— Don Locke —

A Teachable Moment

*You come to realize that life's irritations are just things
that happen. They only become irritations
if you supply the irritability.*
~Robert Brault, rbrault.blogspot.com

I n my sophomore year in college, I took Psychology 202, Human Growth and Development. It was a required course for a teaching certificate, and I was learning a lot.

One day, Dr. Simpson was lecturing, and we were dutifully taking notes. He stopped and fixed a cold stare on a scruffy-looking student in the second row.

The student stared back, crossed his arms over his chest, and lifted his chin defiantly.

"What is your problem, young man?" the professor demanded.

"You," the student replied.

"Me?"

"Yeah, you and the (expletive deleted) you're teaching."

I sat in terror. I had never seen a student be so rude to a professor. Sure, we had minor dust-ups in high school, but this was college. There were never any discipline problems.

"Get out of my class!" Dr. Simpson thundered.

The student snatched up his books and headed toward the classroom door. He glanced back once to hurl one final insult.

"If you want back in the class," Dr. Simpson said, "you'll have to get permission from the dean."

With that, the door slammed shut, and Dr. Simpson continued his lecture.

I didn't hear a word he said. My complete attention was on the student who had stormed out of the room. Was this an automatic failure? Could he apologize and get back in class? What had Dr. Simpson said that set him off like fireworks on the Fourth of July?

Five minutes or so went by. Dr. Simpson stopped his lecture. He scanned the class and seemed to be his regular, jolly self.

"What have I been lecturing about for the last five minutes?"

I didn't know. Nobody knew. The class was silent.

Then, Dr. Simpson said, "John, go tell Fred that he can come back in."

As Fred was making his way back to his seat, Dr. Simpson thanked him and complimented him on an excellent acting job. As it turned out, they had cooked it up ahead of time.

We sat in stunned silence.

And then, Dr. Simpson said something I will never forget.

"You weren't listening to my lecture. None of you were. You were all thinking about Fred and our little dust-up. Remember that when you start teaching. Any time there is a disruption in class, you have lost your students' attention."

It was one of the most useful lessons I ever learned in college.

Over the years, my class was interrupted by fire alarms, students getting into a scuffle, and other distractions.

Every time I lost the class's attention, I flashed back to the lesson Dr. Simpson taught me that day. I gave my students five minutes to discuss what had happened and then said a cheerful "Let's get back to today's lesson plan!"

— Lila W. Guzman —

Sometimes, It's Just a Can of Beans

*On an important decision one rarely has 100% of the
information needed for a good decision no matter
how much one spends or how long one waits.*
~Robert K. Greenleaf, The Servant as Leader

My son had just turned five, and my husband and I were fretting about which school to send him to. We started investigating and visiting schools, and then we started writing lists of pros and cons of each school we visited.

Still, we felt uncertain about which school to choose. In the midst of this indecision, I called my friend Shannon. I'm blessed to have a circle of wise female friends whom I can lean on when I need to, and Shannon is one of them. In fact, she's the one I lean on most when I'm struggling with parenting decisions. She has a son who's ten years older than mine, so she's gone through all the stages I'm still going through.

"Shannon, I'm so worried about picking the wrong school," I told her.

"Jeanette, before I give you any advice on the individual schools, let me tell you this: Quinn is loved by both of his parents, and both you and Kyle are good parents. Loving your kid and being involved in his life is more important than picking the 'perfect' school."

She let that sink in before she continued. "Now, I know you have narrowed it down to two choices, right?"

I nodded. "Well, they're both good schools, right?" she said.

I nodded again. "This doesn't have to do with schools, but let me tell you a story about choices," Shannon said. "I remember one night when I was doing some late-night grocery shopping because that's the only time I could get to it between work and parenting. I was overtired and worried about my budget, and I stood in the aisle of beans. One can was twenty cents less than the other, but it wasn't quite as good as the other. I stood there undecided for at least twenty minutes."

Shannon let that sink in before she continued. "It finally occurred to me: It's just a can of beans. In the long run, whether I picked brand A or brand B can of beans, it didn't matter. Sometimes, it's just a can of beans."

Shannon made me laugh so hard that I almost cried. "Now, choosing a school for your son isn't the same as picking out a can of beans for dinner, but because you are good parents, whatever school you pick is the right school. And, besides, you can always pick another one if it doesn't fit."

I felt a lot better after I hung up the phone with Shannon. My husband and I were able to pick a good school for our son. Now, whenever I'm in the midst of dithering over something — whether it's an activity for my son, a job decision or even picking out a mascara at the beauty store — I ask myself this question: "Is it just a can of beans?"

And, usually, it is.

Sometimes, it's just a can of beans, and you have to just move forward and make your decision. And if it turns out to be the wrong can of beans, you can always go back to get a different one.

— Jeanette Hurt —

Words to Live Large By

Behind every young child who believes in himself
is a parent who believed first.
~Matthew Jacobson

The tall woman stooped down in front of the bench where we were sitting and asked, using sign language, "What's your name?" My four-year-old son Aaron answered by touching his thumb to his temple, the A hand shape.

He'd been only a few months old when I noticed that he didn't turn his head toward sounds. However, none of the tests using blood, X-rays or electrodes stuck to his head showed anything but perfectly formed cochlea and every other sign of good health. No otolaryngologist or pediatric geneticist could come up with an explanation for why my child couldn't hear.

Audiology. Speech therapy. Total Communication. Language, language, language. I didn't want Aaron to miss out on anything. We visited churches and only got blank stares when I asked if anyone there could sign. But I kept searching until we found a place where Aaron could learn the stories and songs through an interpreter. What a relief to meet Gail. She would know that if Aaron tucked his thumb between his pointer and middle finger and twisted his wrist, he needed to go to the restroom.

Gail, I learned after introductions, had two sons, nearly grown, both of whom were deaf. So she knew what it was like to try to get the attention of a child who was playing in the farthest corner of the back yard. Her kids didn't look up when a fire truck screamed up the street, and they couldn't talk to Grandma on the phone.

I waited for Gail to pat my arm and say, "Yeah, I know how it is." Maybe she'd even have some tips for me. But Gail wasn't there to commiserate. She didn't even offer a list of dos and don'ts. Her counsel was given in less than a dozen words. "He's a regular kid," she said. "That's how you need to treat him."

No one had ever said that before: "He's a regular kid." Not the audiologist, speech therapist, school or my mother.

It took some time for Gail's words to sink in, but she was right. My son was a sturdy, curious, smart and funny four-year-old boy — who happened to be deaf. Of course, his education, future, health, and relationships mattered. But his needs were pretty much the same as those of any other child.

Gail's advice was liberating. Watching Aaron choose his own friends and develop his own interests was a joy, even if he did bring home snakes and snails and wanted to keep them in his room.

I'd like to report that, from that day forward, I was the coolest mom, offering support and encouragement without being overprotective. I'd have to lie. Mainstreamed in the fifth grade, Aaron made a new friend. Danny learned to fingerspell immediately. The boys had conversations right under my nose, fingers flying so fast that I couldn't hope to follow. They were talking about Little League baseball, which Danny wanted Aaron to sign up for. Seriously? Sure, Aaron had asked for a bat for Christmas. We played catch in the yard. But team sports? How would he know if the ump called a ball or strike? I'd heard about a mom who attended her son's football practice so she could interpret. It hadn't gone well.

Then there was the time when Aaron was in seventh grade. After dinner, he came downstairs wearing dress shoes and a button-down shirt. I asked Aaron if he was going somewhere. "Yeah," he said, "to the school dance."

Dance? As in, to music that he couldn't hear? Aaron ignored the doubt on my face and walked out the door. He had a great time at the dance — just like he loved playing baseball all the way through high school. If he stood out at all, it was when his throw from deep right field put the runner out at home in a playoff game. I'd almost not given him the chance to find out how much he loved the game.

By the time he was in high school, I didn't even question whether Aaron would take Spanish. Or chemistry or trig. Aaron got his driver's license. He hunted and fished. He mowed lawns for spending money and to pay for his speeding ticket. No one expected him to get a pass on the hard stuff.

I didn't find out until it was over about the assignment in Aaron's health class. Students were given electronic dolls to care for. They were programmed to cry at all hours of the night for food or a dry diaper. The exercise was supposed to make teenagers think twice about becoming parents. Aaron didn't get a doll. The teacher decided a bawling baby wasn't something a deaf guy could do anything about, so he excused Aaron from the assignment.

When I picked up the phone, intending to have words with the teacher, Aaron asked me to let it go. Most of the kids had figured out how to quiet the doll without losing sleep anyway. The silly assignment wasn't worth going to the mat over. I have no doubt that when Aaron does have a baby, he'll figure out how to care for it.

Even if I or a teacher dropped the ball from time to time, underestimating Aaron's ability or expecting him to forego choices, Aaron believed the world was as much his oyster as anyone else's. Without Gail's startling words, would Aaron have explored Alaska by himself, earned a Ph.D., or married a brainy and beautiful wife? Maybe. He's brave and resourceful. But, many times, those words kept me from standing in his way.

—Janice Preston Horton—

Just Ask

If you don't ask, the answer is always no.
~Nora Roberts

couldn't believe the offer I was reading. "Yes, I'd love to do your TV show," I typed. Months before this e-mail conversation, I wouldn't have had the confidence to have asked for the opportunity.

My convoluted journey began as I undertook a nearly impossible mission to re-create my father-in-law's military history. All his records were gone. His medals were gone, his citations had disappeared, and, to add insult to injury, the Army records center in St. Louis, Missouri, had suffered a fire, destroying Dad's records. I wanted to fill in the blanks for my husband and his siblings, but Dad was no longer with us to give me information.

When Dad died, we stayed at the family home during the services. My husband George searched the cedar chest in his parents' bedroom for evidence of his dad's military service. He returned to the kitchen with a small, tattered book so worn that one could barely read the title. Putting it in a plastic sandwich bag, he tucked it in his suit-coat pocket before we left for the funeral.

George was unusually quiet, so I asked him, "What is that?"

"A prayer book that Dad carried through his time in the Army during the Battle of the Bulge and the Rhine crossing, the turning point of World War II," he answered.

"Oh wow! It is special," I responded.

"More than you know. Dad gave it to me before I left for basic training in 1961. I carried it during my tour of duty." His eyes glistened with unshed tears.

The light dawned. "I know what you're going to do with that," I said.

George nodded. "I have to, you know."

I nodded, thinking of our only daughter getting married the same day as her grandfather's funeral.

Later, in a small evening ceremony at Fort Drum, New York, George and I watched as our daughter Margie and her fiancé exchanged vows two days before he was to deploy for Mogadishu, Somalia, with the 10th Mountain Division. The newest member of the family would be the third in line to receive the fragile prayer book.

Meanwhile, after a full year of research, with the help of surviving veterans who served with Dad, I was able to gather all his missing Army records. With the help of our Congressman, I was able to get Dad's medals restored. Two three-ring notebooks held the documents detailing the day when Dad left for basic training until he was honorably discharged. We discovered a hero we didn't know who seldom spoke about the war. The family definitely had a keepsake. I thought my mission was completed.

When our son-in-law returned home, having survived what became known as Black Hawk Down, he returned the prayer book to us in an emotional account of how it had saved his life.

The re-creation of Dad's military history now had another amazing story within it. Over fifty years, three generations of service members had carried the same prayer book. From the battlefields of World War II in the 1940s to the dusty street fighting in Mogadishu, Somalia in 1993, the prayer book was in their pockets.

I held the newly returned military missal in my hands and said, "If only you could talk." Then, I had an epiphany. Maybe I could be the voice of the pocket missal. What if the missal became an animated narrator of the story?

Eight years later, *Guiding Missal* was published. Who knew that this historical fiction novel would evolve from digging into Dad's military history? Writing a book is hard work, but it's only the first step for an author. Marketing and publicity are equally difficult but necessary.

Developing my concise response to "What is your book about?" was the first step. A well-known marketing expert helped me work up a "pitch sheet." I knew I had a well-edited, unique book, but I wasn't quite sure how to sell it and myself. Prepared with business cards, pitch sheets, and a biography, I was ready. I was only lacking confidence. Learning to "toot my own horn" to promote *Guiding Missal* was a challenge. I shared with my writing group that I was reluctant to approach newspapers, magazines, TV, and radio personalities for fear of being rejected.

My wise friend, Cynthia, advised, "If you don't ask, you don't ever allow anyone to say yes. What's the worst thing they could say? No? Get lost? But what if they say yes?" Others in the writing group agreed.

My son, Tim, equated my dilemma to a sports metaphor. "Mom, you'll miss 100 percent of the shots if you don't take them."

My daughter, Margie, wisely commented, "Mom, the answer is always 'no' if you don't ask."

I took their advice and contacted the host of a local TV show who I'd met in a social setting. He loved my story and said he wanted me on his show. Two months later, *Guiding Missal* and I were on his TV segment, which he called, "The story of a book about a book."

I pitched a radio talk show, and they loved the idea. Since then, there have been newspaper and magazine articles, interviews, and podcasts.

How did it happen? I simply asked.

— Nancy Emmick Panko —

Keep It Simple

The question to ask of any day is, "Did I make
some complicated thing simple — or did I
make some simple thing complicated?
~Robert Brault, rbrault.blogspot.com

"Hi, Dad. It's your favorite daughter." Dad squeezed my hand and opened his eyes.

"What are you doing here? Uh-oh, I must be dying. The jail nurse is here." Dad was referring to his surgery many years ago when I stayed with him in the hospital. I had "strongly encouraged" him to cough and deep breathe. As he reluctantly took a deep breath, he had mumbled, "You should work in a jail." It had been an ongoing joke between us.

Now, I choked back tears. *Oh, God, Dad. You are dying. You still have your sense of humor. I am not ready for this.*

My mother was standing next to the hospital bed. She gave me a stiff hug and said, "You're here." She seemed relieved. "Dad looks pretty good, doesn't he?" Actually, I was shocked by how much my dad had deteriorated in just two months.

I needed to be here, even though my mother had discouraged me from making the trip. "Dad will think he is dying if you fly home." I fretted for two days and then bought the airline tickets.

Over the next several days, my dad alternated between a deep sleep and periods of alertness.

My mother stayed with him during the day. I took the night shift.

He slept restlessly. I dozed.

On the fourth evening, my mother met me in the hospital hall. "Your dad has been quite talkative today. He will probably sleep well tonight. The doctor told me that he is improving a bit and may go home this weekend."

I pulled the chair up to Dad's bedside. He was wide awake. A nurse walked into the room, and Dad introduced me to her. "My daughter, the jail nurse."

She laughed. "Oh, Mr. Mac, she just wants you to get better."

Dad and I talked a bit, but his voice became so soft that I could barely hear him. As dusk turned into night, I settled down in the uncomfortable recliner with my book. Then I noticed that Dad's eyes were open.

I will never know what possessed me, but I heard myself asking, "Dad, do you have any words of wisdom for me?"

His voice got stronger, "Hell, no. You have all the education. I had to quit high school just before graduation and go to work." We bantered back and forth for a few minutes.

Then, he began to reminisce about high points in his life, the births of his daughters, and "my visit to Mission Control at NASA." I laughed and asked, "Nothing else?" He dozed. I tried to read.

Sometime later, he said my name, asking if I was there. "Yes, Dad. What do you need?"

"Keep it simple."

"Dad, keep what simple?"

"You know, don't complicate stuff. Some things just are. You don't need to change everyone and everything." In my mind, that pertained more to my mother than to my dad.

I thought he was dozing, but then he said, "Be who you are. Not everybody will like you. That is okay. Just be comfortable with yourself."

I thought, *How true, Dad, but so hard.*

"Oh, and love your kids. They are God's gift to you." Immediately, I was taken back to my early childhood. Dad read a story to me every night. How tired he must have been at times. Then there were the endless checker games and coloring-book sessions.

Another few minutes of silence.

"Don't forget to laugh, especially at yourself."

"Dad, you always teased my friends. Remember? They loved it. You taught me to laugh. Anything else?"

"Guess that's it for now. When are you flying home?"

"In the morning, but I'll be back to see you."

My dad smiled.

Later, I realized that smile was a goodbye.

Back home, waiting for my luggage at the airport, I was paged over the loudspeaker.

I knew.

Now I am older than Dad was when he died so long ago.

I have often thought of his words when my life gets complicated. Sometimes, I forget.

When those memories return, I am filled with gratitude for his simple yet profound words: Keep it simple.

—Rosanne Trost—

Allow Yourself an Enemy or Two

*If people throw stones at you, pick them up
and build something.*
~Author Unknown

The *Seventeen* magazine article I read more than four decades ago concerned high-school social life, but I no longer remember the title or the author. I only remember a single line of advice from it that has stayed with me ever since: "You have to allow yourself an enemy or two."

Back then, I spent an inordinate amount of time trying to make peace with kids at my school who either hated me or, worse, held me in contempt. Attempts to engage or reconcile went nowhere time and again. I'd have been happy for the bullies to just leave me alone, but unfortunately even that seemed out of reach.

One girl loudly and openly mocked me whenever the teacher stepped out of the classroom or study hall for even a minute. One day, this bully even grabbed my purse and threw it out the second-story window of a classroom!

Fortunately, a girl I knew slightly was walking down below, cutting class as she often did. She picked up my purse and threw it back to me. Of course, I shouted my thanks down to her, and she likely forgot all about it. But I remembered that incident several months later when it was time to elect the prom queen and her four princesses, and I voted for her.

She didn't win, but neither did the bully. Maybe she wasn't as popular as she thought! Some of her minions may have only followed her lead because they were afraid to cross her. They didn't want to risk becoming another target for her ridicule, but since the prom-queen vote was by secret ballot, they could express their actual feelings.

Time passed more slowly than I would have preferred. Some of the mean girls moved away, dropped out of school, or at least simmered down. I also made some good friends from the grades immediately before and after my own — girls whom the bullies probably didn't know. I still see several of those friends when I'm back in town, but for some reason I have never attended any of my own class reunions.

To me, that advice about enemies from *Seventeen* goes beyond the more familiar "You can't please everyone." If the cause of their dislike turns out to be some misunderstanding, then reconciliation can be attempted. Otherwise, keeping my distance if I can do so without conceding, defusing the situation in a calm and firm manner if that is possible, and fighting back if I absolutely have to remain my only options.

I had the opportunity to "pay it forward" with this advice when I received a fund-raising letter from a new charitable organization staffed with idealistic young people who wanted to make a difference. The director mentioned in his letter that these young staffers felt discouraged by the vitriolic hate mail they sometimes received.

I wrote back (with a small donation) that they needed the advice I'd lived by for so long: They must allow themselves an enemy or two! The hateful attitudes coming into their mailboxes and over the wires spoke more about the writers than the recipients. They needed to stand their ground and stay the course, remembering that far more people, myself included, liked them and appreciated what they were doing. I received a personal letter back from one of them, thanking me and saying that I'd really helped her and her coworkers put it all in perspective.

I hope they've kept that advice in mind for whatever they're doing now, since I often need to refresh it in my own mind. I sometimes find myself slipping into appeasement behavior at work, with family and in-laws, and even in some volunteer work that I do.

Unless I want to live close to the ground and stuck in the dirt like a soggy mushroom, someone will be envious or spiteful. Victor Hugo told his friend Abel Villemain that enemies are "the cloud which thunders around everything that shines." He recommended that Villemain "be happy, be cheerful, be disdainful, be strong."

His friend listened but expressed doubt that he could do that. Maybe I can't always, either, but at least I don't abandon the arena. I've come to believe that it's more honorable to fight and lose than to run and hide, so I need to hang in there to show both the world and myself what I've got.

Not everyone out there wants peace, and some people seem to run on anger and hate. But the rest of us can stare them down and push them back if we allow ourselves a few people we cannot get along with, no matter how hard we might try. We may not be able to neutralize their toxicity directly, but we don't have to let their malicious words and behavior block out our light.

—Maureen R. O'Donnell—

A Forever After Moment

To shine your brightest light is to be who you truly are.
~Roy T. Bennett

S ome years ago, my partner Amy was feted by her school board as Administrator of the Year. Our son Rhys, our daughter Ceily, and I would be seated at the head table with her and the Superintendent of Schools, several board members and the mayor.

It was a great honour for Amy and clearly a very prestigious event.

Of course, Ceily had left the choice of outfits until the very last minute. Now, "What shall I wear?" became the quintessential sixteen-year-old's plea. She had lain several outfits across her bed. All were dresses or blouse-and-skirt combinations. All were equally appropriate and would suit her perfectly. She tried this with that. She sat, she stood, and she walked back and forth across her room.

Her brother would have no such problem — grey slacks, white shirt, dark tie and new black loafers to replace the sneakers that he seemed to wear to every and all occasions in his adolescent life.

And me? I would not be faced with Ceily's problem. Both my social and professional lives were spent in a variety of shirts, jackets and slacks. I did, however, own one dress. It was a lightweight navy blue with three-quarter-length sleeves, a nipped waist and a loose-fitting skirt. *Perfect,* I had thought when I made the purchase, *for any time when I feel that there is a dress-code assumption to be more conventionally dressed.* At that time, skirts and dresses were still the preferred female attire.

On went the stifling pantyhose — carefully as I only had one pair. A slip — my grandmother had called them petticoats. And, finally, the navy-blue dress with the three-quarter-length sleeves, a nipped waist and a loose-fitting skirt. The bedroom mirror told me that I had met the expectation, and the results, though not particularly pleasing, would have to do.

From my room, I stepped into the hall where my perfectly dressed daughter was waiting. There was a pause, a tilt of her head and then, "It's an okay dress, Mom, but why do you always feel that you have to wear it and look sort of uncomfortable, not at all like yourself, whenever you go somewhere special?"

It was said kindly, but, most importantly, it was said honestly.

She was right, and the dress was wrong.

Off came the stifling pantyhose. Off came the petticoat. Off came the navy-blue dress. On went a white, pleated-front dress shirt. On went my navy-blue business suit.

"Yes!" said my daughter with a nod of her head and a smile of approval.

She had given me a very special, ever-after moment when I truly became who I am.

— Robyn Gerland —

Pretty Dark

You yourself, as much as anybody in the entire
universe, deserve your love and affection.
~Sharon Salzberg

When my ma worked late on school nights, Granny would make sure I was ready for the next day. She would help me pick out my outfit, and then wash and braid my hair. The next morning, she'd straighten my hair with a hot comb and style it into loose pigtails to wear for school.

"There, don't you feel fresh?" she'd ask. "And you look so pretty, too!" She'd fluff my hair in the mirror and marvel at her work. I did feel pretty; she always made sure of that.

At around eleven years old, I started liking boys, and there was one, Davonte, on whom I had a huge crush. He was funny and cute, and he had a caramel complexion that passed as light-skinned. I mustered the courage to tell him how I felt and dared to ask him what he thought of me.

Surely, he would think I was cute, too. Right?

"I mean, you're cool, but I don't date girls darker than me. Plus, I only like girls with light eyes," Davonte scoffed, laughing at the thought of us ever being a couple. Never mind that he was only a few shades lighter than me.

I'd never known I was too dark for some people, and the thought had never crossed my mind before then. My family had always told me that I was beautiful. But now, I wasn't so sure.

As I got older and integrated more into the predominantly Black community around me, I heard comments like these more often. It became ingrained in my young mind that I was never going to be the first choice or the girl whom some people deemed pretty.

Neighborhood kids always mispronounced my name. Each time, I politely corrected them, but it didn't take long for me to realize that they were intentionally making fun of my name, my skin, and anything else they could poke fun at.

"Your nose is too big."

"Your legs are too long."

"Your hair is nappy."

"You're so black."

One time, I cried after being left behind for a trip that some friends had planned without me. I felt so isolated by the people who looked like me yet never seemed to accept me.

"What's the matter?" Granny asked.

With her age came wisdom. Therefore, she understood my pain, my frustration. She took my hand and led me to the kitchen where she set me on top of the table.

"Some people," she started, "just ain't never gon' like you."

That truth stung my tender heart. I didn't understand how this could be. I looked at her with tears brimming in my eyes, and she gently wiped them away.

"There won't be no reason why," she continued in her thick Southern accent. "And you coulda been very nice to these people, but they just ain't gon' like you." She gave me an encouraging smile. "But if you keep bein' the sweet and kind person you are, I promise that some folk'll come 'round an' see how special an' beautiful you are."

I know now that this was her gentle way of telling a small Black girl from the west side of Chicago that the society we lived in wouldn't always accept me. They wouldn't like what color my skin or eyes were. They wouldn't like my coiled hair. They wouldn't like what gender I was. They wouldn't like where I was from. All this was bundled up in a few sentences that a delicate little mind could comprehend.

Over the years, I continued being kindhearted like my grandmother had told me. I tried not to let the people who made fun of me get under my skin. I even made it a point to stick up for other kids whom I saw getting bullied, even if that made me a target, too. For a while, no one really acknowledged or loved me the way I once thought they would.

But then I met Matt.

Matthew was two years older than me with hazel-green eyes and chocolate-brown hair. His skin was sun-kissed and lightly freckled. He was beautiful, really, perfect by American standards. I remember when we first started hanging out, and I thought he was just some white boy who would never fully understand me or my deeper issues. He would never have to face the same judgment that I had endured for years by that time. Still, at some point, we became good friends. He accepted me.

We were walking to a nearby restaurant, and I commented on a girl's blue eyes and what, I assumed, would be considered pretty.

"Her eyes are okay," he said.

"But you've got green eyes. I wish my eyes were anything other than just plain, old, dirty-brown," I half-joked.

"Brown eyes are pretty, too," he said with a nonchalant shrug, as if this was the most obvious information in the world.

Before I knew it, I was laughing. Maybe I laughed much harder than I should have, but I couldn't believe that was what he truly thought. He furrowed his eyebrows, gazing at me with curiosity.

"What?" he asked.

"You think brown eyes are pretty?"

"I think they can be cool sometimes, beautiful even." He looked at me with a goofy smile and then began to blush. "I think you're very pretty, too." My heart fluttered and leapt into my throat as he took my hand into his own. I noticed the stark difference in our skin complexions, but he didn't seem to care.

By then, I had started to believe my grandmother had lied to me all those years ago. I had begun to think Granny only told me I was beautiful because she was supposed to. I thought no one would really like me, not like my family did. No one pursued the dark-skinned, dark-eyed, dark-haired girl, but they willingly ogled all my lighter skinned, lighter-eyed girlfriends.

Matt and I grew closer after that. He always made it a point to tell me how beautiful I was and how much he appreciated my kindness. It was the first time I felt loved by someone outside my family. It didn't feel fake or forced. He gave his love to me openly and freely regardless of what society thought. Our relationship lasted for a few years before distance pulled us apart. He needed to go back to his home state where the rest of his family was, and I needed to stay with mine. We don't talk much now, but I'll always remember that my dark skin, dark eyes, and dark hair were pretty enough for someone.

My grandmother wasn't wrong. Over the years, I did find more people who did like me for who I was. Her advice made me cautious of people at first, but now I'm very thankful that she never sugar-coated the real world to me and prepared me for it. There are people who will never like or accept me, but there are also people who will appreciate how special and beautiful I am. Those are the people who matter most.

— Zirrina Maxwell —

Be Grateful

Curbside Promises

Gratitude is as important for feeding your soul
as eating is important for feeding your body.
~J.L.W. Brooks

itting on the curb outside the church, I felt empty. Tired. The laughter inside the building somehow added to my burden. I mindlessly plucked a piece of grass and stroked it between my fingers before looking up at the setting sun as another day faded away.

Another day when I plastered a fake smile across my face, assured people that I was okay, and sang songs with the kids under my care as a children's pastor. Another day when I tried to get back to living but couldn't pull myself from the depression of miscarriage and infertility. Just another day.

Birthday celebrations stung.

Baby showers hurt.

Some friends of ours came outside. Their son was in mid-rambunctious-toddler mode.

"That kid is going to drive me crazy," she said. "He's into everything all the time."

Her spouse laughed, but she was serious. The kid seemed to have gone from rolling to running overnight.

My husband wrapped his arm around my shoulders to try to share some of the burdens he knew I was feeling. I ripped up the blade of grass in my hand and reached for another. Our child should have been the same age. We would have given anything to have a rambunctious toddler. We promised we would never complain about our kids. We would never take a day for granted. We would never forget how blessed we were if we were in their shoes.

About three years later, I carried my first child to full term. She was a tomboy and princess, a tree climber and butterfly catcher, and she was also the most fragile thing I'd ever seen. Not just because she was a baby, but because she was sick.

From acid reflux that kept us up all night, to being born without the sucking reflex, to urinary reflux that had us going from doctor to doctor for the first year of her life, the pediatrician labeled her with Failure to Thrive by seven months old. She was a huge blessing, but those constant screams of pain that Mama couldn't fix grew overwhelming.

But I loved her. With all my heart, all my soul and all my energy, I loved her.

As she got older and healthier (and I let go of much of my fear and some of my control issues), she became a daredevil. She would climb on anything, jump off everything, and test my patience every day.

From infancy to preschool, I constantly had to remind myself of those curbside promises:

I would never complain about our kids.

I would never take a day for granted.

I would never forget how blessed I am.

The motto worked pretty well until I received a call from the school when my daughter was in kindergarten.

"Ms. Richardson, the principal would like to speak to you," the receptionist said.

"Is everything okay? Is my daughter injured?"

"No, nothing like that. There was…" she paused, huffed, took a deep breath, and continued. "There was an incident in class. Your daughter is fine, but we really need to see you as soon as you can get to the school."

The incident in question was that my lovely tomboy of a daughter had just disrupted class by doing a cartwheel mid-lecture.

A cartwheel. In class.

So, there I was, a grown woman called into the principal's office...
just me, the principal, the teacher, and my daughter. Both women
in authority looked at me like they wanted to ask, "So, what are you
going to do about it, Mom?" I turned to my daughter.

"Why did you do a cartwheel?" I asked.

Her innocent smile faded as her face tightened into a ready-for-battle
snarl that was more adorable than scary on her tiny, six-year-old face.

"I wooked at da wules," she said. Her fingers counted off each
memorized item as she recited, "Don't touch fings that ain't yos. Listen
willy good all da time. Do yo bestest all da time. Be nice all da time.
But dare's nuffin' about not doin' cartwills. Nuffin."

Stuck somewhere between annoyance, pride, bursting out in
laughter, and embarrassment, I immediately thought back to that day
on the curb and my adamant "we would never" judgment.

While I would still (try to) never complain about my kids (too
much), I would still (try) not (to) take a day for granted, and still (try
to) never forget how blessed I am, I had to add a new rule: I will keep
my judgments to a minimum.

Don't judge the principal and the teachers who are doing the
best they can with what can only be organized chaos with a class full
of six-year-olds. Don't judge the child who actually took the time to
examine the written rules before breaking the unwritten ones. And
don't judge the parent who wants to laugh at the fact that her kid just
got kicked out of a fancy private kindergarten.

My daughter has since graduated high school. Her two little
brothers are currently in high school. Since the cartwheel caper that
lives on as family lore, I've had many occasions where I could see my
parenting style being judged by others, and even more cases in which
I could have come down harshly on the crazy things my not-so-little
ones have chosen to do. But I have to remind myself to stay calm and
not judge too quickly.

There's no judgment in love. And love is what makes the curbside
promises work.

— Jamie A. Richardson —

11

The Advice I Didn't Want to Hear

Gratitude is the ability to experience life as a gift.
It liberates us from the prison of self-preoccupation.
~John Ortberg

Sometimes, life throws you a curve ball, an unexpected turn of events that will change your life. Mine came when my husband of thirty-nine years was diagnosed with terminal brain cancer. Nothing can prepare you when you are confronted with devastating news like that.

In a matter of minutes, our lives were changed forever. The cancer door had been opened, and there was no way to close it. I wanted to run, to scream, to cry, to turn back the clock, but nothing was going to change the path that we were on. I needed to focus on what I *could* control by ensuring my husband's last months would be as enjoyable as possible.

After being with him for two-thirds of my life, I struggled to find my way after his death. It was a dark period, because in less than four years I lost my husband and both my parents. Clinically, I know I was depressed, but I refused to accept pills to cope.

I openly talked about losing my husband and my grief. I know now I was searching for comfort from anyone who would provide some encouragement, even if it was fleeting. Then one day, while attending a presentation at the local library, a participant said to me, "I don't know why you are so sad. You should be happy for what you had, not sad for what you lost. I will never have such a long and loving relationship."

I stood there stunned. My immediate reaction was fury. I thought, *How dare you! You don't know me! You don't know what it was like. You aren't widowed. Easy to sit on the sidelines and give advice.* I wanted to lash out, but instead I turned and walked away. I retreated to my vehicle. Tears streamed down my face as I drove home.

I agonized over that unsolicited advice for days. Something in my subconscious was eating at me, and the words echoed endlessly. *I don't know why you are so sad. You should be happy for what you had, not sad for what you lost. I will never have such a long and loving relationship.*

The lady didn't know me, that was for sure, but maybe she was right. Maybe I had wallowed in my grief too long. I woke up one day and decided to take what she said to heart.

Her words became my salvation.

I reflected on what I had enjoyed in my marriage and started to think and talk positively about my husband and our life to anyone who would listen. It felt like the sadness was frozen in time from that point forward. Not that I didn't still have minutes, hours, and days when grief would creep in, but I now used positive reflections to keep the grief at bay.

Changing my outlook gave me the strength to look through the windshield of life rather than through the rearview mirror. Viewing my loss through a positive lens enabled me to step back into life. With my new positive outlook, I found the courage to explore possibilities for the next phase of my life. Eventually, I had the confidence to start dating.

I became active online, engaging with other widows, and joined local grief groups. Whenever I could, I shared the lessons I had been taught about appreciating the life I was fortunate to have had, rather than focusing on my loss. I still share my experience with other widows in the hopes that they, too, can benefit from a new perspective. My advice is always the same: Do not confine your existence to looking backward, to having regrets. Embrace the here and now, and celebrate every day and who and what you have in your life.

I am now remarried, and together we enjoy a rich, full life.

— Wendy Portfors —

12

Three Good Things

*Never let the things you want make
you forget the things you have.*
~Sanchita Pandey

always hoped that I gave my students more than an introduction
to classic literature and an understanding of where to put com-
mas in their writing. I wanted to impart some life lessons that
would help them live productive, happy lives.

Ironically, it was a student who taught *me* a valuable life lesson,
one that still shapes my attitude and actions thirty-five years later.

I began that day as I had begun most days that school year:
stressed, exhausted, and burned out. The staff was dealing with several
issues affecting teacher morale. One of my classes was particularly
challenging, and I was tired of trying to motivate a group of students
who seemingly did not care about school. In addition, my two-year-old
son had been sick so often that I was considering the need to remove
him from his child-care situation. I did not know if I could continue
to teach, and I was not optimistic about my future.

By third period, I was already looking forward to the three o'clock
dismissal bell. Near the end of the class, I was returning graded essays
to my eleventh graders while they read an assignment. After I handed
back a paper to Jill, she looked it over, read my comments, checked
the grade, smiled up at me, and said, "This will be one of my three
good things for today."

I had not heard that expression before, so I asked her, "What does that mean?"

She explained, "Every night before I go to sleep, I think of three good things that happened that day. No matter how bad the day has been, I can always look back and find three good things. A good thing does not necessarily have to be something that would seem big or important to anyone else, just to me. It can be a good grade on a test or a really good meal or a fun time after school with my friends. What matters is that I end my day being thankful for my blessings and focusing on what is positive, not negative. I usually wake up the next morning looking forward to the day."

I stood in the aisle near her desk thinking about what she had just told me. "Thank you so much for sharing that with me," I said. "That sounds like a great idea, a really good habit that encourages you to see that there is good in every day, and in life, even if some things are not going well."

Honestly, I was a little embarrassed. A sixteen-year-old student had just taught me a life lesson that I badly needed. I had always been someone who assumed that things would work out for the good. When had I become this person who saw only the problems in her life?

I decided right then to start practicing the "three good things" habit. That night, before I went to sleep, I was surprised to find that I had no trouble coming up with three positive things that had happened that day. I thought about the insightful discussion I had with a group of seniors about a book we were reading, the gorgeous rainbow I saw after it stopped raining, and the afterschool stop at the park with my children. Focusing on those things was so much better than replaying all the things that had gone wrong during the day.

When I woke up the next morning, I was not quite as pessimistic as I had been the day before. I was looking forward to finding my "three good things." During the next days, the more positive things I looked for, the more I found.

Throughout the years, I have continued to work on being positive and grateful. When I have time and energy, I write in a gratitude journal. But even on days when I don't write anything in my notebook, I try to focus on "three good things." During even the hardest times,

I can usually find them. As I have grown older, when life has given me challenges and difficulties, I have faced them with a more positive and hopeful attitude, thanks to some good advice from someone who called me *her* teacher.

— MaryBeth Wallace —

13

The Power of a Thank-You Note

*"Thank you" shows respect, which is
the foundation of all relationships.*
~Maxime Lagacé

"Did you write your thank-you notes?" I asked my younger son, Jon.

"No, not yet, Mom," Jon replied, rolling his eyes. "I'll do it when I get back from Kim's house."

"Sorry, that's not going to happen!" I snapped. "You're not leaving this house until you've written a note to everyone you came in contact with during your interview."

"Even the receptionist who was rude to me?" Jon asked with a bewildered expression.

"Especially her!"

Jon was home on Christmas break from college and had just finished interviewing with his first-choice company in Cleveland, Ohio. It was a rare opportunity considering that jobs were in short supply in 2008.

The power of a thank-you note is something I drilled into our boys from the time they were old enough to hold a pencil. It didn't matter if it was for a birthday, Christmas or graduation. Every gift had to be acknowledged with sincere gratitude within twenty-four hours.

Growing up, my mom was a stickler for thank-you notes. But she couched it in such a way that it came across not as an ultimatum but as a privilege. She'd say, "Your words of sincere gratitude have the power to change someone's life for the better — even if it's just for a moment." Her advice changed my life, and it was my hope that it would change Jon's life as well.

After an hour, Jon emerged from his room and handed over eight thank-you notes. To my delight, they were all sincere and heartfelt — even the one to the receptionist who had been less than friendly.

Before Jon left to visit his girlfriend Kim he turned to me and announced, "Mom, I'm pretty sure that a thank-you note to the CEO or the receptionist isn't going to land me this job. But if it makes you happy, then it's worth it."

"We'll see about that," I said, smiling.

Jon was twenty-one years old, and I felt foolish telling a grown man what to do, but I also didn't want him living in our basement for the rest of his life!

Ten days after the thank-you notes were mailed, Jon received a call from the company that he had interviewed with. When his cellphone pinged for the second time, I asked, "Jon, why aren't you responding?"

"Oh, they're just calling to let me know that I didn't get the job," Jon lamented.

"I'm sorry to disappoint you, but they don't offer that courtesy," I explained. "They only give you a call when you get the job."

For days, Jon had been moping around the house feeling the weight of his school loans coming due after graduation and not having a job lined up. He had thoroughly convinced himself that he didn't get the job, but I knew better.

"Jon, it's almost 5:00 P.M. You need to call them back ASAP."

Jon finally gave in and went into the next room to make the call. I pressed a water glass next to the wall and could hear everything he was saying. "Yes, I'm still interested," he said matter-of-factly. There was a long pause, and then Jon cleared his throat and added, "Yes, I look forward to receiving the welcome packet in the mail, and thank you again for this opportunity."

I tried to pretend like I hadn't eavesdropped, but I'm not that good of an actress. I grabbed Jon's arm, and we danced around the kitchen chanting, "Gainfully employed."

Over a decade later, Jon is now at the peak of his career in marketing — building on the success of his first job. He's now the one who does the hiring and firing. On a recent trip to visit him and his sweet family, I asked, "So, how do you know who to hire?"

"Oh, that's easy, Mom. It's the one who writes me the best thank-you note," he replied with a wink and a smile.

What I never shared with Jon was the fact that my first job out of college was attained by one simple act — writing a thank-you note to everyone I met during the interview. Two weeks later, I received a personal handwritten note from the CEO that brought tears to my eyes — along with a letter stating: "Congratulations, you're hired."

And I'm pretty sure that, one day, Jon will be having the thank-you note conversation with his children, "Never underestimate the power of a thank-you note!"

— Connie K. Pombo —

14

Coming Out of the Chains

I've been embraced by a new community.
That's what happens when you're finally honest
about who you are; you find others like you.
~Chaz Bono

"Good will not accept you in paradise if you're homosexual." It was a lesson I had been taught time and time again. Religion and faith were important in my Christian household. I had known since I was a child that being anything other than heterosexual would throw our family off-balance, so realizing at the age of twelve that I was bisexual was no gift, at least not then.

The rumors at school were running rampant by the time I was thirteen. My personality seemed too much to handle for my peers, leading me to an abyss where the only way out was faking it. Growing up in Costa Rica, a heteronormative society in Latin America, didn't leave room for much hope that things would get better. Having to lie to the mirror, friends, family, and everyone who so exhaustively questioned me about my sexuality was the greatest irritation.

Then, I had an epiphany at age fourteen.

Ashley was one of those friends who just got me, with a bond so strong that she could hear any of my truths without judgment. The day I came out to her, my headache threatened to make me faint. But that day, my life took a turn.

I base my life around a straightforward rule: After 10:00 P.M., no secrets exist, and there is only frankness. My brain has no filter for lies at a certain point. Something I would have considered a weakness would end up freeing me from the lies I had been holding onto for the past two years.

Half-asleep, we had texted each other for at least an hour. The conversation was getting intense. My confidence in myself and appreciation of Ashley grew with each text message. My heart raced when I recognized it was time.

I had come to terms with myself about who I was. I wasn't able to hide from it anymore. Even if I knew my secrets and was true to myself, holding a secret from the world was no picnic. I knew I had to do it. I felt an impulsive urge to let things go. I figured it wasn't society that had me chained down, brainwashed, and ripped from reality. It was me. I was the antagonist who had put myself down for so long.

"Ash, I've got something to tell you." Those five words conveyed there was no going back. I continued. "I'm bisexual."

I had done it. I was naked, vulnerable. I was real. I was me. I was me for the first time.

"It's okay," Ash said. "I don't think you should have to live in fear of who you are, you know? I mean, the people who accept you are those you should care about. Anyone else is simply not worthy of you."

Something lightened in me at that instant. Tears started gushing from my eyes while an ear-to-ear smile spread across my face — a happy cry. I was free.

I realized something that night: God isn't the only one I should seek love from, but from myself, too. There was no fear left. Life was just what I would make it. I had been the only one obstructing myself from acceptance. Accepting myself had to come from deep inside, from the core of my soul.

I planted a seed that day — a seedling that would persist, growing as I continued to live. To my astonishment, no friend of mine has left me for being bisexual. No insult, cruelty, or iniquity has been inflicted on me.

I am thankful for finding myself. I liberated myself from my mind's prison, and I feel empathy for that twelve-year-old me, crying myself to sleep for being born "this way."

—Ander Fernán—

15

Love's Lens

Relationships are based on four principles: respect,
understanding, acceptance and appreciation.
~Mahatma Gandhi

sat down at one of the breakroom tables to eat my lunch and made my usual call to my fiancé. "Hi, beautiful!" He answered the phone as he always did — with a compliment.

"Hi, baby! How is your day going?" I inquired.

"Same, same. Just another day at the shop. Brake job and oil change now. Have an alternator to work on next. How about you?"

"Same, just another day. Glad it's Friday. Definitely ready for the weekend." I sighed with relief. Only a few more hours and we would have an entire weekend to spend together.

"Oh, yeah, I got you a present from work today!" he exclaimed, with great enthusiasm in his voice.

"Oh, really?"

"Yes! I just know you will love it. Can't wait to see you in a few hours! Love you," he said enthusiastically on the other end of the phone.

"Love you, too, baby. Excited to see you soon!" I exclaimed before we hung up, and I proceeded to finish the remaining few hours left in the workweek.

When I got home, my fiancé was as giddy as could be about the gift he had gotten me from work. I was excited yet curious at the same time; after all, my fiancé was a mechanic. What kind of gift would he have gotten for me from one of his tool vendors?

He had me cover my eyes, and when I opened them, he handed me a black, square bag. I unzipped it and did not understand what was inside.

"Uh, what is it?"

"It's a jumper box!" he exclaimed. "You charge it, and then you can keep it in your car. If your battery ever dies, you don't need jumper cables and another car to start yours. This will jump your battery for you, all by itself!" He was toggling and maneuvering the device around, explaining to me how it worked, just like a child showing me a new toy at Christmas. "It's already all charged up. I charged it at work today. Come on outside, and I will show you how it works!" He just about bolted out the front door as the telephone rang.

"I'll be right out, babe!" I called out the door to him as he unlocked the car, and I ran to answer the phone. It was my mother.

"Hi, Mom. How are you?" I answered. I told her that I would call her back because I needed to learn about my gift.

"A gift? How sweet. What did he get for you?"

"It's some jumper box that will start my car battery if it ever dies without needing jumper cables and another car," I explained.

"You don't sound too excited about it."

"Well, I don't really get it. I mean, it's sweet, and I appreciate his gesture and excitement, but it's just a car thing," I responded.

"Well, were you hoping for flowers? Or a necklace?"

"No, you know I am not into all that."

"He is excited because this is his way of taking care of you," said my mother. "You mean the world to him, and this is a gift to give him a little peace of mind in making sure you are safe when he can't be with you."

My mom surprised me with her wisdom. "You know, I never looked at it like that. Thanks, Mom. I will call back in little bit. Love you!"

"You are welcome. Love you, too!" My mom's words sunk in as I hung up the phone and went outside to join my fiancé.

He started showing me how to use the battery pack and all I could do was smile and gaze at him. When the demonstration was over, I gave him the biggest hug. "I love you, baby. Thank you so much. This is the best gift ever!"

My mother's wise words really flipped a switch, both in my relationship with my husband, as well as with friends, family, and others. I realized that no one acts or shows love exactly the same way, so it is important to take a step back and look at others' actions through a lens of love.

— Gwen Cooper —

16

Just Like Us

Be present in all things and thankful for all things.
~Maya Angelou

'm grateful to have a roof over my head, food in my belly, and the ability to take care of my family. This is why I try to help the homeless and those in need whenever possible.

Here are a few examples of words from some unfortunate souls that changed my perspective about what's really important in life.

1. One hot day, I was sitting on my front porch enjoying a cold beverage when a young gentleman who was obviously homeless strolled by my house.

"Hi, there. Would you like something to drink?" I asked.

"No, thank you," he replied as he took another few steps and then stopped. "What I'd really like more than anything is a clean pair of socks."

His response really struck a chord with me, hitting me right in my heart and soul. I have a whole dresser drawer overflowing with clean socks, and he just wanted one pair. Along with a bag of these warm foot coverings, I gave him some cash, and he was so grateful. Now I can't look at my socks without feeling blessed.

2. Another time, I was coming home from work on payday with a huge bonus in my pocket. I found myself stuck at a stoplight during a normal commute. I saw something common: a man in shabby clothing holding a cardboard sign that read, "Need work or food. Anything helps."

Most will say not to give money to panhandlers, but I just couldn't help myself given my recent windfall. I have a full-time job, and this unfortunate soul had practically nothing. So, I honked my horn, rolled down my window, and gave him a rather large bill.

"Thank you so much," he offered politely and then stated, "Seriously, I really need a job." I gave him a couple of leads on possible employment opportunities in the area and went on my way, hoping his luck would change for the better. Now I'm even happier about my reliable employment.

3. Stopping by the corner store on my way to work another day, I heard a friendly voice asking me, "So, how are they doing this season?"

I'd completely forgotten I was wearing a hat with our football team's logo. We chatted about the last few games, and he was sweet, nice and polite.

It became apparent that he was homeless due to his belongings around him. He seemed to be camping out in the parking lot. During our conversation, I noticed some customers scowling at him and making cruel comments.

I asked if I could get him anything at the store, and he politely replied, "No, thank you." However, I still felt the need to get him something — almost anything to brighten his day as he did mine.

Inside the store, I asked the cashier about the young lad in the parking lot, and her response was epic.

"I don't know why everyone gives him such a hard time. Basically, he's a good guy who doesn't bother anyone and usually just keeps to himself, minding his own business."

"I know what you mean," I replied. "Would you mind if I buy him a hot meal (something microwavable) and some water?"

"That's very kind," she responded. "I have no problem with that. He's welcome here."

Most homeless folks are people like us. They're just enduring an unfortunate part of their journey through life. They are not all alcoholics and drug addicts. They deserve our respect and admiration in overcoming their everyday struggles. They're just people who might need a helping hand from their neighbors and not judgment and rude behavior. Now I'm grateful that my life didn't hand me enough bad luck to end up in their situation.

—D.J. Sartell—

17

Living Life at 90-9

Gratitude makes sense of our past, brings peace for today,
and creates a vision for tomorrow.
~Melody Beattie

I was in my mid-forties when I bought my house in a quiet, older neighbourhood. It didn't take me long to realize that, even though I was in my forties, I was the "youngster" in the area. Most of my neighbours were well into their eighties and nineties. Within the first couple of weeks, most of the neighbours wandered over to welcome me. My next-door neighbour, however, seemed indifferent to my presence. Heading off to work, I would often see her sitting on her porch in her rocking chair, and I would offer a cheery "Good morning," but never receive any acknowledgement.

I had lived there for nearly a month when there was a knock at my door. It was my indifferent neighbour. She was carrying a plate of freshly baked cupcakes, which were painstakingly decorated with beautiful pastel flowers. I stood in my doorway distracted by the screeching of her hearing aid. She seemed quite unaffected by it, but I was having a hard time understanding what she was saying as she competed with that high-pitched squeal. She seemed to sense the problem and removed her hearing aid.

She informed me that her name was Kay, she was ninety years old, and she was deaf. She also explained that if I ever needed to tell her something or ask her a question, writing a note that she could read would be appreciated. I invited her in for coffee, but she responded,

"Yes, it is nice to meet you, too." And off she went.

Over the years, I learned to approach Kay from an angle where she could clearly see me, and I would exaggerate my lip movement when having a conversation with her. Kay was able to lip-read to a certain extent, and we soon found our own ways to communicate. Kay was clearly a wise woman. She had owned her own business and had been on a church council. She was also a great source of information on baking, gardening, canning or any domestic task.

She was also very agile for her age. She would squat in her garden and carefully pluck every stray weed or piece of grass. When she was done, she would stand up and walk back to her house as though she had just been out for a leisurely stroll. I would practise weeding by squatting as Kay had done but found I either lost my balance after a few minutes or could hardly straighten my back again if I did manage to persevere for a bit longer. Kay later explained that she was Ukrainian and had started Ukrainian dancing when she was just a child. She still regularly participated in Ukrainian dancing at the senior center. She was so grateful for being able to stay active by participating in something that she still loved.

When I arrived home from work one day, Kay waved and motioned for me to come into her house. She had made perogies and wanted me to join her for supper. The supper was delicious, but the squealing hearing aid was very distracting and annoying. I tapped my ear and then pointed to her to indicate that her hearing aid was squealing. I wasn't sure she would understand, but she removed it, and the squealing stopped.

Then she put her hand on top of mine and said, "Dear, do you ever wonder why I wear a hearing aid even though I am deaf?" To be honest, I had often pondered that question. She clearly could not hear no matter how loudly anyone spoke, so wearing a hearing aid seemed a bit pointless. I nodded, and she proceeded to explain.

"Every once in a while, if I turn my head, and the wind happens to come from the right direction, my hearing aid squeals." I rapidly nodded in agreement. She continued, "And there are times when I can hear that squeal. In a life where deafness has become my reality,

I love the moments when, even for a few seconds, I can hear again. It is the most wonderful feeling. The next time you hear an annoying noise like the neighbour's dog barking, some kid squealing tires, or a loud machine running, don't be annoyed. Count it as a blessing. Like me, the day may come when you would give anything to be able to hear those noises again."

Another time when I came home from work, Kay was sitting on her porch as usual but clutching her purse and watching the driveway. I walked over to say hi, and she explained that her daughter was coming to pick her up for supper. She told me that she loved Wednesdays. When I asked why, she said, "Because every Wednesday, my daughter and I have supper at a nice restaurant, and then she takes me to the park."

I questioned, "Park?"

She said, "Yes, I love to swing at the park. Did you know that when you swing, the wind on your face feels exactly the same when you are ninety as it did when you were nine?" I shook my head. I had never really thought about it. She smiled and said, "It does, and every Wednesday, I get the chance to feel nine years old again."

I would now be classified as a senior citizen myself, and when I get frustrated at events in life, I take Kay's advice and go to the park to swing or fly my kite beside some quiet country road. My day-to-day cares disappear as I feel the wind on my face, and my nine-year-old self emerges. When I sit in my yard and listen to the birds chirp, I am grateful for the sounds that not everyone gets to enjoy. I have also learned to be grateful for the things that are annoying because I am still well enough to be annoyed by them! Each time I go for a walk now, instead of focusing on who has the nicest house, I focus on the fact that I am still able to walk around my neighbourhood.

I am so thankful for my wise neighbour, who was able to give me a better perspective on what is truly important in life.

— Brenda Leppington —

Chapter 3

Face Your Fears

18

Walk This Way

Fear is only as deep as the mind allows.
~Japanese Proverb

As a lifelong dog owner, I have taken many to the kennel for boarding, but nothing prepared me for the terrifying scene that unfolded one early summer morning.

It was a quick weekend beach trip to Ocean City, New Jersey, but Maggie, our one-year-old rescue puppy, would be away from home for the first time. In the nine months since we had adopted her, this sweet and spunky black Lab/Pointer mix had become a cherished family member. She had separation anxiety, and we hated to be away from her and our five-year-old, equally adored Pit/Lab mix, Barkley. But, after a year of postponed travel plans, my husband and I and our two sons needed a post-pandemic night away.

I was confident in our veterinarian's kennel, which provided expert care and would give Maggie a spacious run next to her brother. This one-night stay would prepare her for a longer one mid-summer. Although Covid protocols didn't allow us to accompany her, I thought she'd trot right in after she saw Barkley walk inside.

But as we approached the glass doors, Maggie resisted. Suddenly, in one swift motion, she twisted backward out of the harness and collar. Cars whizzed by at forty miles per hour on the road at the end of the parking lot. I dove toward her into the concrete as my boys and husband watched in horror.

Blood gushed from deep gashes in my legs as Maggie charged

past everyone in her path toward the busy road. I panicked, thinking how traumatic it would be for my ten- and fourteen-year-old sons to lose our beloved puppy. Maggie was the most lovable girl with the sweetest spirit.

She was a few feet from the road when my quick-thinking boys jumped out of the car, beckoning her to return. She froze, saw Kyle and Tyler with the open car doors, and miraculously pivoted mid-sprint to race into the safety of our SUV.

Once we all recovered from the frantic close call, it took a stressful thirty minutes, the entire kennel staff, and our car pulled up to a back-entrance door to get her safely inside.

While my physical wounds healed, our emotional scars deepened. Maggie was now afraid to leave our house. I lost confidence in my ability to keep her safe on a leash, so we no longer took walks. The veterinarian prescribed calming medication for our next visit. An hour after our scheduled appointment, I still couldn't coax her into the car.

The next time, I secured her in a crate and enlisted a team to help carry it safely into the building. My husband said it looked like the disturbing scene from *Silence of the Lambs* — and he was right.

Maggie and I had become prisoners to her intense fear. Her increasing reactivity triggered anxiety for Barkley and me. Both charged the fence aggressively at dogs passing by, so they were no longer allowed to run and play freely. A dog sitter wasn't an option because of her worsening fear of people. Even regular guests were met with ferocious barks and growls.

I was overwhelmed by this dilemma. And it wasn't my only problem. My mind swirled with the worries that come with preteen and teenage children but also those that come with aging parents. Several family members were facing heartbreaking and debilitating illnesses. To top it off, bloodwork revealed a genetic cholesterol issue that meant I was at risk for a fatal heart attack. My cardiologist recommended reducing stress, but too often during the day and night, I was consumed with fears.

Determined to implement a soothing bedtime reading ritual to calm my racing mind, I stumbled upon a much-needed solution in

Chicken Soup for the Soul: Think Positive, Live Happy. Amy Newmark's "Facing the Fear" spoke to me as the strategy I desperately needed. Her method for dealing with waves of intense fear of cancer recurrence was to decide she was only allowed to think about it between 8:00 and 8:10 each morning. If she wanted to think about all the scary stuff that day or night, she'd have to wait until 8:00 the next morning. Of course, she never ended up having such morose thoughts at 8:00 in the morning.

I practiced on the walk home from my son's school. This time was now dedicated to processing my feelings of anxiety. Afterward, I'd let them go until the same time the next day. It took practice and discipline, but soon I enjoyed the exercise and therapeutic release of my fears as I breathed in the fresh morning air.

I loved my daily walk, but I longed for my high-energy companion to be able to face her own fear and relish it alongside me. Our neighborhood bordered a breathtaking, tree-lined, five-mile trail. I knew the exercise would be good for both of us.

After thorough research and some trial and error, I found the right dog trainer. When I learned Heather was committed to effective recall because her first dog slipped out the door and was hit by a car, I knew she was meant for us. She was also an in-home pet sitter who could reinforce training while we traveled. I studied her informative Instagram feed, #HandfulofLeashes, and decided the investment of time and money would be my priority. During our entire first session, Maggie barked and growled any time Heather came close. I felt hopeless, but she reminded me that training was a journey that required many small steps.

Progress was slow, but with daily practice on a leash in our back yard over the next few months, a less anxious dog and a more confident owner emerged. Armed with the proper tools, I learned to trust myself again. Finally, using a prong collar to control her reactivity, an e-collar to ensure recall, and a double leash with extra hooks (for my peace of mind), we cautiously went on our first walk in nearly a year.

In the six months since, we haven't missed a day. Our morning therapy walks are our dedicated time to face our fears and release them. Maggie and Barkley run and play in our back yard and recall obediently when told. They accompany us on frequent weekend trips to Ocean City, and Maggie's my happy sidekick as we explore miles of the beautiful town on foot. She is unruffled when barking dogs pass by and happily wags her tail as people approach her. Maggie is the calm and confident girl I knew she could be and living the full life every dog deserves.

Her anxiety will always be a work in progress, but aren't we all? A daily ritual as a result of a shared story has been life-changing and perhaps life-saving. Our determined path on a gorgeous, colorful trail brimming with fall leaves allows us to face our fears one step at time.

—Jennifer Kennedy—

The Next Right Thing

*Having spent the better part of my life trying either to
relive the past or experience the future before it arrives,
I have come to believe that in between these
two extremes is peace.*
~Author Unknown

Twelve years after we began our journey to build our family, eight years after our first adoption, six years after our second, and mere months after a heart-wrenching miscarriage, I sat, stunned, in the reproductive specialist's office. Not only was I pregnant, but we'd just heard the heartbeat.

We were in uncharted territory. At the age of thirty-six, I was experiencing my first viable spontaneous pregnancy. Our hearts and home were already full with our two sons, and the idea of adding a miracle baby seemed like an embarrassment of riches. It almost seemed like too much to hope for. The long, winding road of pregnancy stretched out ominously ahead of me, a woman with significant reproductive challenges. A lot can go wrong in a pregnancy. Would we get to meet this little miracle?

I was an anxious person by nature, so the prospect of successfully navigating forty weeks of pregnancy seemed completely daunting. My anxiety invented imaginary catastrophe after catastrophe.

Now, as I sat in my doctor's office, shame crept into my voice as I confessed my fear. My doctor, a pragmatic man, listened to my concerns and replied gently, "There is no way to predict what the future holds, and trying to won't do you any good. The only power you have right now is in your choices. Do the next right thing."

The next right thing.

The next right thing, he explained, included taking my prenatal vitamins, going for walks, staying hydrated, resting when I could, and nurturing my body throughout the pregnancy. That was something I could control.

And that is how we walked through the pregnancy. Weeks of nausea and vomiting turned into months, and I battled dehydration by doing the next right thing. My high-risk pregnancy meant extra tests and frequent trips to the doctor. The next right thing. The pregnancy progressed slowly… and perfectly. As our little one developed and grew inside me, I beat back my fears of something going wrong by doing the only thing I could. The next right thing.

At exactly forty weeks, I gave birth to our baby, our third son, Rowan. He was, and is, perfect.

Years later, we took all three boys to see the animated film *Frozen 2*. In the film, Anna sings a song entitled "The Next Right Thing." Listening to it, with tears in my eyes and a lump in my throat, I felt immense gratitude, not just for my three sons, but also for the gentle advice given to an anxious expectant mom by a caring doctor.

We cannot always do everything… but we can do the next right thing.

— Kelly A. Smith —

20

Two Roads Diverged

*Embrace uncertainty. Some of the most beautiful
chapters in our lives won't have a title until much later.*
~Bob Goff

At age thirty-four I was left standing in the middle of the kitchen while watching my husband of sixteen years walk out the door. He left me and my two daughters to forge on without him.

I had married him right out of high school and gotten pregnant the next year with our first daughter. We decided together that I would be a stay-at-home mom. Four years later, our second daughter came along, and we lived the idyllic life. Or so I thought.

Then the fairytale vanished, and I awoke in real life. My work experience consisted of one year as a bank teller right out of high school. So, I stumbled along with low-paying jobs, stress and self-doubt.

Three years later, while working at a community college, I became friends with the president's secretary. She was a certified teacher just waiting to be hired by the local school system. She encouraged me to take classes and get a teaching degree. I wrestled with the idea for several months and finally enrolled in one class that fall.

To my amazement, I loved school. I loved learning. So, in the spring, I enrolled in two classes while working full-time. I doubled up on classes, even going in the summer months. I won't say it was easy. I still had all the responsibility for two teenage daughters, making my house a home, preparing meals, planning social events, making sure their homework was done, and finding time to do my own homework.

In one of my low moments, as I questioned whether to continue with my education, my fifteen-year-old daughter strolled into the room.

"Whatcha doin'?" she asked nonchalantly.

"Trying to decide if I want to pursue my education and get a degree or not," I replied despondently.

"Why are you wondering?" she asked.

"Well, I'll be forty by the time I finally get my degree." (Forty seemed so old at that time.)

"You'll be forty anyway," she said matter-of-factly. "Do you wanna be forty with a degree or forty without a degree?"

And then she walked out of the room.

I stared after her incredulously. Out of the mouth of babes! In that moment, my life changed. I wanted to be forty *with* a college degree!

I don't know what got me to the finish line, but four months after my fortieth birthday, I walked proudly across the stage to receive my Bachelor's in Education. Three years later, I received my Master's in English.

At the age of sixty-five, I retired from teaching high-school English. That one decision I made so many years ago gave me a life filled with wonderful memories of students, colleagues, football games, University Interscholastic League events, pep rallies, and even parent-teacher conferences. It opened doors to new worlds that I had never dreamed of before. It changed my life in the most beautiful way, filling it with joy, happiness, laughter and fun.

And that made all the difference.

—Darlene Carpenter Herring—

21

Chicken Soup
for the Soul

You Can't Strike Out

Thinking will not overcome fear but action will.
~W. Clement Stone

With all the great books out there, who would have predicted that the one that changed my life would be *How to Pick Up Girls* by Eric Weber? I was shy growing up and wanted to have a girlfriend. I had one date in high school, and that didn't go well, so I was desperate when I picked up the book.

I thought it was a bit corny, but there was one piece of advice that really resonated with me. Near the end of the book, the writer suggested trying out what I had just read but to pretend it was like the preseason in a sport — when the games didn't count. It didn't matter if you won or lost or, in my case, met a girl.

I don't know why the suggestion to pretend my attempts didn't count resonated with me other than the fact I grew up loving sports. When my teams would lose during the regular season, I couldn't bear to watch. But when they lost in the preseason, I didn't care.

Somehow, this new way of thinking worked for me. I could use it to my advantage if I didn't take rejection personally. All I had to do was pretend it didn't count.

After reading those words, I could go up to anyone I found interesting and ply my words with no fear of striking out — to use another sports reference. It was empowering to know the results didn't matter because this was the exhibition season when I was practicing what I had learned before the real games started.

Fear is like a snake tightening its body around you as you struggle to breathe. You can't just shake it off. I was taught at a young age to be afraid rather than to experience life. Don't ride a bike because you might get hit by a car. Don't swim because you might drown. That's why I was initially afraid to approach girls. They might say no — how could I live with that rejection?

Besides meeting girls, I discovered there were other ways to use this new tool. If the outcome of a try didn't matter, I could go after anything in life I wanted to pursue.

It allowed me to have a successful sales career, even though I heard the word no hundreds of times. It was part of the business, but I didn't let it get me down. I turned a negative into a positive by reasoning that every time I heard the word no, it meant I was one step closer to yes. It's amazing how empowered you feel when you eliminate the fear that stops you from going after what you want in life.

While sales was an avenue to a successful life, it wasn't what made my heart flutter. That was sports. With no fear of going after what I wanted, I reached out to different websites and papers dedicated to sports and asked if I could write for them. After all, what did I have to lose? If I didn't get the answer I desired, I would go on to the next potential opportunity.

Being able to say I was writing for a particular sports site gave me the impetus to reach out to the local pro sports teams in Chicago and say I would like to go to the game to cover the team. More often than not, I got a positive response.

Before I knew it, I was sitting in the dugout with Chicago Cubs manager Dusty Baker and a slew of local media as he did his pregame press conference. I asked him questions I thought fans would want the answers to. They were tough questions, but he respected my knowledge of the game, and we became close.

I went to spring training the next season and interviewed him for a paper I wrote for called *The Heckler*. I was doing it on a freelance basis, and Dusty spent twenty minutes talking with me while several of the beat reporters and media types that covered the team for a living waited for us to finish. At the ballpark not long after the regular season started, a writer for the *Chicago Tribune* who was president of the Baseball Writers' Association of America (BBWAA) told me that Dusty talked to me longer than anyone else that spring.

I was doing what I loved and having a blast at the same time. I covered both the Cubs and the Chicago White Sox, and I was there as media on a regular basis when the Sox won the World Series in 2005. I interviewed their mercurial manager, Ozzie Guillén, that year for the paper. Aside from baseball, I covered the Chicago Bulls for fifteen years when I had free time.

What's funny was that I was afraid to ask girls out way back when, but I was never afraid to ask players, coaches, managers, and general managers tough questions at the games.

I still worked my sales job, and we had a lot of high-school and college students working at the store. I would talk to them about sports, as well as pass on the advice that I learned many years ago, which allowed me to go after what I wanted in life without fear of failure. I encouraged them to utilize that idea for whatever they wanted to achieve.

Who would have thought it would come full circle, and I would end up teaching a class called "How to Talk to the Opposite Sex" later in life?

My life took a completely different direction after I read that book. A seemingly irrelevant suggestion had a profound impact on my being. I wish the writer knew how much his little piece of advice — to pretend the results didn't matter — could be so powerful and change lives like it did mine.

— Darrell Horwitz —

22

Sometimes Laughter Isn't the Best Medicine

*Sometimes you have to kind of die inside in order to
rise from your own ashes and believe in yourself and
love yourself to become a new person.*
~Gerard Way

"**H**ave you ever thought," she said carefully, "that perhaps you use humour as a defence mechanism?"

I scoffed and rolled my eyes. She wasn't the first person to have said this to me, and I very much doubted that she'd be the last.

"I'm just funny," I replied. "My whole family is. We had to be."

"What do you mean by that?"

"Well…" I paused, thinking of how to try and explain it. In the end, I settled for a cliché or two.

"My mum always used to say that if it wasn't for bad luck, we'd have had no luck at all. Our family motto is 'If you don't laugh, you'll cry.'" I snorted.

When I saw that she'd stopped writing and raised her eyebrows at me, I took a deep breath and steeled myself. When a therapist looks at you like that, it means that you're about to do some unpacking, and things are going to become real uncomfortable.

I hadn't been lying when I told her that we're funny. Okay, it can be a bit sarcastic and dry, and that's not to everyone's taste, but we're a funny bunch.

When I think back, I recall the after-school karaoke when we would deliberately sing the wrong words to put each other off, the jukebox that loved to come to life on its own with James Brown's "I Got You (I Feel Good)," or the pranks that we used to play on each other. It's very easy to gloss over why we were doing that. We were singing karaoke to drown out another argument.

That afternoon in the therapist's office, I wasn't unpacking but unfurling myself. Once I'd started, the floodgates were well and truly open. I found myself telling her about the bedroom so cold that I could see my breath in the mornings, the asthma brought on by living in a house full of smokers who didn't open windows, and the time my mum took off and we didn't know where she was for three weeks.

I could feel the therapist looking at me and realised that I'd been talking to the floor the entire time. I looked up at her.

"You've been through a lot," she said. "I think your problem is that you need to let yourself feel."

I stared at her. I'd spent the past fifty minutes spilling my childhood angst to her, and that was her advice — that I needed to "feel"?

She could tell that I wasn't impressed.

"What I mean is that you don't let yourself feel anything whenever something 'bad' happens. You automatically go into humour mode. You make jokes, play the clown, and downplay how things really make you feel because you don't know how to deal with your emotions."

She could see that the cogs were starting to turn for me, so she took the opportunity to push further.

"I'm going to set you a task," she said. "I want you to think about and write down how it really made you feel when your mum left for three weeks and you didn't know where she was. No jokes. No quips. Just how you felt. Then, next week, we can read through it together."

So, that's what I did. It took me a while to get started, but when I did, I thought I was going to burn a hole through the paper. I wrote about how I felt like she'd abandoned me. How I was scared that she might never come back, and how part of me didn't want her to come back because I was angry at her. I wrote about how insignificant and invisible I must be for her to have left me without a second thought. I wrote about how I still hadn't managed to shake off the feeling of being unloved and how I wasn't sure that I ever would.

I wrote down everything that I could just like she'd asked me to. If I didn't write it down, it's because I couldn't. There were some things that I just couldn't describe. There were feelings and emotions that I didn't even know the name for. As much I hated to admit it, she was right. I'd convinced myself that I was "just funny" when my humour was a façade, and it had stopped me from feeling anything. It was actually quite sad.

The fact that I'd been referred to a therapist in the first place should have given me a clue that maybe my coping mechanisms weren't the best, but I've always been stubborn, so it was going to take some doing to get me to realise it. I did get there in the end, though. Now, when people ask me if I have any advice I live by, I tell them that laughter isn't always the best medicine.

—Ashleigh Russell—

23

The Reluctant Traveler

Teaching is the one profession that creates
all other professions.
~Author Unknown

My teaching colleague Margie and I had just read the last book about Midwest pioneer life to our third graders. We started to discuss what project to do next with the students. But then she said to me, "Why don't you travel to all those places we read about?"

Me, travel? I was a Hoosier homebody. Sure, I enjoyed seeing other people's photos of faraway lands. But the farthest I traveled was driving to my mom's in Missouri, my home state. I certainly didn't possess any of that pioneer spirit of taking off into the unknown, as I called the rest of the Midwest. Besides, that lengthy journey would take money for travel, lodging, and meals. Unless someone paid for all those necessary items, that road trip wasn't happening anytime soon. (This was in the days before GPS and online booking, when you used a paper map and phoned to reserve a hotel room.)

But I couldn't get her advice out of my mind. I imagined actually being at all the places I had only read about, like picking wildflowers on the Kansas prairie, wading into Plum Creek, and stepping inside a one-room cabin in Wisconsin.

Not long afterward, by the teacher mailboxes, I noticed a brochure advertising a teacher creativity fellowship program for the summer. This fellowship was for teachers like me who had taught for a number of years and needed a new spark for continuing our teaching careers. I read over the application and the ideas for projects, which would be funded with $7,500. One of the examples mentioned travel to domestic locations to study literature and history.

I talked over the program with my family and Margie as well as my principal. Other teachers told me that the grants were very competitive and receiving one on my first try was a long shot. I wrote up my idea, outlining my plan of traveling through eight states, journaling, and sending postcards to my students. Not expecting any success, I went ahead and mailed in my application. Two months later, I learned my project was one of eighty selected from hundreds of proposals. Margie was so excited for me, and I was swept up in the local publicity, celebrations with the staff, and enthusiasm from my family.

Then, reality hit me. I was going to be traveling! All alone! For an entire month! How would I find my way around? What if I got lost? Where would I stay? I had just won this fellowship for teacher creativity, and I was reluctant to take the first step of the journey. Over the next three months, I never expressed my doubts about this summer adventure to anyone. I went through the motions of packing, preparing my car, and giving myself pep talks. I forced myself to set up an appointment with a travel agent, and we spent long hours booking hotels near the sites I wished to visit.

With a smile on the outside and fear on the inside, I waved goodbye and hit the road. I arrived late in the night at the first hotel, in southern Missouri. I couldn't sleep. I seriously thought about getting back in the car and going back to Indiana with my head drooping down in shame. What was I doing when I decided to take Margie's advice about traveling? What did she see in me that I didn't see in myself?

I grabbed the books I had brought, the ones my third graders had read with me. The pioneers had experienced hardships, difficulties along the trail, and separation from family members just to explore new territory and make a better life. As for ungrateful me, I was trying to adjust to a hotel pillow and a lumpy mattress.

I opened a biography that Margie had given me before school was over. Inside the front cover was an inscription she had written:

"For the teachers and students at school, you are our feet, but we will go with you in spirit wherever you go!" If I couldn't travel using my own courage, I could at least give it a try, keeping in mind that those at school were counting on me.

I can't say that the fear left me altogether, but I rested that night and started on my travels the next morning with a new purpose in each step. Yes, I finished my adventure. I'm not sure the pioneers would have been proud of my navigational skills throughout the Midwest or my lack of a can-do attitude, but I met new friends along the way and continued using all I learned in my lengthy teaching career. Ever since that trip, I travel to unfamiliar locations and give presentations about my fellowship. My life changed due to a wise and creative teacher who gave some inspiring advice to this reluctant traveler.

— Glenda Ferguson —

24

I Could Never Do That

Strength will always be with you; you just have to find it.
~Ann-Marie Hevey

remember the conversation as if it occurred yesterday. My friend Betty was caring for her father-in-law during his terminal illness. He had moved in with them several months earlier when his cancer prevented him from living independently. Most of his physical care became her responsibility, although her husband helped as much as he could.

"I could never do what you're doing," I told her. "At least you're a nurse. You're used to caring for people like this. Not me."

"Never say never," she said, her voice quiet but reinforced with resolve. "When God calls you to a God-sized task, He gives you God-sized grace. But He does not give it ahead of time."

That sounded nice — even spiritual. But I knew better. God might indeed give me God-sized tasks, but I was certain it would not be *that* kind of task. Maybe someone else, but not me. It wasn't something I was equipped to do, and He and I both knew it.

Twenty years later, I found myself caring for my mother-in-law, Nan, at home during her battle with a host of illnesses. She suffered from heart disease, diabetes, lung cancer, and Alzheimer's disease. As her dementia worsened, it became a daily struggle to provide her care. My husband helped as much as possible, but many of her physical needs required the attention of a woman.

The burden of Nan's care was made heavier by the change in her nature. The sweetness that had characterized her disposition seemed to disappear in an instant. She became suspicious of our motives and actions. Anger permeated her every word. Her dementia prevented us from reasoning with her, and she soon retreated into a fantasy world where we could not follow even if we wanted to.

Our care for my husband's mother began as a labor of love, but it was quickly becoming an unmanageable weight. We needed grace and strength from a source other than our own efforts because our own efforts were wearing thin.

As difficult as this was for me, it was more painful for my husband to watch his mother transform from a gentle parent into a hostile stranger. We had agreed to look after her at home, but with each passing day, I wondered if we would be able to keep our commitment. The strain of caring for her began to affect our marriage.

Then Betty's words, spoken so many years earlier, came rushing back. "When God calls you to a God-sized task, He gives you God-sized grace. But He never gives it ahead of time."

If there were ever a period when my husband and I needed the ability to handle a situation bigger than ourselves, it was then. I asked God to pour out His grace on us and to give us an extra measure of His patience and strength. Most of all, I asked Him to help me see this stranger who was my mother-in-law through His eyes.

I won't pretend life became easy overnight. Nan's physical and mental health continued to deteriorate. The demands of her care intensified. We were exhausted, yet somehow each day our strength was equal to the task.

More importantly, I began to see this difficult situation from Nan's perspective. As frustrating as these circumstances were for me, it was even more so for my mother-in-law. Her own mind had become her enemy. Past and present often collided without warning. She didn't know who or what she could trust. The result was constant fear and confusion.

My heart ached for her. We could not give her physical healing, but we could surround her with love — the one constant in her bewildering world.

Once again, I thought of my words spoken in such determined haste decades earlier. Love a stranger—a hostile stranger? I could never do that. I was partially right. I could never do that… in my own strength. But, by God's grace, I could become the vessel through whom His love would be poured over her.

As I surrendered to loving someone who was no longer able to express love to us, something unexpected happened. I learned, in a tangible way, the true meaning of unconditional love. I was reminded of God's love for me, especially when I am unlovable—and I don't have dementia to blame! And I realized that the truest form of love is expressed when the other person is most unlovable.

Some weeks were easier than others. Most days found me clinging to the Lord for all I needed to help Nan feel safe and secure. Despite the fact that neither people nor possessions were familiar to her, I could still meet her most desperate need. Through total dependence on someone greater than myself, I could wrap her in love—both God's love and ours.

We were privileged to care for my mother-in-law until she left Earth for a better place. Through it all, I realized the Lord had, indeed, given me God-sized grace for a God-sized task.

— Ava Pennington —

25

Do Something About It Every Day

When you do the things in the present that you can see,
you are shaping the future that you are yet to see.
~Idowu Koyenikan, Wealth for All

After a very happy childhood and young adulthood, I encountered some setbacks: failed relationships, career and money problems, and a life-threatening illness. With support from my family and friends, I stumbled through a tough year. By my thirty-first birthday, I could see the light at the end of the tunnel. I was thankful and grateful, but I was feeling quite vulnerable. My old confidence had yet to return. But then I met a man who would change my life. With his encouragement and support, I pushed through and completed the work necessary to earn my master's degree. By the time I marched up to get my diploma, I was newly married and ready to take on the world.

We had many choices open to us, so we decided to relocate to be closer to my husband's son. I was excited about the prospect of starting our lives together in a new place, but I was anxious about getting a job. He was able to transfer with his current employer, but I was not. So I whined to him, "I really need to get a job in my field."

What he said in response was stunning in its simplicity: "Do something about it every day."

Not "Fix your resume," or "Call thirty people," or "Go to the career center at school." None of the old standards. Oh, doing those things would certainly be a good investment in time. But they are part of the reason why finding a job is so daunting—the tasks themselves are daunting. So, what is *not* daunting? Doing something about it every day. "Something" can be as small as making a list, telling one person you are looking for a job, or deciding which font to use on your resume. (Never use comic sans.) Each of these little activities can really add up toward solving a problem or achieving a goal.

As I reflect on his advice, I realize that part of the reason it changed my life is the spirit in which it was given. My husband was older than me, and he had lots of experience. He had changed jobs, changed careers, been self-employed, been retired, and returned to the workforce after retirement. One could say that he was an expert in job changing. But he didn't try to fix my situation. His advice showed me that he cared about me. He recognized my anxiety, and he showed his love and support. But he also showed that he trusted me to know what I needed to do to accomplish this goal for myself.

It freed me from having to instantly do everything on my long list. It even encouraged me to try a few things that weren't on the list. Perhaps it was one of these things that made the difference. I was much less anxious. I was able to relax and enjoy the anticipation of moving to a new place and starting a new life. I found a great job in my field at a location an hour away from my stepson and his family. We started our new life full of optimism.

Do something about it every day. It is so simple, which is why it is such great advice. It has all the elements of a smart goal. It is specific, measurable, achievable, relevant, and time-bound. So why didn't anyone ever share it with me before? I'm not sure. But I have passed it along to many others. And, each time I do, I remember my dear husband.

—Jan Comfort—

26

The Long Way Around

Look well into thyself; there is a source of strength
which will always spring up if thou wilt always look.
~Marcus Aurelius, Meditations

I stared at the steep, rocky climb ahead and knew I was finished. Even the fresh bear tracks pressed in the recent snow couldn't entice me to take one more step. I stared at my husband and felt too weary for tears.

"Leave me. Get help. Come back for me. I can't move my legs," I said as I rubbed my pregnant belly. "My pants are soaked. I think my water broke."

Earlier that day, my husband David and I had set off on a short trip with my brother-in-law and a friend of ours who would act as our guide. Our friend said it would be an easy two-hour loop through the Carson-Iceberg Wilderness between Yosemite and Lake Tahoe to see the rare Paiute Cutthroat Trout in its natural habitat above Llewellyn Falls. We couldn't wait. Although I was seven months pregnant and huge, I'd spent spring, summer, and early fall hiking with my husband in the mountains while he reveled in catch-and-release fly-fishing. I'd felt confident I'd have no trouble on the hike.

Right off, we found ourselves traveling over a snow-covered ridge, and the terrain seemed rougher than average to me. When two hours came and went, it seemed our friend had made a huge mistake. We had not reached the falls, but he insisted it wasn't much farther. Accompanied by snow squalls and howling winds, we continued on our way.

By the time we reached Llewellyn Falls, it was late and we were pooped. But not too tired to enjoy the thrill as we gazed upon the iridescent pinks, greens, and copper colors of this beautiful fish swimming in its native habitat. As late as it was, we could only rest and enjoy the scenery for a short while in order to make it back to the car before dark. Our friend assured us that we'd find the rest of the hike easy and short. But it wasn't. It was the steepest terrain we'd faced so far.

Already weary, as I climbed my huge, swollen belly felt like a ton of cement. It was so steep that each step I took crammed my legs into my stomach. My legs were cramping as we ascended and my knees were in agony on the descent. We thought the climb would be the last, only to find another grueling peak ahead of us. With darkness upon us, my legs reached the point where I couldn't move them at all.

My husband told the other two to keep moving; we'd follow shortly. He took my hands in his and squeezed. "I'm not leaving you. It's almost dark. We need to keep moving. I'll help you."

"I can't," I said as the tears pooled in my eyes.

"You can. Just take one tiny step at a time. Don't look at the mountain. Keep your eyes focused on your feet and on me."

David never let go of my hands as he continued to encourage me. "Just one tiny step," he repeated as we climbed together, my legs in agony.

Some of my steps were so minuscule that we hardly moved at all, but I clung to the power in his words. Eventually, we did make it over the ridge, grateful to find that it was the last formidable obstacle in our way. By the time we reached the car, we had been gone over eight hours and would learn later that our friend had led us on one of the most difficult and longest loops through those mountains.

Early the next morning, at the doctor's office, I learned that my water had not broken. The baby was safe and sound, which was a huge relief.

Almost thirty-two years have passed since that hike, and David's words have continued to be a lifeline for me. Although I am usually an optimist, during those times when I feel paralyzed I remind myself that I don't need to conquer my mountains all at once. It might take me a little longer, but one tiny step at a time will eventually get me where I need to be.

—Jill Burns—

Chapter
4

Get On with Life

27

Choosing Joy over Grief

The pain passes, but the beauty remains.
~Renoir

When I drove my sister from Michigan to Arizona to start her junior year of college, I didn't realize it would be the last time I'd see her alive. Four months later, when she was traveling back to the Midwest for winter break with four of her college friends, the driver of her car fell asleep. The car went off the road and rolled over several times. Miraculously, no other vehicles were involved, and her friends suffered only minor cuts and bruises. My sister, however, wasn't so fortunate. She was thrown from the car and died within minutes.

As a nineteen-year-old away at college myself, I was already dealing with my own confusion and uncertainty about where my life was headed. I had thought I wanted to become an engineer, but the related courses I had taken left me wholly uninspired. Now, with the emotional pain and struggle from my sister's sudden death, I knew leaving my family to return to school hours from home would only heighten my despair and confusion. Yet, when my parents expressed their belief that Connie would've wanted me to return to college (she was going to be the first in our family to earn a college degree), I knew they were right.

During the first semester following her death, I felt like I was navigating through a personal fog in a rudderless boat. I couldn't say I was *off* course because I had *no* course. I was aimlessly drifting, fearful of what lay beyond the horizon. My grief consumed me as I continually questioned how the college courses I was taking would affect my life or whether I even wanted to continue in college. And, more important, I missed my sister. Born just ten months apart, she had always been there for me. One time, our younger brother rushed home from the playground and shouted as he ran into the house, "Some big guy stole Marvin's bike, and now he's beating him up!" My sister, who had been in the back yard sunbathing, sprinted three blocks down the middle of the street in her bikini, arriving at the scene before my mother in her car or even the police! Yep, my sister always had my back.

When I began my junior year, I still hadn't declared my major, but I signed up for one particular class for personal reasons: "Death Education and Suicide Prevention." And, despite the class title, or perhaps because of it, the professor did a wonderful job of making the subject matter interesting and, in some instances, even humorous.

One day, the professor had a guest speaker come to our class. I have no recollection about the topic of the presentation. I don't remember what the speaker looked like. I don't even remember if the person was male or female. I only remember one thing about that day. At some point during the presentation, the speaker said, "Joy shared is joy increased. Grief shared is grief diminished." The speaker explained the saying by breaking it into parts, saying, "Joy shared is joy increased. If you don't believe it, go into a closet and tell yourself a joke. It isn't funny unless you share it with others." I'm sure the speaker spoke more on the topic, but he or she could've started speaking a foreign language or singing, and I wouldn't have noticed. I was locked in on "Joy shared is joy increased. Grief shared is grief diminished."

I silently repeated this message to myself over and over again, trying to absorb these words into my being. I instantly felt that the speaker's purpose for being in that classroom was specifically to tell me this. A strange feeling stirred inside me. Perhaps it was my sister's spirit connecting with me through this speaker and this message, telling me that it was time for me to move forward — that she wanted me to be happy and live my life to the fullest.

After that day in class, I began journaling about my sister. The professor had recommended journaling about death, loss and grieving, but, until then, my heartache got in the way of putting pen to paper. Now, my painful emotions, joyful memories of my sister, and questions about death — and her life — began pouring out of me. I had never sought out college professors during their office hours before, but I started dropping in to talk with my "Death Ed" professor, rarely for academic reasons. And, over time, with help from a college professor, a compelling guest speaker and a timely, poignant message, my grief diminished.

So, I finally knew what I wanted to do with my life. I wanted to help others cope with their grief and despair. That same semester, I took my first psychology course. That course resulted in me declaring a psychology major. And that psychology major eventually led to a master's degree, which then morphed into a career as a psychotherapist. And I like to think, with the help from my sister and two people who showed up at a key point in my life, I've helped many others overcome their personal struggles, lessen their grief, and learn about the power of joy.

— Marvin Yanke —

28

The Power of Yes

Make the most of today. Get interested in something.
Shake yourself awake. Develop a hobby. Let the
winds of enthusiasm sweep through you.
Live today with gusto.
~Dale Carnegie

My friend Laura thought I would enjoy pickleball and invited me to play on her homemade court. "Yes, I'll give it a try," I responded when she mentioned she even had an extra paddle for me to use.

We volleyed at the end of her cul-de-sac after sweeping the fall leaves off the chalk lines while her mobile net swayed in the brisk New England breeze. And I loved everything about it, from hearing the *bonk* of the whiffle ball hitting my ping-pong-like racquet to practicing short shots called dinks.

She taught me the basics of the sport, which is typically played as a foursome, including how to apply the double-bounce rule, how to stay out of the box around the net called the kitchen, and how to observe the unofficial no-sorry rule.

"There's no saying you're sorry in pickleball," Laura said emphatically. She went on to explain that while nobody intends to hit the ball out of bounds or into the net, it's natural to want to apologize to your teammate when it happens during a game. Since you can only score when your side is serving, it's even worse when your serve goes awry. "Everyone knows it's not intentional, so there really is no need to apologize. It's part of the game," she said, knowing I would likely feel pressure to do well when playing with people I didn't know.

And she was right. For someone who doesn't like letting people down, the no-sorry mantra was a healthy reminder that we all make mistakes in life. Since I'm usually pretty hard on myself, it's good for me to remember that we can't always anticipate our opponent's next move or make a winning shot. It's part of the human experience to make missteps and drop the ball; it's what we learn along the way that helps us grow.

Who would have thought that a forgiving sport I started playing right before the pandemic began would rescue me at a time when I needed it most?

I had lost my longtime boyfriend, Robert, to brain cancer the previous year and I was still grieving when the pandemic hit. Since we had been active members of our local dance community, I missed having a fun, recreational and social hobby almost as much as I missed him.

During the lockdown, I couldn't help rehashing some of our more stressful moments, and I routinely analyzed what I could have said or done differently. Robert had been in a hospice facility for almost three weeks, and I thought I had made it a point to tell him everything I wanted to while he was still conscious, including how much he meant to me.

So, I was extremely disappointed when I still felt regret for things left unsaid after he was gone. This added frustration to the weight of my grief and began to adversely affect my sleep.

I finally decided to write him a letter to anchor the thoughts swirling around in my mind. It helped a bit, and I've continued to add numerous postscripts over time. I also spoke to a professional grief counselor for several weeks who validated my feelings and allowed me to release some pent-up emotions.

She reminded me to be gentle with myself, to relinquish having specific expectations, and to practice being more mindful. When she asked if I had any hobbies or interests to help create balance in my life, I was grateful to be able to say that I had taken up pickleball.

Pickleball gives me something to look forward to, and it helps keep my mind occupied and my body active. I was pleased to discover there are eight outdoor pickleball courts at a park less than one mile from my condo, too.

I recruited my retired friend Ken to play in the evenings on the lighted courts. His tennis background made him a natural, and soon we were playing every Wednesday against Dave and Cathie, a couple we met at the courts.

While a pickleball court is smaller than a tennis court, the sport still provides a great workout, and we were all glad to be getting fresh air and good exercise. We also liked the fact that the game is more about strategy and shot placement than power. No wonder many of the older set have taken to this sport.

After I'd been playing for about a year, my town introduced a six-week Saturday afternoon social league. Each week, we were assigned a random teammate and played against all the other four randomly assigned teams that day. As a result, I connected with several like-minded players who were also interested in meeting new people and playing for fun. I knew I was in good company when we went out to celebrate the end of the league at the local yacht club and decided to continue playing as a group every week.

We even found a place to play indoors during the snowy winter months. The nights I played were the highlights of my week because I was now working remotely fulltime. I would have felt pretty isolated without my new pickleball community. I relished the friendships, camaraderie and laughter — not to mention the food and music we often added to Friday-night play.

Now I participate in two different groups, usually playing three to four times per week. We use a scheduling app to keep track of who is playing on any given day. And I can hardly pull into the parking lot without seeing someone I know whose life has been positively affected by the sport.

Playing pickleball is the way I met sweet blue-eyed Ed, who con-founded his doctors by mending his heart issue through the consistent cardio exercise of the game. Now we're enjoying a fun and fulfilling off-court relationship and looking forward to a future together.

I've learned that answering a simple invitation with one small word — yes — can change my life in unforeseeably big ways.

— Kay L. Campbell —

29

Why Didn't I Realize That Sooner?

To forgive is to set a prisoner free and
discover that the prisoner was you.
~Louis B. Smedes

I grew up with a single mother who had plenty of demons of her own to wrangle, including addiction, anger issues, and depression. She was abusive to me in just about every way that a parent can abuse a child, from physical to verbal and emotional abuse (the worst by far for me) and even sexual abuse when she "loaned" me out for the night to her sleazy lover's buddy who was crashing at our house, drunk.

As any child would, I tried harder. I wanted so desperately to be worthy of her love. She was the only family I had, my only security in a scary world. I kept telling myself that if I could just become more this, or better at that, she would finally love me, and all would be well. Needless to say, it never worked. And believing that it was my fault she didn't love me because I was not good enough to be loved was actually part of the abuse she inflicted on me my entire life.

Once I was in my forties, married with two children, I started seeing a wonderful counselor who helped me work through these issues and begin to understand the abuse for what it was. It took more than two years of very hard, emotionally taxing work, but I finally accepted that my mother was the one to blame, not me, and the best thing I could do was to stand up for myself and refuse to accept any further abuse from her. So, a few months later, when she was yelling and screaming at me and calling me vile names on the phone, I simply hung up—and vowed that I was done at last. I would no longer allow her to treat me like the worthless piece of trash she always told me I was.

I told my counselor what I had done, and he told me the next step was to try and forgive her for all she had done. My reaction was one of pure shock. I asked him, "You just told me I did the right thing by refusing to accept more abusive treatment. Now you're telling me to go back for more?" The words he said next will stay with me for the rest of my life as the best advice I have ever received and the most powerful lesson I have ever learned.

He said, "Forgiveness is not the same as permission. You can and should forgive her, for your own good. You need to move on without bitterness or regrets. You need to let it go. You will never fully achieve that unless you forgive her. But that does not mean you have to let her back into your life or give her access to you in any way. Forgiveness does not equal permission."

Wow. I had never once even considered that. I pondered it, prayed about it, wrote in my journal about it… and weeks went by. Weeks that turned into months. And then, one afternoon, as I was out for a walk, I suddenly realized that I felt free for the first time in my entire life. Free, lighthearted, and truly happy. And it was because I had forgiven her. I had allowed myself to feel that, despite all she did to me for more than forty years of my life, I was okay. The abuse was not okay; *I* was okay. And I could let it all go.

This literally changed my life. Now, I can think of the few good moments we shared in my childhood. I can even pray for her happiness and wellbeing. But, other than that, I have let it all go. I have a wonderfully blessed, joyous life with my husband and children that is completely untainted by my own suffering because I have healed. And forgiveness was a huge piece of that healing. Forgiveness, not permission.

—Stephanie Schiano Wallace—

30

See How Much Is Left

If you look the right way, you can see
that the whole world is a garden.
~Frances Hodgson Burnett, The Secret Garden

Two years ago, my life changed dramatically. The things that happen to "other people" were suddenly happening to me.

My seemingly healthy twenty-one-year-old son was suddenly transported by ambulance to the nearest university hospital and underwent life-saving surgery that would leave him without his large intestine.

No, not his spleen. Not his appendix. Not his tonsils, for goodness' sake. Nothing that the body can easily live without. No, it was his *entire* large intestine.

And, let me tell you, life changes drastically when you lose something like that.

Many hospitalizations followed. No sooner had he recovered from one surgery, we were back having another. And then, once the surgeries were over, the adjustment came: trying to live life in this new state. Many hospitalizations would come from that, too. One time, his weight plummeted to 110 pounds (he started this process close to 190), and we truly almost lost him. Had it not been for the intervention of a PICC feeding line, we would have. A year to the day before, my son had been out playing basketball with his buddies. Now, I was looking down at his shriveled body in a large hospital bed being kept alive by a milk-like substance being pumped directly into him.

I was scared. I didn't want to lose my son. I kept it together at the time, of course. I kept putting one foot in front of the other and doing everything that needed to be done to keep my son with me. That's all that mattered.

Soon after, we came to understand that the life-saving surgery was not the cure we hoped it would be. What had been diagnosed as ulcerative colitis, a disease that would end with the removal of the colon, was later deemed to be a severe case of Crohn's disease, which would affect the entirety of his digestive tract. A disease that had no cure.

My son would have a lifelong fight ahead of him — on top of everything he had already been through.

At some point, I stopped being scared. That fear started to morph into something else: anger.

Oh, yes, I was mad. And, once that anger set in, there was no letting it go. It was behind everything I did. Every word that came from my mouth had an underlying tone of anger. There was the question that everyone asks when something like this happens — when you have to watch the person you love more than anything go through so much pain and loss. The question we all ask when we don't understand.

WHY?

I'm not sure that question will ever be answered. None of us has the capacity to understand why things happen the way they do.

But I do remember vividly the moment my anger started to ease.

One of the things I did to try to maintain some semblance of sanity through all my son's hospitalizations was to read. I've always been the type to grab a book when my own life gets too heavy so that I can quietly fade away into someone else's. Feeling a fictional character's pain and loss is easier than feeling my own. Once the last page is turned, it's over. There's an ending. As the book finishes, so do their troubles.

For many nights, as I sat by his bedside, I'd have a book in my lap. What little sleep I did get was fitful, interrupted by the nurses coming in to check on him or just by my own scattered brain. So, I'd fill the hours with books.

And I'll never forget when I read the line that somehow changed me. That line has stuck with me to this day and comes back into my mind as often as I need it to.

The book was *The Storyteller* by Jodi Picoult. In one part, a woman is remembering when she walked in on her grandmother as she was coming out of a bath. She had recently undergone a mastectomy. The woman remembers her childhood self seeing that for the first time and recounts it as follows:

> "It's missing," I said.
> My grandmother smiled... "Yes," she said. "But see how much of me is left?"

I remember reading that like it was yesterday. Before I even had time to fully process what I was feeling, I had to lay down the book and wipe away my tears. That sentence felt like a punch—a good punch but a punch nonetheless. Here I was, mad at the world because so much of my son was missing. So much of his life was not going to be the same. So many of his plans were derailed, and all because of what was taken from him. What was "missing."

And yet.

See how much of me is left?

In that very hospital where I sat, all around me at any given moment, mothers and fathers were saying final goodbyes to their children. To their loved ones. To the ones who lost everything, not just a piece of themselves.

See how much of me is left?

I still had my child. He still had his life. He was here. Right here in front of me.

See how much of me is left?

So very much was left. He has years ahead of him. He'll have treatments to undergo, sure. But he'll be here to undergo them. Life will go on. He's *here*.

My baby is *here*.

See how much of me is left?

This has become a mantra for me in many ways. I've applied it to situations other than the one with my son. Anytime I lose something,

I do my best to remember what's left — to focus not on what's gone but on what remains.

This simple sentence in a novel somehow redirected my thoughts.

Of course, I'm human. Sometimes, I fail and lose a little time focusing on what we don't have anymore. But I always climb back out of it. And I do so with those words on my mind. I look at my son and see a warrior. A strong fighter who has battled in his own war for almost three years now and is still so full of life. So full of hope and a future. I look at my baby, and I hear those words coming from him over and over again.

See how much of me is left?

Yes, I do, son. And there are no words for how grateful I am for that. Go out there and show the world why you're still here. And know that your mother will be smiling in the background, filled with so much pride and gratitude for how much of you is left.

— Melissa Edmondson —

31

Falling Down

*Our greatest glory is, not in never falling,
but in rising every time we fall.*
~Oliver Goldsmith

My dad struggled to get up and out of the recliner. It was too soft for him. He used his arm muscles and pushed, twisted and turned to angle his upper body into a position so that his limp legs would follow. He reached for the arm of the wheelchair, but the brakes were not set. My seventy-year-old "rocket scientist" father slid down to the carpet with an undignified thud.

I tried not to gasp at what had just happened as my brother quickly came to my dad's aid, reached under his arms and lifted him up into the wheelchair. My dad settled in with a sigh.

"Daddy, what do you think about when you fall down?" I asked him.

My dad looked up at me with his steady, clear blue eyes.

"I think about getting back up again."

Over the years, I have thought about my dad's words many times. That simple phrase was, hands down, the best piece of advice I ever received.

"I think about getting back up again."

It doesn't really matter what happened to me nor what will happen to me. What matters is how I react to what happened. What will happen *next* matters so much more than what hand of cards this life has dealt me.

My dad began to work at age sixteen to help support his single mother and two sisters. He was in the Army when he met my mom, who was a nurse during the war, on a blind date. They married and had four children. My dad built his first house with his own hands. When his estranged father reentered his life many years later, he welcomed him into our family with open arms. Grandpa even lived with us the last few years of his life.

My dad worked as a "rocket scientist" and corrosion expert as a civilian for the Navy most of his career. As a chemist, he specialized in developing customized coatings to mitigate corrosion events. Often, the Navy sent my dad out to troubleshoot rust problems on battleships and aircraft landing gear stationed around the world. He helped formulate the chemical compounds that coated the heat shield of spacecraft capsules to guard against burn-up during reentry to Earth's atmosphere.

Our garage looked like a scientific laboratory. It was furnished with workbenches filled with beakers, compounds, centrifuge equipment, Bunsen burners and the like. Dad went to work Monday through Friday, but Saturdays were usually spent with him working in the garage, writing down notes and doing experimental work.

My dad was strong and healthy, and he worked several years past the typical retirement age. Then, one day, he started walking with a limp. Then, at work, he fell down. And then he fell down again. And again. He finally went to the doctor after my family's urging.

Late-onset multiple sclerosis. Dad knew he couldn't work much longer and that, in his case, he would get progressively worse. He retired with little fanfare and decided to make a plan and goals. My mom and dad loved traveling in the past, so now they went to Europe, Hawaii, and on cruises to Mexico and Alaska. Dad planned the trip of a lifetime to Australia, but they never got to go. However, in the three years after Dad was diagnosed, they made many happy memories.

At that time, Dad could still walk a little, and my mom purchased new, smooth dress shoes for him. She waxed the bottom of his shoes with a candle so they could glide on carpets, keeping Dad upright and mobile for as long as possible. We bought Dad cool-looking canes and then a walker, along with the wheelchair. Dad faced each new obstacle with courage and strength.

Dad kept his mind sharp. He loved when family came to visit, especially when the grandkids came over for an afternoon. He was an avid reader, and one year he decided to learn Spanish. He read his English-to-Spanish dictionary from cover to cover. He watched the Spanish-speaking telenovelas (soap operas) and learned to be quite fluent. He was also totally immersed in the dramatics of the characters.

Dad also kept his humor sharp. He will always be one of the funniest people I have ever known. He could keep any tense situation manageable by the right remark to defuse anger. Dad would always come up with just the right thing to say. If someone in the family was mad, and Dad said something funny, and they angrily retorted, "Dad, that's not funny!" Dad would say, "Come on, that's a little bit funny!"

"I think about getting back up again." It doesn't matter so much about what has already happened to me. There are always people in life who have it better than me or worse than me. That's not as important as what I do now. The future is the only uncharted ground I have.

Dad was a funny, strong man with a sharp intellect who taught me many things. He was an overcomer. He used his brain when his brawn ran out. He was a deep thinker, and I like to believe I picked up some of those traits.

Dad's been gone for many years now. My now-adult son looks like him and has inherited my dad's sense of humor. I hope I have instilled in my son the importance of getting back up again in all the tough situations that life will offer. After all, it doesn't matter if we fall down; we all will fall down in some way. What truly matters is getting back up again. And again.

— Laura McKenzie —

32

Heeding Her Words

*Darkness cannot drive out darkness; only light can do
that. Hate cannot drive out hate; only love can do that.*
~Martin Luther King, Jr.

The answer to a significant problem I'd been struggling with
for years appeared right before my eyes in *Chicken Soup for the
Soul: The Forgiveness Fix.* In her story "The Clean Record" L.Y.
Levand shares how she resolved a similar dilemma. Her advice
enabled me to let go of the past and recover a loving relationship with
the mother of my great-grandson.

Though the author's story is about her strained relationship with
her mother-in-law, her quandary was surprisingly similar to mine.
She was keeping a record of her mother-in-law's wrongs, including
perceived wrongs.

When my grandson's wife decided to leave the marriage to pursue
a relationship with someone else, I couldn't forgive her for choosing
him over her husband and their young child. That, coupled with
comments she'd made blaming our family instead of accepting her
responsibility, provoked me to focus solely on her wrongs.

Their sweet boy, my great-grandson, spent the majority of his
time in my care since his parents both held down full-time jobs. Over
time he began to spend more time with his mother on the weekends.
By the time he was ready to begin school, I could see how much he
loved his mother, and I knew she loved him as well. But I couldn't
get over what I considered her past wrongs — something I honestly

wanted to overcome.

Coincidentally, a couple of my friends had stories published in that *Chicken Soup for the Soul* book and I'd received a copy as a gift. I knew I'd found the solution to my dilemma the moment I read Ms. Levand's story.

The author shares words uttered by the Bible class teacher: "Love doesn't keep a record of wrongs." At that moment, she realized that was exactly what she had been doing regarding her mother-in-law. I definitely could relate to her story as it was what I was doing with my great-grandson's mother.

In an attempt to remedy the problem, Ms. Levand made a list on her computer of all the wrongs that had bothered her. One by one, she highlighted each wrong on the list, prayed about it, and then deleted it until the record was wiped clean.

That clean slate enabled her to put the reboot button on her relationship with her mother-in-law. She interacted with her without the overhang of past resentments, and that made it possible to appreciate her good qualities.

It was the best advice I could have read. Heeding her words, I immediately did the same thing to rid my mind and heart of every wrong I perceived that my great-grandson's mother had done in the past. Using my computer, I listed each wrong, highlighted it, and then deleted it to wipe the record clean.

It worked, and a huge weight was lifted from my shoulders!

I am now able to love and appreciate my great-grandson's mother, and accept that the things she did were not meant to hurt others. I also realized that I was not entirely blameless for the strain on our relationship. We may not always agree on everything, but that is fine.

She calls me Grandma, and I consider her one of my granddaughters. We see each other frequently and chat openly. Most importantly, my great-grandson is blessed to be loved by his mother, father, and a large extended family who respect and care about each other.

— Connie Kaseweter Pullen —

Do Something Small

Magic and mystery lies on the edge,
just outside the comfort zone.
~Amit Ray, Peace Bliss Beauty and Truth:
Living with Positivity

'**ve spent my life avoiding uncomfortable situations. I've always sought safety in the path of least resistance, opting for comfort, routine, and predictability.

A work-from-home mother of three, I wore my safety net as a cozy fleece blanket. My days were spent ushering backpack-laden children out the door each morning and then going about my routine. I'd check my e-mails, go to the same gym, shop at the same store, and walk the same neighborhood route. I'd work in the afternoons and have dinner on the table by 6:00.

One fall morning, I was out on a routine walk with a trusted friend. This woman is independent, brave, and capable. I often seek her out for advice, relying on her wisdom and level head. As we fell into a brisk pace together, I broached the subject of fear. I confided in her that I felt trapped, living a life of fear. I knew I was avoiding situations that pushed me out of my comfort zone and had witnessed how I was creating my own padded prison. I admitted that I felt trapped by my commitment to familiarity but didn't know how to be brave and branch out.

The advice she gave me changed my life. "Start small," she said. "Starting today, do something every day that terrifies you."

Knowing that something in my life needed to shift, I took her advice and committed to embracing fear. It began with making conversation with the cashier at my regular grocery store and deviating from my usual order at my favorite lunch spot. I gave myself permission to explore new and intimidating opportunities.

My profession as a health coach typically centered around working with individual clients in the comfort and safety of my home office. When approached by the PTA to do a presentation on healthy eating for the school board, I took a breath. Every part of me wanted to say no. They were asking me to put on an entire presentation in front of my peers with slides and handouts! Just the thought of it quickened my pulse and made my stomach turn. But I'd come to recognize those as signals not to shy away from but as a time to say yes to growth, learning, and overcoming my own limitations.

My venture to seek out fear transformed me into a person who said yes. Yes, I will give a guest sermon at church. Yes, I'll teach a corporate seminar on mindfulness. Yes, I will update my resume and apply for this new job position. My wise friend's advice became my life's mantra. It motivated me to look past my impulses and to be intentional with my thoughts and actions. In the years to come, following this advice upended my life and opened doors I didn't even know had been closed.

Years of practicing being brave meant that bravery became easier and easier. My resilience strengthened, and I felt confident and capable for the first time in my life. This newfound bravery of mine was challenged one day when my husband, ever the dreamer, presented me with the real possibility of moving to a foreign country. For years, he had dreamed of moving our family overseas to pursue a different avenue for his career. "No, thank you," I'd always said. "I'm fine staying right here." Held back by fear, never before would I have considered taking this giant leap of faith. But, this was the new me who didn't back down from a challenge. I was capable of anything.

"A position has opened up in Turkey," my husband told me. "Should I put in for it?"

Heart racing, palms sweating, and stomach churning were once signs that signified danger. Now, they were the signs I'd come to recognize as opportunity. My answer? "Yes."

I knew the moment I said it that we would be moving to Turkey.

Every day leading up to the moving trucks arriving was filled with opportunities to practice embracing fear. Fear of the what-ifs and unknowns. Fear of experiencing the new and saying goodbye to the old. Fear of failure, discomfort and pain. But what I had learned in my years of exercising bravery in the face of fear was that no matter what happened, I would be okay. Six months later, we unpacked our bags in our small city apartment and showed our children the view from their new bedroom window.

One year into our life abroad, the days are still exhilarating, complicated, beautiful and terrifying. Every day presents a new challenge and requirement to be brave. In a country where I don't speak the language, know the rules of the road, where to get the toilet paper I like or what an item on the menu is, I get to try and fail, feel fear and choose to be brave every single day.

Embracing, accepting and even seeking out opportunities that scare me has empowered me with the knowledge that I can do hard things. I have learned that regardless of my place in the world or the comfort of my surroundings, I will be okay. Fear is a teacher. It is a gift. Without it, I'd still be at my regular drive-through asking for the chicken sandwich instead of sitting in a café telling the waiter to "surprise me."

— Emily Rusch —

Chapter
5

Choose Your Battles

34

Loving or Right?

Choose your battles carefully. Peace is often far better
than proving someone wrong.
~Katrina Mayer

My friend Barbara waved at me from the other side of the park lawn as I pulled into the parking lot. I slid out of my truck, grabbed my lunch pail, and headed toward the picnic table where she sat.

Every few weeks, I met Barbara at the park on my lunch break, and I always looked forward to our conversations. Barbara volunteered for the non-profit I managed. At work, I taught her. But, in our friendship, she taught me. At twice my age, she had a lot of life experience to share. I was drawn to her gentle wisdom, grounded in our common faith.

This week, I'd had a conflict with my husband. Michael and I had only been married a few months, and we were still navigating newlywed life — discovering our flaws, learning to communicate, and adjusting to sharing a household. I told Barbara about the incident between bites of my sandwich.

"So, what do you think?" I asked.

Barbara pushed back a strand of wispy salt-and-pepper hair, pausing before she spoke. "I learned early on to let go of the need to be right. It changed my marriage."

I propped my elbows on the table and rested my chin in my hands, letting her words sink in. It wasn't the answer I'd expected nor the one I wanted to hear. If only it were that easy.

I had an opportunity to implement Barbara's advice later that same week. I failed miserably.

On Thursday morning, as I went through my morning routine in the bathroom, Michael appeared over my shoulder wearing the plaid flannel shirt that I liked. He wrapped his arms around me from behind and looked over my shoulder at me in the mirror.

"I love your brown eyes," he said.

I brushed a few more strokes on my teeth and then spit in the sink. My eyes weren't brown. How could my husband not know the color of my eyes?

The words leaped out before I could stop them. "Thanks, but they're hazel."

I saw Michael's face tighten. He released his embrace and reached for the hair gel. I remembered Barbara's words and immediately regretted my thoughtless response. If only my mouth had still been full of toothpaste. Maybe then I would have swallowed those words instead of speaking. My husband had been trying to pay me a compliment, and instead of receiving it, I had corrected him. In a matter of seconds, the atmosphere had changed, filling the air with tension.

I walked down the hall to the bedroom to escape the guilt. Pulling a sweater from the closet, I slipped into the sleeves. But it didn't warm me from the chill in the air. If I was right, why did I feel so wrong? In the past, my pride would have prevented me from apologizing. I would have brushed off the uncomfortable feeling and pressed forward. But not this time.

I slunk back to the bathroom and leaned against the doorframe. Michael was running his fingers through his hair, smoothing down his dark curls. I crossed my arms.

"I'm sorry. You were trying to say something nice, and I shut you down. Will you forgive me?" The words felt foreign and forced.

Michael rinsed his hands under the faucet, swiped them on the towel, and then pulled me into a hug. "Yeah. Thanks for saying that."

That was the first of many apologies I would make. I apologized more in that first year of our marriage than in my whole life previously. I'd learned to be polite in public, but Michael experienced the real me — the one who cared more about accuracy than his feelings. Letting go of the need to be right was a hard habit to kick. Sometimes, I'd get defensive over some insignificant detail before I even realized it. In my job, it was important to get things right. I dealt with numbers and words and other people's safety, so accuracy was of the utmost importance.

But it went deeper than that. When I held Michael and others to the same standards of perfection that I imposed on myself, they experienced judgment instead of grace. I didn't know how to extend that grace to myself, let alone others.

When Michael held up the mirror, I faced a choice: Did I want to be loving or right? Often, I couldn't be both. I didn't want my desire for correctness to come at the expense of my relationships. So, I started learning to bite my tongue when the urge arose. When Michael remembered a story differently than I did, I didn't correct him in front of others. When he got a date wrong, I let it slide. When he misspoke or mispronounced a word, I just smiled. When he made mistakes, I tried not to point them out unless necessary.

Michael and I are no longer newlyweds. I credit Barbara's advice, in part, for our lasting marriage. Have I let go of the need to be right? No. Every day I still fight the urge and face the choice — loving or right? I like to think that now, more often than before, I choose love.

— Sarah Barnum —

35

But It's Only...

*You never get people's fuller attention
than when you're listening to them.*
~Robert Brault, rbrault.blogspot.com

I was exasperated with my sixteen-year-old son Anthony. I stormed out of the house, letting the door slam shut behind me. Standing on the front porch, hands on hips, I sighed deeply. I saw my elderly neighbor, Clara, on her knees working in her flower beds. Shaking my head in frustration, seeking sympathy, I stalked across the street.

Clara glanced up at me, an amused little smile tugging at her lips. "Anthony again?" she asked. "You look madder than a wet hen." She giggled. "But I can't say that I've ever seen a wet hen."

I sighed and sat down in the grass beside her. "It's his hair again," I said, shaking my head and frowning. "Have you seen him? All that mass of tangled curls hanging down over his shoulders! But just mention a haircut, and he gets that same stubborn look in his eyes that I've seen a million times before, and I know that the argument is over before I get a half-dozen words out. And his clothes! Why does he have to wear black all the time?"

Clara glanced up at me, a small smile tugging at her lips. I dropped down on the grass beside her and continued my indignant rant. "If we aren't arguing about his hair, we're arguing about his clothes, or his messy room, or his loud music."

I looked at Clara, and that little smile was now a full-blown grin.

She chuckled softly and patted my knee. "It's only hair, Liz. It isn't drugs. It isn't alcohol. It isn't gang membership." She took my chin in her hand and turned my face to hers. She spoke slowly, emphasizing each word. "It's… only… hair."

The smile slipped from her face, and her eyes grew serious. "I learned many years ago when I became a widow with three young kids that I had to put everything in perspective if I were to survive. I learned how to say, 'But it's only.' But it's only a bad day. Tomorrow will be better. But it's only another late bill. I'll catch up when I can. But it's only a dead battery. My old car can last a few more years. But it's only a bad day my boss is having. He'll be in a better mood tomorrow." She nodded her head emphatically. "You get it, don't you, honey? Everybody has enough heartache and trouble in their lives without wasting time and energy on the 'it's only' things that come their way."

I walked back across the street to my house with Clara's words echoing in my head and settling into my heart. I went into the kitchen and baked a batch of brownies, Anthony's favorite treat. By the time the brownies had cooled, Clara's words had become my new creed.

I carried the brownies to Anthony's room where I was greeted as usual by a firmly closed door. I rapped gently. "Can I come in, honey?"

I heard a low groan, followed by mumbled words. "Not if you're going to harp on my hair again."

I pushed the door open and held out the brownies. "Not one word. I promise."

He eyed the plate of brownies greedily, but there was still a glint of suspicion in his eyes. "Not one word about my hair?" He looked at me challengingly.

"It's only hair," I said, holding the brownies out to him. "And it's *your* hair. Not mine."

He managed a grin as he took the plate of brownies. "That's what I've been trying to tell you."

"Yes, you have," I said. "But I thought that you were just putting up an argument. Now I realize that you really didn't want to fight with me. You just wanted me to hear the point you were making."

I reached out and brushed his hair back off his forehead. "Honey,

I finally heard you."

Anthony shot me the best smile he had given me in a long time. "Thanks for finally hearing me, Mom. And thanks for the brownies."

Now, whenever I feel a frown pulling my face down, or feel anger or impatience boiling up inside me, I pause and ask myself: Is this just an "it's only" moment? My life has been much more peaceful and less plagued with stress and frustration since I took Clara's words to heart. And, best of all, it certainly improved my relationship with Anthony. Now that I have learned to let the "it's only" situations go, he is more willing to listen to me when I have a legitimate concern. Being focused on the things that really matter has led to an unexpected bonus: Anthony has actually come to me for advice on a few occasions now that he knows my judgment isn't clouded by trivial issues. I have taken advantage of these situations to teach him about the "but it's only" moments that cause us so much anxiety and frustration but resolve nothing.

—Elizabeth A. Atwater—

36

Be What's Missing

He who refreshes others will himself be refreshed.
~Proverbs 11:25

Where was that cashier? Irritated, I glanced at my watch. I barely had enough time to eat my tacos—if I ever got them—and then dash back to the hospital where I worked.

Once again, I'd cut it too close, trying to get too much done in too little time. But I could still make it back to work in time if people would cooperate. I looked around the nearly empty fast-food restaurant but the cashier was nowhere in sight. A woman whom I guessed to be about my age stood wiping the far end of the counter with a towel. When she thought I wasn't looking, she scrutinized me with sad, dark eyes.

I waited, drumming my fingers on the counter. The woman with the towel pushed a wisp of gray hair from her lined forehead and attacked the counter with renewed vigor.

This was ridiculous. I'd been standing there, the only person in line, for at least three or four minutes. I could understand if they were busy—where was that cashier?

I glanced again at my watch. Management was going to hear about this, I decided. I planned to write a scathing letter about the lack of service in this place.

But just as I mentally formulated my letter, I had a memory of Rosie, a former coworker of mine. Standing there, frustrated, I heard her sweet voice admonish me: "Be what's missing."

"What do you mean, 'Be what's missing'?" I had asked the first time I heard her use that phrase.

"Whenever you find yourself in an unpleasant situation," she explained, "just think about what is missing."

Rosie smiled at my blank stare. "It's really simple when you think about it. If someone is mean, then kindness is missing. If someone is inconsiderate, then thoughtfulness is missing. If someone is hateful, then love is missing. If we will be what's missing, then we'll provide whatever the situation needs."

I had frowned as I contemplated her words. "That makes sense," I admitted. But, I added, "It sounds simple, Rosie, but it's definitely not easy to do." Yet I had to admit that I admired her ability to live what she verbalized.

And here I was in an unpleasant situation. How was I supposed to "be what's missing"? What was missing was service. Maybe I should just jump behind the counter and take my own order.

But then the haggard woman who had wiped the counter until it shone laid down her towel and ambled slowly toward the cash register. With tilted head, defiant eyes, and deliberately paced words, she asked, "May I help you?"

My emotional temperature jumped off the chart. Before I could respond sarcastically I again heard Rosie's voice: "Be what's missing."

I took a deep breath. Looking at the woman more closely, I was struck by our differences. I was well-dressed and had driven up in a late-model car, clearly visible through the restaurant window. And it was clear I was in a hurry to be waited on — by someone who was, no doubt, overworked, underappreciated, and underpaid.

The woman looked tired. She probably felt that life was unfair, which it probably was for her.

I recalled my anger that morning at a physician who had treated me poorly. "Just because he's a doctor doesn't mean 'his lordship' shouldn't treat me like a human," I had fumed to a coworker.

With Rosie's words ringing in my head, I gave the woman my order... and smiled. "How are you today?"

My question seemed to surprise her. She eyed me suspiciously for a second before answering. "Not too good. It's been a lousy day."

"I'm sorry," I said. "I hope it gets better — starting right now."

She almost smiled as she looked at me. "Thanks. I hope you're right."

I mused as I ate my tacos. *We're all the same, really. We have problems and irritations, we feel mistreated, we get tired, and we hurt.*

And we need to be nicer to each other, I concluded.

When I finished eating, I placed everything in my tray and wiped the table more thoroughly than usual. After emptying the tray and replacing it neatly on the stand, I walked toward the door. Midway, I stopped and glanced back toward the counter. The cashier was watching me. But, this time, a broad smile replaced her frown. She waved an enthusiastic goodbye as I pushed open the door.

"Be what's missing." It worked.

— Kitty Chappell —

37

Pick Your Battles

*Life isn't measured by how many times you stood up
to fight. It's not winning battles that makes you happy,
but it's how many times you turned away and chose to
look into a better direction.*
~C. JoyBell C.

t started with a parenting course I took when my three sons were in elementary school. The class consisted of eight two-hour sessions and included reading and homework assignments. We had to put into practice what they preached! And then we had to report back on how the advice worked in a real-life situation. The basic message weaving its way through all eight sessions was "Pick Your Battles." Another piece of advice that went along with that was "Remain Flexible."

The class was not advising parents to step away and not be the parent. It was not suggesting that you be your child's friend so he would "like" you. You are, after all, the parent. Some things are important and need to be dealt with, especially when the decisions involve the welfare of your child. You need to give guidance and teach good values and a sense of right and wrong. You need to provide structure and say no sometimes. But not all the time. "No" shouldn't be the first word out of your mouth! Think first... then speak. Some decisions, while they could be important on some level, don't need your input. You can step back and let your child sort it out. By doing that, you teach your children independence and to be able to deal with different situations on their own.

What started out as parenting advice went much further than that and has guided me to this day. After taking the class, when a situation presented itself, and if there were two differing opinions, I would stop and think. I had to decide if the outcome was worth a battle or worth even the time it took to discuss it. If my son wanted to wear the same superhero shirt to school three days in a row, did it really matter? No. I would have been more comfortable if he had worn a clean shirt each day, but he was happy. If his friends gave him a hard time about his shirt, he would have to deal with it. It wasn't my issue and he wasn't hurting himself. If I had made plans to have lunch with a friend and I suggested a place to eat and she wanted to go to another place, did it matter? Was it worth a discussion? No. We were spending time together, so it was unimportant which restaurant we were going to.

The "pick your battles" lesson really helped me and became important recently when it involved two of my friends. Their argument started small. But both were equally stubborn and didn't want to give in and so it grew and spread quickly, like a wildfire on a windy day. Each friend tried to get me to see her point of view and to take her side against the other. It was a no-win situation; there could be no winners... only losers, the loss being a friendship. It was not my battle. Any opinion I would give would only fuel the fire. I chose to not get involved, to not take a side. It was not my battle so I remained quiet. I let them sort it out, which they eventually did — without my input.

The class also taught us that flexibility, especially when it involved kids, was key. Was it more important to follow a planned schedule or was it better to remain flexible enough to make changes to that schedule, even at the last minute? Well of course you need to be flexible and make changes. We were with a group a few years ago, driving through the mountains to a small town where we were planning to have a picnic lunch. There was no set time we had to be there; we were just going to a park.

On the way there, we saw that a beautiful new winery had opened. It was not on our schedule. If we stopped it would delay our picnic in the park, but stop we did. And we had an amazing experience. We toured the facility, met the winemaker, tasted some wonderful wines, and, after changing our picnic plans, ate in the winery's beautiful picnic area. Had we not been flexible we would have missed out on that opportunity.

Following the advice that I learned in that parenting class also got me into an argument! A few years ago, a friend of mine actually accused me of being a wimp, of being non-confrontational by always going along with what other people wanted. None of these descriptions could be further from the real truth. I am not a wimp — push me too far and watch out! I'll push back. I will confront you if I think you are being unfair or mean. And I do care passionately about many different things, so in this case I did choose to "battle" my friend by defending myself and my choice to not battle most of the time. To let the small stuff go. Why argue if it's not all that important? What a waste of my time and energy. Going along, if that's what I choose to do rather than leading, doesn't make me a doormat. I have an equally good time doing lots of things, whether I've picked them or someone else has.

I think that parenting class really helped this parent become a full adult!

— Barbara LoMonaco —

38

Right or Nice

Be kind whenever possible. It is always possible.
~The 14th Dalai Lama

My brother and I were spending our usual Saturday with Grandpa, cleaning his house. Like clockwork, Mom would drop us off in the morning. At ages five and eight, Bobby and I would spend the day dusting, mopping, and changing the sheets on his bed.

Grandpa was only in his late fifties, but he had grown up fast. His own dad had died when he was twelve, and Grandpa had to leave school, run the family farm, and raise his siblings. Because of that, his skills consisted of being able to sign his name, read his grandchildren's names, and "cipher" or do simple sums in his head. Grandpa was proud of these skills and always got that famous twinkle in his eye when an opportunity arose to sign his name. He would painstakingly form the loops and swirls that would write out "Paul" and his last name.

I, on the other hand, was an early reader and loved school. As the world opened up to my young eyes, I assumed that everyone had the skills and hunger for learning that I possessed, and that it was my sworn duty to educate anyone who didn't measure up to my exacting standards.

Yet somehow I missed the evidence staring at me from my grandpa's meager home. For, if I had been able to see, I could have better understood the stark poverty and limited opportunities my grandpa lived with. A loaf of white bread, a pound of bacon, and a jar of bread-and-butter pickles were the only items in his small refrigerator. Each week, we'd give him the leftovers from our previous week's dinners. He worked as a night janitor for several companies within walking distance of his home, and the highlight of his week was the reward he gave my brother and me for cleaning.

After we were done, Grandpa would put on his only suit, and we'd head to town. As we walked, Grandpa would greet every merchant he met along the way. Everyone had a story to share, and my grandpa would stand quietly, always smiling, and listen with great appreciation.

When we'd finally arrive at my grandpa's favorite diner, the waitresses would all greet him as a long-lost elder. Waves and grins would follow us to our favorite table as we piled in and placed our orders. Bobby and I split an adult plate, and Grandpa either had a cup of soup or a cup of coffee.

We'd laugh and eat, and Grandpa would brag about how well we cleaned his place, telling anyone who would listen every step of every task we accomplished.

Regardless of who was waiting on us at the time, each of the other waitresses would make sure they came up to say "hi" to Paul and congratulate his grandkids on their work. It may have been a diner, but it was our other home.

When dinner was over, the waitress would bring the check and slide it over to Grandpa. One day it was Gloria, and like always she bent close to him and told him the amount of the check (knowing that he couldn't read the slip of paper).

Grandpa carefully dug into the pocket of his suitpants and brought out a battered coin purse. He carefully laid out the bills and coins. Then he gave Gloria a woefully small tip. I was mortified that he had got it wrong and that he — we — would be embarrassed.

I was about to say something when Gloria grabbed my hands. "Come help me scoop the ice cream, Susie," she said as she led me toward the counter.

"I want you to listen really good, Susie," she began with such quiet and solemnity that I was taken aback. "You are very smart, and that is good, but it's not everything. Your grandpa is a very special man, and we all love him. Your grandpa's tip is a treasure of a gift from a treasure of a man. Do you understand that?" I nodded my head, but I was still unsure what she was getting at.

"If we're talking about math, your grandpa's tip is not enough. But it's more than your grandpa can afford, and it is given with love, so the math simply doesn't matter."

She paused a minute before continuing. "But it's not about that for you, Susie. Here's what it's about: If you have a choice of being right or being nice, always choose nice. It's not your job to 'fix' your grandpa if that fixing will hurt him. It's your job to love him."

I stared into that ice-cream tub for several long minutes. Even then, I knew she was right. I knew it was one of the most important pieces of advice I would ever hear. In that instant, all the pieces of my world rearranged themselves in a new — more compassionate — way.

And I've lived my life that way ever since.

— Susan Traugh —

39

Control Your Second Thought

Edwin Markham said, "At the heart of the cyclone
tearing the sky is a place of central calm." The cyclone
derives its power from a calm center. So does a person.
~Norman Vincent Peale

"You can't control your first thought, but you can control your second thought," the speaker said as she delivered her presentation on the power of a positive mindset. I didn't give her advice a second thought (pun intended) until the following day when I was having a hard time balancing everything I needed to do. I was getting frustrated by all my son's questions on our drive home, and my answers were getting shorter with every "Why?"

My son has an insatiable appetite for learning and asks many of the same questions over and over again. He was getting upset with me for not giving him the answers he wanted, and I was getting upset with him because I felt bombarded and couldn't think. I was about to raise my voice and tell him to stop, but I took a deep breath and told myself, "Control your second thought." I asked him why he kept asking me the same questions, and he told me it was because he liked to talk to me. I felt disappointed in myself for reacting to my first thought so often.

I am a forty-three-year-old combat veteran who is set in my ways. I often feel overwhelmed as I try to figure out how to raise a young son on the autism spectrum. As it turns out, I constantly need to control that "second thought."

Now I whisper it to myself throughout the day, "Control your second thought." There is something empowering about it. The word "control" leads me to more thoughtful and responsible reactions now, after I've had the chance to have that second thought.

Regarding that first thought, well, as the saying goes, "You can't control your first thought." I used to feel guilt and shame for getting irritated too quickly and for the mere existence of my first thought. This insight helped me realize that my thoughts are normal, and they are perfectly alright. Taken together, both parts of this advice told me that my first and second thoughts are not in conflict; they are a natural progression. For the first time in my life, I was able to accept both the existence of my first thought and the responsibility for my second. It was an important lesson for me in my constant desire to be a better father today than I was yesterday.

When I control my second thought, my son gets more. More explanations and fewer dismissals. More experimentation and fewer missed opportunities. More teachable moments and fewer blockades. More laughter and fewer sighs. More resilience and less rigidity. When I control my second thought, my son gets more of *me*. I certainly have not perfected the advice, but I am a better person and father because I reiterate this one piece of advice to myself every day.

— Elton A. Dean —

40

Now I Get It

If you're going to start something — if it's worth
starting — then it's worth finishing.
That's what I live by.
~Marshall Faulk

A t the end of fifth grade, there was a flurry of excitement in the classroom. The school year was almost over, and we would be moving on to a new school for sixth grade. All the girls made autograph books and collected signatures.

As I signed my classmates' books, I noticed their moms had written in them, too. Such sweet thoughts were expressed:

"I couldn't be prouder of you. Can't wait to see how you like junior high!"

"I love you — great things lie ahead. Dad and I are so proud of you."

"You're graduating. Congratulations! We love you and know you have a bright future!"

I asked my mother to sign mine, too. She was busy, she said, but she'd get to it later. I set the book on the kitchen table.

Later that night, she handed it back to me. I was anxious to see what encouraging words she had written.

This is what I found on the page:

When a thing is first begun,
Never leave it till it's done.
Be the labor great or small,

Do it well or not at all.
Mom

My heart sank. That was it? I was crushed. No words of pride or encouragement. It was just a stupid poem — another indication to me that, if I couldn't be perfect, I wasn't good enough.

I held back my tears, not expressing the disappointment I felt. I left the page in but secretly hoped my classmates wouldn't read it.

That page in that handmade book haunted me for years.

Do it well or not at all.

I battled perfectionism and low self-esteem and never felt good enough for most of my life. Many times, I gave up on things after I barely got started. I mean, if I couldn't do it well, why bother?

Do it well or not at all. All I could hear was "You're not good enough."

When my mother was in her eighties and in a nursing home, I gave her a book to fill out so we could know more about her. It had prompts at the top of each page and then blank space to respond. I wanted her to write down her memories and a lifetime of experiences so my siblings and I, along with her grandchildren, would have some precious snippets of her life.

In the beginning, she was very excited. She'd call me to report that she was working on it. I'd cheer her on and say, "That's great, Mom. I love it. Keep going!" After a couple of weeks, though, she stopped mentioning it, so I asked about it.

"Oh, yeah, I forgot. I'll work on it again." I guess it got boring for her. I mean, there was Bingo, puzzles and social things at the home with her peers.

Then, Covid struck, and everything was locked down. I could no longer visit her. We were restricted to phone calls only. Not wanting to nag her, I rarely said anything to her about the book other than an occasional reminder.

"I'll get back to it."

I secretly hoped she'd been working on it all along.

Sadly, my mother passed away from Covid-19 pneumonia. After she died, I was designated to retrieve her belongings. The one thing I wanted more than anything was that book.

I found it and immediately sat down to read through it.

And, once again, I felt disappointment. When I saw she had only filled out ten pages, I snapped the book shut.

Figures, I thought. *Even at the end of her life, she wouldn't put in some extra effort.*

Like all the disappointments in my life, I made peace with it. She was who she was. Maybe one day I would open it again.

It was six months before I revisited the book. I decided that ten pages of memories were better than no pages.

What I found stopped me short. On page ten, the prompt asked, "What's the best advice you got from your mom and dad?"

Her response was what she had written in my autograph book. Even though I'd memorized it years ago, I read it at a slower pace now, seeing it in a new light.

When a thing is first begun,
Never leave it till it's done.
Be the labor great or small,
Do it well or not at all

I've come to see that Mom was passing on something she found valuable in her life. It was written to her by her mother, and she was passing it down to me in the same way. Encouragement to do things well. A gift from her to me.

She was giving me treasured, valuable advice when all I was thinking about were warm, fuzzy feelings. I understand it now.

— Carolyn Barrett —

Live Life to the Fullest

41

One Radio Broadcast Changed My Life

If we all did the things we are capable of,
we would literally astound ourselves.
~Thomas Edison

n 1972, I was a clerk at the Housing Authority in Little Rock, Arkansas, an assistant to a man who was not busy. Truly, Bob Moore didn't need a helper, but I was there for him. My title was Assistant Loan Specialist, but my challenge was finding useful ways to fill my day. Bob didn't call on me very often, so I read books, learned from coworkers, and occasionally processed loan applications. Mostly, I spent my time thinking about my future.

As a newly married twenty-six-year-old, a two-packs-a-day smoker who was fifty pounds overweight with no college degree or money in the bank, there wasn't much promise for a bright future yet. I spent my days daydreaming about what I might do, but nothing was fixed in my mind.

Then, one day, I overheard a radio broadcast in the next room. It was "Our Changing World" by Earl Nightingale, the Dean of Personal Motivation. He was on 900 radio stations around the world, and I heard him say, "If you will spend one (extra) hour each day studying your chosen field, you will become a national expert in that field in five years or less."

"Five years or less?" I was a government clerk. I had eight extra hours each day. I figured I could do this by Thursday!

But I had a new dilemma: At what did I want to become an expert? I didn't know.

The math worked. One hour a day, five days a week, fifty weeks a year for five years was 1,250 hours! That much study in one narrowly focused field would indeed make anyone a national expert. But what would I study?

For weeks, I thought about it. Then, one day, it became clear to me. I wanted to be like the man on the radio. I wanted to help people grow and succeed.

But I had not succeeded, so how could I help others do what I had not done?

It occurred to me that I already had the answer: spend one extra hour each day studying my newly chosen field. Since I was starting without advantages, I decided to devote more hours than required. I literally became fanatical about studying motivation. I bought or borrowed every major book on the topic. Luckily, there were only a few such books in 1972. I listened to audio recordings, attended seminars when I could, and sought out successful people in order to learn from them.

Within a few months, my world began to change. My circle of friends evolved. Those who weren't committed to success drifted away from me, and fellow achievers were drawn to me. This accelerated my growth. I joined the Jaycees, the Junior Chamber of Commerce, a civic group for young adults whose purpose was leadership training through community service.

As a new Jaycee, I became very active in serving on committees, leading meetings, and volunteering for every position possible in order to learn and grow. During the years 1973 and 1974, I attended 400 Jaycees meetings after work and on weekends. My skills grew, and my confidence soared. I lost fifty-two excess pounds, stopped smoking, and became smarter about managing money.

On the job, my boss and his boss noticed the changes in me. I received a promotion, a raise and, soon afterward, another raise. My coworkers elected me president of the employees' association. My world was expanding.

Harold Gash, a man who sold Earl Nightingale's audio programs to businesses, heard me speak at a Jaycees meeting and recruited me to work with him as a salesperson. In this new job, I was solely focused on personal development, so my own growth soared.

Then, I received an unexpected phone call. The U.S. Jaycees national headquarters called to offer me the job of Senior Program Manager in charge of Leadership Training for the entire 356,000-member organization. I moved to Tulsa, Oklahoma and spent the next two years traveling the country, speaking at large conventions and creating training programs.

The more I grew in my role, the more people with whom I connected. Within a short time, I was in business on my own working with clients throughout the USA in the capacity of motivational trainer and consultant. I was, in fact, a "national expert on personal motivation." By 1977, I was a full-time, self-employed speaker and trainer — literally five years from the day I had heard Earl Nightingale on the radio!

Since then, I have continued my study of motivation. Today, I have written and published twenty-three books, delivered over 3,300 paid speeches, circumnavigated the globe three times on lecture tours, served as president of the National Speakers Association (NSA), been inducted into the National Speakers Association Hall of Fame and the Sales & Marketing Hall of Fame, and received virtually every major award in professional speaking. In September 2021, I received an honorary bachelor's degree in business from High Point University in North Carolina.

In short, I have become a national expert on personal motivation.

One of the great moments in my career came in 1984 when Earl Nightingale himself called me and offered to publish my audio program on "Relationship Strategies for Dealing with the Differences in People," coauthored with Dr. Tony Alessandra. Nightingale-Conant Corporation sold $3.5 million worth of that program in 1984 and 1985.

When I was president of the NSA in 1989, I invited Mr. Nightingale to join me on stage at our convention so that I could interview him about the field of personal motivation in front of thousands of our peers. A few months before that event, his wife Diana called me and said, "Earl has died. We spread his ashes in a private ceremony here at home, but I'd like to hold a memorial for him at your speakers' convention because you are his people."

Naturally, I accepted, and we were honored to have such a special privilege to acknowledge our mentor in this way. Diana asked me to speak at the memorial, but I declined. I said, "This is Earl Nightingale we are honoring. The speakers should be giants of industry and world leaders, not me."

She replied, "Jim, you are the product of what Earl was teaching. You applied his lessons to transform your life. That is why you should speak that day." I humbly accepted.

On the day of his memorial, hundreds of his peers and students assembled at the NSA convention in Dallas, Texas. And the only speakers at the event were Diana, a short video message from my colleague Dr. Denis Waitley, and a live presentation from me.

The day I heard Earl's voice on the Housing Authority radio in Little Rock, Arkansas, was the day my entire life took on a new direction. I will be forever grateful for the inspiration he provided and the imprint his wisdom left on me. I shall also strive to continually be worthy of carrying on the legacy that he and his mentors passed along. One extra hour each day, devoted to studying your chosen field. Try it.

—Jim Cathcart—

42

A Stranger in a Bookstore

A ship in harbor is safe, but that is not
what ships are built for.
~John A. Shedd

I used to go to the World Trade Center a few times per week. There was a large bookstore called Borders that was a great place to study. It sold music and movies in addition to reading materials; and it also had a café. I used to sit there and pretend that I was at a sidewalk café in Paris. When I wasn't studying, I read travel guides. I fantasized about voyaging around the world.

One day, while I was perusing a book about the top sites to see in India, I noticed a stranger smiling at me.

"When are you going?" he said.

I replied, "Excuse me?"

"When are you going to India?"

Cheeks warm with embarrassment, I admitted that there was no trip planned. I was a broke student and could barely afford the train fare to the bookstore. But I gave him a different explanation.

"I don't have anyone to go with. No one that I know wants to travel to the places that I want to see."

This was true. Friends shared my dream of people-watching on Parisian sidewalks, but no one understood why I was excited about spice markets in Delhi or ancient ruins in North Africa. I imagined that I would never travel anywhere exotic even after getting a job. No one that I knew wanted to go off the beaten path.

The stranger's reply changed my life forever.

"You should just go by yourself," he said.

I had never considered doing such a thing. I pictured the horror on my mother's face if I told her that I was going on an overseas trip by myself. Just two years earlier, at age twenty, I had flown to Florida to meet up with friends from high school. I remember hesitantly mentioning the vacation to my mother and bracing myself for her reaction.

I finished my study session and returned to my apartment. The conversation was all but forgotten.

Medical school was followed by an internship and a residency. Then I spent three more years doing specialized training. A full decade passed after that brief conversation in the bookstore. Many events took place during the intervening years. The bookstore was destroyed on 9/11. The world had become a scary place. But I remained hopeful and escaped the harsh realities of life by fantasizing about travel. I kept reading about other cities.

When I finally finished my education and got a job, I was thirty-two years old.

For my first vacation, I took my mother to see the beautiful Caribbean island where she was raised. I knew that the trip would be the first of many. We looked at the electronic flight map on the airplane ride home, and I fantasized about where I would visit next. A few months after that my friends were too caught up with careers or kids to travel with me during my infrequent breaks from work. Mom was not interested in traipsing around to places where she doesn't speak the language or know anyone.

I didn't *want* to travel alone. I worried that it would probably cement my family's fear that I would be single forever. I even mused that traveling alone would make people think that I had no friends. I imagined that I would be scammed — or worse!

But my childhood dreams had morphed into something bigger. I yearned to see new places and try novel cuisines. Living in one of the world's most international cities did not satisfy these desires. New York fanned the flames by teasing me with Tibetan restaurants, Nigerian movies, and Indian nightclubs.

I started exploring the world tentatively. I went to Los Angeles and the Grand Canyon alone. Baby steps. I quickly became an addict. The excitement of scrolling through travel websites was matched only by booking flights and hotel rooms. Packing was not a chore. Planning my wardrobe around my itinerary gave me a thrill.

In those days, it was almost unheard of, but I toured the world alone as a single female. I stayed in hostels with college students, in upscale hotels, or with strangers who I met via hospitality websites.

I began to mature in unexpected ways. I became conversant in several languages. Cultural differences were accepted and welcomed.

My spirituality was also nurtured through my travels. I prayed at the Western Wall and in Gethsemane. My awe of nature was renewed while climbing volcanoes or floating down jungle rivers.

Work even incorporated itself into my voyages. After the destructive 2010 Haitian earthquake, I volunteered my specialized skills in Port-au-Prince. I spent the winter holidays of 2011 providing medical care for an isolated Guatemalan orphanage. During one week in 2013, I was the only doctor in a rural Ghanaian village that lacked basic amenities such as running water.

Looking back, it is fascinating that a passing comment from an inquisitive stranger changed me in more ways than I can imagine. I realized that I don't have to wait for life to unfold in a fairy-tale narrative. I can fulfill my dreams even if things are not going as planned. Solo travel taught me what it means to be brave. Visiting the world alone made me learn how to be a creative problem solver. My encounters with new cultures and unexpected challenges have made me stronger and wiser.

To my mother's delight, I even met my husband during a solo trip to Canada! She had nothing to worry about after all. As a couple, we have visited Latin America and Europe together. When our son is older, we hope to show him the Taj Mahal and the pyramids of Giza.

Twenty years later, I still feel immense gratitude to that nosy stranger in the bookstore who gave me the advice that transformed my life. It was the best advice that I have ever received.

— Cherry March —

43

The Price of Every Decision

*The price of anything is the amount
of life you exchange for it.*
~Henry David Thoreau

Every decision has a cost. In business school, they even teach you about "opportunity cost" — the loss of value or benefit incurred by engaging in one activity, relative to engaging in an alternative activity that could offer a higher return.

I first started thinking about the price of important family decisions in my thirties when I was considering leaving corporate America and launching a business as an executive speechwriter and advertising copywriter.

I had a good job. No, a great job — in the marketing division of a Fortune 500 company. I was a creative writer in the sales-promotion department and an incentive-travel planner for sales-contest winners. So, besides developing much of the sales and marketing literature for the company, I coordinated travel trips for top salespeople to Hawaii, Spain, and the Caribbean on the largest cruise ships in the world. Why would anyone want to leave this dream job?

After working for this first-class company for fourteen years, I got to thinking about what it would be like to design a job around what I enjoyed most, while using my strongest skills. The theory being, spend the next stage of my career doing what I loved most and spend more time with the people I loved most, my wife and sons.

My wife was a stay-at-home mom, so I would sacrifice our only income and insurance for nothing more than a pipe dream. Yet, after conducting extensive research, reading books on how to launch this type of business, calling the authors for additional details, freelancing for ad agencies and design firms to ensure I could write on any subject, and purchasing insurance, this goal slowly developed from impossible to probable.

I realized then that author Henry David Thoreau was on to something when he said, "The price of anything is the amount of life you exchange for it."

At thirty-seven, I had a window of opportunity to chase a dream — to run a home-based business and spend more time with my family. Now, I had a decision to make. How much more of my family life was I willing to "exchange" for a corporate career? I pulled the plug — and launched my advertising and executive speechwriting business in June 1991 — thirty-one years ago.

Looking back, Thoreau's quote is, in reality, advice that changed my life. Leaving corporate America was one of the best decisions I've ever made. And, while working with myriad clients, sharpening my writing skills on multiple subjects, and winning twelve writing awards, including Best of Show, I had the privilege to add these sacred accomplishments to the resume of my life. I watched my sons grow up for ten years, played hundreds of unscheduled backyard baseball games, learned it's more fun to play football in the rain, relished ice-cold Cokes from a gas station vending machine (glass bottles, of course) on steamy August afternoons after a close game, enjoyed countless spontaneous father/son chats while walking around the block, rediscovered the world of pretend, achieved "kid status" bike riding with them as the wind blew through our hair, realized that young boys will share what's on their hearts over an ice-cream cone, and taught the essential principle of operating a successful Kool-Aid and cookie stand: Don't eat the profits.

How would I have benefited if I had never taken a ten-year break from my corporate career? It's a question I've asked myself before. The answer? I'd have a larger 401(k) plan and more money in the bank — but I would also have a major deficit in my memory bank.

Life provides windows of opportunity — but they close quickly.

For me, to remain in corporate America during this "window" came at a price too high. Thoreau was right; I wasn't willing to exchange more of my family life for my professional life.

—James C. Magruder—

44

Let Yourself Fly

*I want to be improbable, beautiful and afraid
of nothing, as though I had wings.*
~Mary Oliver, "Starlings in Winter"

I f my husband hadn't left, taking all my dreams and my dream house with him, I never would have met the woman whose advice saved my life. Robin showed up one day on the playground near my new place in Boulder, Colorado and sat down next to me on a bench. We shared our stories. While we watched our daughters play together, my new neighbor told me we had to grasp the present moment because time goes so fast. Robin said to look forward, not backward, and make new goals.

"You're free now! Have fun! Let yourself fly!"

When I couldn't think of any goal besides begging my husband to come back to me, she groaned audibly and told me that I couldn't control *him*, but I could control *me*. She coaxed me into running with her.

She encouraged me. I had never run even a step, but soon Vando, a Brazilian marathoner, showed up on my doorstep to make my training plan. I started by walking twenty minutes, and then twenty-two minutes, until I got to thirty minutes and could add some running. Robin called or showed up every day to make sure I kept going. She bought a green T-shirt for me that said, "Behind Every Successful Woman Is Herself," and on those days when I felt too sad to lift my head from the pillow, she'd pound on the door until I gave up being grumpy and went running with her. Then she decided I needed a goal: to run with her in a Halloween 10K Race. Now, Robin had run plenty of races, but this 10K would be my first one.

At her insistence, I dragged myself to the racecourse for the Eerie Erie. There Robin stood in a cheerleader outfit. She had little bat wings waiting for me.

"Put these on," she said. "I knew you wouldn't remember to bring a costume."

"Costume?" I said.

"Yes," she said. "Everybody's in costume. It's Halloween, silly. We're supposed to have fun."

I turned around with reluctance and let her pin two little bat wings to the back of my shirt. I started stretching — bending, twisting, breathing deeply. Everything in me felt tight.

"You've got two kids who need you, honey, and you're still alive," Robin said. "You have to keep that body moving, keep that heart pumping. Let's get going."

As we started running Robin stayed with me, even though she could run much faster than I could. She said she had a little cold and didn't want to push too hard, but I knew she meant to make sure I finished this race. When we ran up hills, she told me to stretch my legs farther, breathe more slowly. On the down hills, she said to loosen up.

"Don't hold back!" she exhorted. "Let yourself fly!"

I ran my best that day, but at the end of the ten kilometers (about six miles), I felt exhausted to the core. Robin wanted to run the race in less than an hour, but I didn't think I could do it. She'd been a runner for more than a decade. I felt like a novice, holding her back.

"You go on up ahead," I said. "I'll make it."

"Well, all right," she replied.

I saw her strong legs surge under her bright red cheerleader skirt as she turned the corner ahead of me. She had such strength, such beauty, and she kept smiling. For Robin, life meant pleasure. I trudged along slowly, alone.

When I turned the corner, too, I got the surprise of my life. Robin leaped out from behind a pickup truck on that last block of the run, and she started cheering for me as if she were my own personal pompon girl.

"Go, go, run run run!" she said.

She flung her arms up in the air and kicked her legs up and danced around me, then ran behind me, cheering the whole way.

"I'm right behind you," she said. "Now, you know you'll beat somebody in this race!"

I laughed as I crossed the finish line. I made it in sixty minutes, and Robin made it in sixty-one. She gave me a big hug.

"You flew! I knew you could do it!"

It was my blessing to be able to run and laugh with Robin for the next seven years. When she was diagnosed with stage four melanoma, she brought her eight closest friends together for a long weekend in Breckenridge. We did yoga and cooked together, talking late into the night. One friend had known her since kindergarten, and she had changed all our lives for the better.

"I want you all to have each other," Robin said. "I love you so much."

A group of us, her best buddies, formed a Round Robin Inner Circle and took turns being there for her through the cancer journey, giving her husband a little respite. On the way to one of her chemo appointments, she told me to drive faster.

"Get in the fast lane," she said. "I don't know why they even have that other lane."

Robin always lived full out. Everybody thought she would kick that cancer to the curb. When I shared Mary Oliver's "In Blackwater Woods" with her, she told me she wanted me to read it at her memorial service. I told her she had to live so she could read it at mine.

Cancer kept coming at her, and soon she couldn't run, bicycle or kayak. Later, she couldn't walk. Her last words to me were, "I love you." Too soon, she couldn't speak at all. I sat next to her and sang "Somewhere over the Rainbow" at the last Round Robin potluck before she passed away.

Robin died at home in a hospital bed set up in the living room. We in the Round Robin didn't mind doing all we could for her because of all she'd done for us. She hadn't been able to smile for a few weeks, but she died looking toward the sliding glass doors, outside to the stars. Somehow, she had a smile on her face the next morning, and a beautiful, peaceful expression — her last gift to us. Three friends dressed her and made her ready for the next transition. I walked with her body to the hearse and gave her one last kiss on the cheek.

At her memorial service, I read the words by Mary Oliver that meant so much to her:

> *To live in this world*
> *you must be able to do three things:*
> *to love what is mortal;*
> *to hold it against your bones*
> *knowing your own life depends on it;*
> *and, when the time comes*
> *to let it go,*
> *to let it go.*

She told me to keep running. Today, I lace up my running shoes. I step onto the trail, and in my heart I hear Robin's voice, cheering me on.

"Don't hold back! Let yourself fly!"

I feel Robin, flying far beyond me. I take a deep breath. And I fly.

— Kiesa Kay —

45

Bookends of Wisdom

A lifetime isn't forever, so take the first chance,
don't wait for the second one!
~C. JoyBell C.

F resh out of college and newly married, my husband and I started our life together in an economically challenged Canadian community. Leapfrogging from one temporary job to the next, we squeaked by with the hope of purchasing a home someday, but it was a dream firmly planted in a distant future. The idea of assuming a mortgage at the risk of losing everything had no appeal, so we scrimped, saved and bided our time.

We took advantage of the free things in life that filled our souls with happiness, like time spent camping, hiking, and swimming. Our love for the great outdoors provided an escape from the daily grind and, by rare chance one day, an opportunity. During one of our outings, we spotted a for-sale sign advertising a snippet of paradise along the shoreline of Lake Superior. It was a little chunk of land to call — well, not quite home but the next best thing — camp.

This untamed waterfront property had just listed on the market for a relatively inexpensive sum. It offered a view to die for, along with a mountain of work to whip the uncleared land into shape. But we were young, with plenty of energy and time to burn. Still, with our limited funds, could we afford such a venture? Then again, could we afford not to take advantage of an opportunity? We were conflicted. For objective advice, we turned to Steve's uncle.

Uncle Joe was an accomplished, kindhearted man whose opinion we valued. He had provided Steve with sound advice in the past. "Take all you can get out of life… and more," he had once told my husband. When Steve frowned at what appeared to be a self-centric view, Joe qualified his statement. "I don't mean greed. I mean prosperity in the vast sense. Pursue the things that will make your life rich and prosperous in all things and pursue them with enthusiasm. Make informed decisions that lead to happiness as well as prosperity."

After dwelling on the fear factor of purchasing the shoreline property, Steve sought his uncle's advice again, explaining that assuming a large debt was a huge risk for us.

Uncle Joe smiled reassuringly. "Well, Steve, my advice to you is simple. If you wait until you can afford to take a risk on something, you will never take a risk on anything. So, ask yourself this: Will I regret it later if I walk away now?"

We looked at each other. "Yes, we would."

The next day, Steve and I scraped together enough for a down payment. Delighted with our first big purchase, we wasted no time clearing a meager path to the waterfront. We spent every possible moment at the lot, camping, swimming, having fun, and building dreams. That pursuit gave us the courage to take on a bigger project. Two years later, with secure employment, we used the lot as collateral to purchase our first home.

A few years passed, and another downturn in the economy made it a struggle for us to maintain both properties and remain employed. Facing relocation for employment meant selling everything and taking an even greater risk. Joe's advice echoed in our minds, along with a few clichéd proverbs: "Nothing ventured, nothing gained" and "Go big or stay home." Since staying meant losing our home, we decided to go big. Florida had a booming economy and wonderful weather. So, after much debate and research, we decided we would move from one end of the I-75 highway to the other. Why shovel snow if you have an alternative?

A few things were needed before we could leave. First, we had to advance our educations and prepare our home and property for sale.

A little planning and preparation ensured a successful relocation and a future filled with prosperity. We squeaked out a living at odd jobs while pursuing our dream, and two years later, still adhering to Joe's original advice, we made the ultimate leap. We moved from the great white north to the sunny south. It was an enormous risk but one that paid off. Steve and I settled into advancing careers, a new life in a new home, and time walking the soft sands of sunny beaches — another paradise found. Eventually, we even celebrated becoming American citizens.

By our twentieth anniversary, Steve and I had accomplished most of our goals because of a few simple, sound words of wisdom. But there is always a flip side.

When the recession hit Florida, and property values dropped, we faced another rare opportunity. This time, we debated if we should purchase a neglected, undervalued condo to fix up as an investment property. It would devour our savings but offer a potential rental-income source for the future. We agonized over the pros and cons, weighing possibilities and outcomes. Steve once more turned to his uncle for his thoughts, expecting to hear familiar words. Instead, Uncle Joe surprised us.

Over the speakerphone, Steve voiced our concerns: "We understand it's a great opportunity for a retirement nest egg when property values rise, but a condo is always additional work that can gobble up free time and money, especially if renters damage the property. Still, the price makes this a great opportunity, one that seems too good to pass up."

Joe listened and then politely dispensed his advice. "Well," he said. "Opportunities come along all the time. So, ask yourself this: Will you regret passing on this one? Possibly. But there is also something to be said for the peace of mind in getting a good night's sleep."

His lack of enthusiasm floored us, so we took a moment to consider Joe's counsel and realized he made sense. We passed on the opportunity and chose instead to reduce existing debt by refinancing at a lower rate. Eventually, the savings allowed us to purchase another snippet of paradise property to savor for retirement. A short time later, we learned that the condominium board had made some special assessments that owners had to pay. We had narrowly dodged a money pit. Grateful for an uncle's wisdom once more, we realized a good night's sleep was also a worthy pursuit.

While Uncle Joe's gems of wisdom on matters of risk may appear contradictory, they are in fact bookends of the same thought. When you have nothing to lose, a risk to chase your dreams makes it a worthy goal. But if your pursuit could cost you everything should it go astray, it is likely best to pass it up and rest easy, knowing you have lost nothing. And, above all else, take all you can get out of life... and more.

— Cate Bronson —

46

The Flying Train

Perhaps imagination is only intelligence having fun.
~George Scialabba

t is always a shock when you come to realize that you might be the crazy one in your family! That happened to me not long ago when I was left in charge of my six-year-old nephew for the day.

It was a cold, rainy morning, so my nephew and I had started our day with a trip to the Main Street Diner for the all-you-can-eat pancake breakfast special. Then we were off to the local cinema for the early showing of the latest Disney animated movie.

Later, my nephew and I settled in back at home for an afternoon of intense playtime. We were working together to build a wooden train railroad set-up that wound around the living room floor. And we had a number of unusual passengers lined up waiting for a ride, including a group of superhero action figures, a community of Lego people, and a herd of plastic, glow-in-the-dark dinosaurs.

I watched as my nephew struggled to connect two pieces of track attaching the drawbridge to the train tunnel. "That's not right," I said, taking the track out of his hand. "The bridge and the tunnel wouldn't go together. That wouldn't make any sense. We'll put the tunnel over on the other side of the set-up."

My nephew sighed as I moved the tunnel attachment to the far end of the tracks.

"What is going on here?" I asked, pointing to the toy tugboat parked next to the train station. "The tugboat belongs over by the river bridge, not with the train station."

My nephew nonchalantly shrugged his shoulders and slid the tugboat over to the bridge.

Eventually, the set-up was so big that it wound under the coffee table, along the front of the fireplace and past the couch. The railway finally came to an abrupt end at the door to the dining room when we ran out of pieces of track.

"This set-up is awesome," said my nephew.

Then he quickly loaded the passenger car with his Luke Skywalker action figure and a neon-green T-rex and began pushing the train along the lengthy track. When he reached the end of the line, he picked up the engine and the train cars and loudly announced: "Now it's time for the train to fly back to the station!"

"Whoa, whoa, whoa, trains do not fly," I insisted. "You have to back the engine up until you reach the turn-around. Then you can drive the train back along the tracks to the station."

Still holding the train in mid-air, my nephew shook his head. "Uncle David," he asked with a perplexed look, "you do know this is make-believe, right?"

I opened my mouth, but I had no reply. A six-year-old had left me speechless. And, I sadly realized, he was right; he was using his imagination. It was make-believe.

The train tunnel could be connected to the lift bridge. The tugboat could dock at the train station. After all, this was a train carrying a Jedi knight and a dinosaur, for goodness' sake. It was just make-believe, and I had forgotten to relax and let my nephew's creative imagination govern the play.

Sometimes, even though it is difficult to put the reality of the world on hold, it is essential to embrace youthful imagination and allow it the opportunity to flourish in a child's world.

Even the Nobel prize-winning scientist and physicist Albert Einstein once said, "Imagination is more important than knowledge."

Sometimes, it just takes a little kid with a flying train to remind us of that.

— David Hull —

Permission to Say No

Always remember: You have a right to say no
without having to explain yourself.
Be at peace with your decisions.
~Stephanie Lahart

t was a Sunday morning following church services, and I was slowly walking through the gathering of congregation members enjoying fellowship hour. I was looking for familiar people whom I could ask to join my team.

A few weeks earlier, my pastor had called upon me to be one of ten team leaders to assist with the church's upcoming fundraiser for building improvements. I wasn't thrilled about serving on the project, but I knew that it was a much-needed campaign.

Each team leader needed to recruit five to seven people who would call upon other church members personally to ask for pledges to the building fund. Though I said yes, this was definitely outside my comfort zone. Asking people for money was very difficult for me.

I already had three team members recruited, and I only needed a couple more. Scanning the crowd, I noticed Beth. Our sons went to school together, and they both played for the Praise Band. I had never worked with her before, but I did know that she had recently retired. I thought she might have time for the project.

We went to a quieter place in the narthex, and I explained everything to her. She listened respectfully and agreed that the church needed some remodeling, and then she said something that changed my life

140 | Live Life to the Fullest

forever. "I will happily donate toward the improvements, but I am giving myself permission to say no to calling other parishioners. That is way outside of my comfort zone."

I stood there shocked by her response. I wasn't upset about her refusal. Instead, I was completely awed by the way in which she put it. "I am giving myself permission to say no." It had never occurred to me that I could say no when asked to help out or volunteer for a project. Beth had just opened up an entirely new world to me, and I realized it was time that I gave myself permission to say no as well.

First, I analyzed why I had always been afraid to say no. I had to admit that I didn't want to jeopardize my relationship with the person or organization that was asking for assistance. A people-pleaser wants to be liked by everyone. I was afraid that by saying no, they would think less of me. So, I took on some tasks begrudgingly and then didn't have sufficient free time to pursue volunteering in the areas I liked. I realized that my time was limited, and while I have a strong sense of service, it was sometimes taken advantage of or put me in a situation that made me anxious. I was never at my best when that happened.

The next time I was asked to assist in a project that I didn't feel was a good fit, I declined, just like Beth had taught me. I discovered that there were no hard feelings or repercussions when I said no, and it gave me the necessary free time to do a better job with other projects. These were the things my pastor called "joyful heart moments." I discovered that I could better serve my church and work with the extra time I found in doing those things that made me the happiest. The surge of energy and satisfaction that comes with completing a project or task is truly a "joyful heart moment" for me now.

I spoke to Beth several months after our conversation and shared with her how eye-opening her response was to me and how I was implementing it myself. She laughed and then said, "I was so overworked and underwhelmed by all the projects I said yes to following my retirement that I realized none of them was getting my best work. By narrowing down the areas I said yes to, I had more time and a better attitude about doing them." She added, "After being stressed-out at work, I didn't want to stress out again in retirement." I was truly inspired by her thoughts and realized that it's okay to gracefully decline and still contribute in other ways. Saying no was difficult, but it truly got easier with practice!

I still say yes to some projects that may be outside my norm, but I only say yes after I have fully researched the project and felt that I could either learn something new from it or contribute in a way that I know will have a lasting impact.

Luckily, I did find my final two team members at church, and the fundraising campaign was a huge success. We are all enjoying the new improvements done to enhance our Sunday school classrooms and sanctuary. I feel good that I was instrumental in making that happen, but it is not a project that I would take on again. I am giving myself permission to say no but will also ask, "How can I help or contribute in other ways?"

—Adrienne Matthews—

48

Banned? Me?
I Don't Think So

Live life to the fullest because it only happens once.
~Maddi Jenkins

ords of wisdom from my Grandma Dore: "Grab life by the…" Well, you get the picture. Gram was a fireball. I adored her. She loved doing new and fun things, and she encouraged me to always go for it.

First of all, let me make a disclaimer. I'm officially "you look good for your age" years old. Even so, I have a bucket list, and I'm determined to put checkmarks on it. I'm forever chastising my friends when they miss opportunities to live on the edge. But, frankly, I talk a lot of smack for someone who tips over when putting on her underwear.

Anyhoo, I had the occasion to call my own bluff when I went on a cruise vacation a few years ago. Did I ski down a mountain? No. Did I drive a race car? No. But when I had the chance to get on a jet ski in the blue Caribbean water, I took it.

First off, I had to don a bathing suit and meet up on the beach with the others in our tour group, who were all half my age. I didn't pack a bathing suit because I had no intention of swimming, so I had to borrow one from my travel mate. She's larger than I am, so the crotch of the suit hung almost to my knees. I don't even want to talk about what the top looked like. Okay, maybe I will. It looked like I had taken a hard fall on my front and smashed both of them flat, but they were still in there moving around alarmingly free. My plan was simple: I'd keep both arms by my sides so nothing would pop out. And as for the crotch problem, I threw on a pair of dark panties under the suit and hoped no one would really notice. Of course, when you pretend something isn't happening… just know that it still really is happening.

So, I walked across the sand to the meet-up area with mincing steps to keep the crotch from swaying to and fro and with my arms pinned rigidly by my side to hold my boobs in place. Yeah, I got stares. No matter because my adrenaline spiked when I saw that gorgeous, sleek, black and shiny jet ski waiting for me.

After listening to the safety lecture, the next chore was to mount the machine. It hadn't dawned on me before, but I had to lift my leg dog-on-a-hydrant style to straddle it. I also had to let go of the bathing suit to use my arms. I'm tall with long legs, so when I sat I looked like a grasshopper on a black leaf. I'm pretty sure I heard cell-phone camera clicks, but there was no way I was backing out now.

Finally, we were allowed to give it the gas and speed off into the blue ocean. Okay, the rest of the group sped off. I was puttering off. But I was off, gosh darn it. The instructor felt it necessary to ride next to me, like I was some kind of invalid. He shouted instructions to me, but over the sound of the engine, I didn't hear a word he said. I just nodded and made a shooing motion for him to leave me alone. "You're embarrassing me," I yelled to him. Like I hadn't done that to myself already.

At that moment, I recall being sort of grateful and amazed to be upright and not tipped over into the water, and it boosted my courage. I gave it a little more throttle and headed out to where the rest of my group was gathered. And, no, they didn't wait for me. I felt like the middle piece of bread in a club sandwich when I really wanted to be the bacon.

No matter; I puttered all over the lagoon solo, feeling quite free and exuberant. I was having so much fun that I decided to give it more gas. The machine responded quickly to my lightest touch. I began to go faster and faster, with my hair and suit — and maybe other parts of me — flapping in the wind. It was the closest to flying I'd ever done, and I was thoroughly enjoying myself. I was caught up in the thrill of accomplishment. Eventually, the rental time ran out, and I saw the signal to come back to shore, so I headed in. But I was really moving now.

Turns out I didn't hear, or maybe I didn't absorb, the instructions on how to proceed back to shore in some kind of safe manner. I sped my way to the beach like a torpedo menacing a small shore town. I was quickly approaching the docking area and the little restaurant that sat on the end of the pier. I was headed toward them like a speeding bullet. As I got closer to the glass wall of the restaurant, I could see people grabbing their plates and scattering. It was like a sci-fi movie where the monster shows up, and people start running for their lives.

Folks on the beach were sending stunned looks my way and began waving their arms. At first, I thought they were impressed by my ability and speed, but it quickly hit me that, if I didn't stop, I was going to crash through the glass. I panicked. *Just let up on the throttle,* my brain screamed to my now frozen hands.

I was getting alarmingly close. There were jet skiers on either side of me now going as fast as I was. I later learned they were trying to catch me to help me, but all I registered is that they were blocking my pathway to turn and avoid hitting the pier. Then, out of the corner of my eye, I saw a red jet ski with a rather large man approaching me at a right angle from the left side. He later said he hadn't seen me because he was watching the restaurant patrons screaming and scattering like rats. The next thing I heard was a metallic crashing sound, and then I felt myself being launched upward and off the machine. I landed in the water with a loud, clumsy plop. I remember bobbing in my life vest and staring at the blue sky while people made their way to what they thought was my cold, dead body.

They brought me up to the same restaurant that I almost smashed into and had me sit. A cold drink was thrust in my hands, and I was very aware of the *tsks* and gawking looks. More cell-phone camera clicks. When my legs stopped being wobbly (traitors), they loaded me into a golf cart and carted me back to the ship.

I was told by the cruise line that I am banned from water activities on that island. Banned?! Humph. Not to worry. Heck, they'll forget about it. Anyway, I know Gram was watching, and I probably made her pee her pants a little. So, next cruise? I'm going zip-lining.

—Jody Lebel—

49

The "Why Do It?" Guy

When you start loving yourself and respecting your
time and energy, things will change. Get to know
your worth, and your value will go up.
~Germany Kent

ommon sense isn't a characteristic often found in the young. Normally, it takes a fair amount of life experience for a person to possess it. So, when one discovers common sense in a person who hasn't yet reached the age of majority, it's an event worth noting and celebrating.

The young man in whom I discovered an uncommonly large reservoir of common sense was named Jim Swihart. I came to know Jim, who was a year behind me, during my senior year at a well-known New England boarding school known as Andover. Jim was in the same dormitory as me and lived just down the hall from one of my close friends, so we had a few brief conversations. I didn't know him all that well, but even from the few conversations we had, I learned to appreciate his obvious intelligence and sardonic wit. In an environment where rigid social conformity was the norm, Jim was clearly a guy who thought for himself. This was refreshing and made me feel well-disposed toward him.

Though I sensed that Jim was also beginning to like me a bit, I was most surprised one Saturday, a bit after Christmas break, when he suggested that we go skating together on a small pond near our dorm. I had not skated even once during my three and a half years at

Andover, nor had I ever discussed skating with Jim or anyone else. I don't know how he even knew that I owned a pair of skates! Nonetheless, I accepted the invitation with pleasure despite my minimal skating ability. Given that I was an extreme introvert, social invitations of any sort were few and far between, and Jim was someone I was interested in getting to know better.

As a skater, Jim seemed to be about average. As for me, though, I performed somewhat better than might have been expected, given that I had only skated twice in the past two years. To my amazement, I even remembered how to skate backward — briefly — the outer limit of my ice skills.

We continued skating for about an hour. Then, after changing back into street shoes, we went down to the Coffee Mill for a cup of java. As soon as we'd been served, Jim asked me, "Do you enjoy skating?"

"No," I said. "Not really."

"Then why do you do it?" he asked.

I had no ready answer available. It would have taken two or three sessions with a sympathetic psychiatrist to bring one up. The truth was that skating had never been my idea; it had been more or less forced on me, as something I'd more or less been expected to do while growing up in a town with several fine skating ponds. At age twelve, I'd been presented with a pair of skates and told, in effect, "Go learn how to use them."

Granted, I had at one time had visions of playing hockey, a sport similar in some ways to lacrosse, which I loved. But my lack of speed and dexterity on the ice quickly laid such thoughts to rest. At best, skating was something I tolerated. I enjoyed being outside on brisk winter days but would far rather have been coasting, riding my bike, or taking a walk through the New Canaan bird sanctuary.

Observing my puzzlement, Jim quickly changed the subject. Though I couldn't produce an answer to his question that day, I had one before the end of the year. I never put on my skates again, and after graduation they found their way to the huge cardboard box destined for the Salvation Army along with a bunch of superannuated sport jackets, torn trousers, shirts with frayed collars, sweaters out at the elbow, and mouldering sneakers.

Although I never had another serious conversation with Jim, his acid test, "Why do it?" is one I have come to apply again and again throughout my life. Most notably, I applied it to jogging, which I took up in my thirties mainly as a way to sublimate the rage built up in a bad marriage. Running around the local track one afternoon a few months after my separation, I asked myself if I was enjoying it. One lap later, not coming up with an affirmative answer, and no longer feeling any rage needing to be sublimated, I stopped and went for a beer.

The next day, I went to a local swimming club and took out a pool membership. Swimming has remained a favorite activity of mine to this day (some thirty-five years after the decision to stop jogging). More recently, I've applied the "Why do it?" test to books I was struggling to read and people I was struggling to understand. It has, indeed, become an integral part of my overall life philosophy. "If you don't enjoy it and are not being paid well for it, why do it?" Indeed. I can't recall any advice I've ever received, as a boy or man, which has served me better.

I understand that Jim later became a career foreign-service officer, as was his father before him. If he applied anywhere near as much practical wisdom to the diplomatic situations he faced as he did to my situation with regard to skating, the United States would have been exceptionally well served.

—Jon Peirce—

50

Courtside Decision

A leader is one who knows the way,
goes the way, and shows the way.
~John Maxwell

"Dave is over there talking about you. Telling everyone how you lost the championship game for him." My husband's words hung in the air as I gazed across the field. I could still feel Dave's arms in a gorilla embrace as he'd greeted me minutes earlier. Now, one of those arms pointed an accusing finger at me. I felt betrayed.

The warm sunshine. The delightful aroma of popcorn and hot dogs. The crack of a ball against the bat. Cheers from parents in the stands. It had been a perfect day to watch Little League baseball, until now.

Unwillingly, I was whisked back to a courtside decision several years earlier. I was Dave's coaching assistant. It was the final minutes of the basketball championship.

Community leagues depend on parent volunteers to coach these pre-high school sports. I am not coaching material, not by a long shot. I can, however, follow instructions, yell encouragement, and track attendance. So, when no one else would, I reluctantly raised my hand.

I admired Dave's style, knowledge, and commitment. He knew how to bring out the best in people, including me. Under his leadership, I earned the boys' respect even though we never hid my lack of knowledge about the sport. Unfortunately, it seemed that our last game together still haunted him.

That basketball season, our group of boys turned into a fairly decent team of talented and not-so-talented players. Dave was committed to fair time on the court regardless of skill. His method to determine the lineup was as predictable as it was unpredictable. It was, however, one-hundred-percent fair.

Whether for practice or a game, each player was assigned a number when he arrived. The first to arrive was number one. It was not unusual for some of our boys to arrive before us. So, our two sons were not always first. Each boy's number was recorded on his right hand and on a spreadsheet with the different positions listed in order. On paper, we looked very organized.

All players played all positions in numerical order. Each quarter, we rotated. The next set on the court stood ready to fill in mid-quarter if needed. With Dave's system, our boys always knew what to expect. Our games were an interesting mix of talent, skill development, and luck. The system wasn't foolproof, but it was fair.

As the season wore on, our players solidified, intuitively anticipating each other's strengths and weaknesses. They became a stronger team — together. As coaches, we couldn't have been prouder. No favoritism. No fighting. No bickering. No parental criticism.

Now, back to that championship game that Dave was still lamenting. Despite a losing season, our team had accomplished the impossible. Our bunch of mismatched players was minutes from securing a championship trophy. Except for three players, one being Dave's son, our team's skills did not merit the coveted prize. And yet, it was within reach.

Just before the final quarter, Dave asked me for a consult.

"I'm not sure what to do," he said. The lack of confidence in his voice alarmed me. "We're only two points behind. However, we have an advantage. They have only played their strong players. They are exhausted. Their legs wobble. Their shots barely clear the rim. I really think we can win this."

Dave's fair-play rotation had preserved our boys' energy. Was it enough to compensate for their mediocre skills?

"Here's the problem. The next set to take court are not our strong players. If we skip them and send in the next string after that, we could actually win this! Our boys can walk out of here with their heads high. What do you think?"

A million thoughts whirled through my brain, bouncing off what-is-best-for-our-team. Slowly, I inhaled, exhaled, and prayed.

"Dave, your system made these kids into a team. They work and think as a unit. They trust you. They know their own skills as well as each other's. The decision is yours, and I will support you. You asked for my opinion. Do you really want it?"

Dave nodded.

"They know the lineup. They know what is at stake. And they know who is next on the court. We expect them to *do* their best, not *be* the best. Dave, listen. Five, ten, or twenty years from now, no one will remember the score of this game. But the boys you skip over will never forget that you thought their best wasn't good enough."

Dave hung his head. "Why do you have to put it that way? As a coach, what you are saying is insane." Dave took a long walk down the hall alone. When he returned, he stuck to the lineup.

Our team cheered from the sidelines. The boys on the court gave it their all. For the first time in the game, we took the lead. Then lost it. Then regained it. The roar from the crowd was deafening. It was a glorious finish.

We lost the championship by two points. There would be no fairytale ending. Why did I encourage Dave to make that insane decision to play fair regardless of the cost? What if I had kept my mouth shut or just said what Dave wanted to hear? Now, that courtside decision still haunted him. And it was my fault.

"Did you hear me?" My husband's voice brought me back to the present. "Honey, did you hear me? Dave is telling everyone about you!"

"Just let it go. Forget it," I muttered.

"Seriously. Do you really think a guy like Dave is going to forget a championship game?"

"Well. Yeah. Kinda. Hey! I don't know anything about coaching. Dave knew that. He was a fool to ask me for advice. And a bigger fool for taking it."

"What are you talking about? Dave admires you. He said your

advice changed his entire perspective on coaching. That's what he's telling everyone over there. Whatever sport he coaches, he is committed to fair play for all players regardless of their skills or the scoreboard."

—Marie T. Palecek—

51

Green Truck Moments

Almost everything will work again if you unplug
it for a few minutes, including you.
~Anne Lamott

I t's been nearly ten years since I read the story, "The Man in the Green Pickup," by Anna S. Redsand, in *Chicken Soup for the Soul: Inspiration for Writers*. No time-management course or self-help book on overcoming procrastination has had as practical an impact on my life as the story of this man who simply used, rather than squandered, fifteen minutes every single day. Every day during his half-hour lunch break, that man spent fifteen minutes eating his sandwich and then spent the remaining fifteen minutes writing on a legal pad in the cab of his truck. In two years of faithful dedication to those fifteen-minute opportunities, he completed a book, which was published.

"I can do that," I told myself, "even if I don't have a green truck." But it soon became clear that adhering to the rigid discipline of his method was more challenging when the "cab of a truck" space was expanded to my home. "Just toss the clothes in the washer first, load the dishwasher, make the bed, and bring hubby a coffee," I told myself. "Answer that text from my friend but try to be brief. As soon as I water the plants, I'll start. Better pay those bills first." By the time I'd accomplished these tasks, I'd already frittered away a half-hour or more.

I couldn't get the picture of the man in the green truck out of my mind, though. It would haunt me until I stopped and went quietly aside to write. I adapted his routine into a more flexible schedule that honored the reality of my day. But I would still set the timer for fifteen minutes and steal away to my desk in the corner.

The pages accumulated; my journals filled shelf after shelf as the years passed. Eventually, they materialized into a first draft of a manuscript. Editing and revision would now become the focus of the precious fifteen minutes a day.

Then the lesson of the man in the green truck spread into other areas of my life. I began calling them my "green truck moments." I learned that, by planning ahead and using as little as fifteen minutes at a time, I could always have my own "fast food" ready. I took a few minutes when I arrived home with groceries to chop fresh fruits and vegetables and package them for easy snacks or quick soups later in the week. I batch-cooked and froze extra portions. When we had day trips out of town for medical appointments, I tossed in small snacks and thermoses of drinks that saved us time as well as money. All took less than fifteen minutes to prepare.

I love receiving mail so I started taking fifteen minutes to write notes or send off birthday cards or small items to cheer my friends with something besides bills in their mail. Friends responded, and now I often find special treats in my own mail.

There are so many areas of my life, from fitness to finances, where a little attention, even fifteen minutes on a regular basis, has made a huge difference. But then there are the other times when the pressure of a crisis or a difficult situation makes me feel I don't even have the fifteen minutes to spare. Sometimes, the idea of having a green truck to sit in, away from the chaos, holds great appeal.

But if I pause, take a deep breath, and look around me, I can usually find at least fifteen minutes to pursue something meaningful. I can find those "green truck moments" to put the tough thing I'm enduring in perspective. And I silently thank "The Man in the Green Pickup" again.

— Phyllis McKinley —

Chapter
7

Make the Effort

Do Your Best

*I wanted to believe that in the end, the universe would
take care of us, and we would end up exactly
where we were meant to be.*
~Julianne MacLean

"**D**ad," I pleaded into the phone, "I don't want to go to
Japan." I stood in one of the Post Exchange phone
booths, just eighteen years old, a little over half a year
into my six-year enlistment in the Air Force. I didn't
have a phone line in my room, and I didn't want to stand in the
hallway of the barracks having an emotional breakdown. I had to use
a pre-paid calling card and find what privacy I could.

"I got my orders for my first base," I told my parents, fighting
back tears. "They say I'm going to Japan. Some place called Kadena,
on Okinawa."

Growing up, I had never left home for anything longer than the
occasional church camp. Those trips took a couple of hours by bus
and lasted a few days.

The flight to basic training in Texas was the first plane I'd ever
seen up close. I knew enlisting in the Air Force meant being away
from home, but there were so many bases and positions in the States,
I just assumed I wouldn't ever go too far.

I left home knowing I would go to California for language training.
I arrived six weeks later in Monterey to learn Vietnamese. School was
challenging but fascinating. Between the beautiful locale and my fun

classmates and friends, I felt really good about my situation.

Then they issued us orders for our first duty assignments.

Japan was literally on the other side of the world. I didn't even understand where Okinawa was before I got those orders. Back then, in 1995, I had to look it up in an atlas.

During technical training, new Airmen could sometimes trade duty assignments on their orders if both of them wanted to switch. I asked around among my classmates but no one wanted to trade. Two of them were headed for Kadena, just like me. The others liked their future assignments in the States.

I started to panic. In the States, a plane ticket to visit home or a road trip in a car would be easy. Overseas flights cost far more.

I found myself out of options and increasingly desperate. One idea remained, a course of action I wouldn't be proud of, but one that might spare me this fate.

"I could fail the final test," I explained to my parents. Even though I enjoyed it, language school was intense and challenging. Students spent eight hours a day in the classroom followed by homework every night for forty-seven or sixty-three weeks. At the end of the course, students would take the Defense Language Proficiency Test or DLPT, where we had to score well enough to move on to learn our military job.

Some of my classmates had already failed and started training for new jobs in the States. I had done well enough up to that point, so I didn't think I could convincingly fail the class.

I laid out the plan for my parents. "My teachers know I'm good enough to make it to the end of class, but they don't control the scores we get on the DLPT. If I do really poorly, I can just say I had a bad day or whatever. Then they'll give me a different job somewhere else."

It would've been easy for my parents to agree, to tell me it was okay to fail. Holidays and vacations would be so much easier to plan and enjoy together. But my dad calmly spoke into the phone. "David, there's an old saying I think fits." He always had favorite phrases and sayings to share. "Do your best, and let God do the rest. If God wants you to go to Japan for some reason, you can't fight it. If He doesn't want you to go to Japan, He can change what happens. You should do the best you can on that test and trust God to work out whatever happens next."

That wasn't the answer I wanted to hear, but I knew he was right.

I went through the rest of class and my final test putting in the effort. I passed the DLPT and went to Texas for a few months of technical training on my way to Okinawa. I wasn't sure what to expect in Japan, but I kept putting in the necessary work to advance through training.

I had no idea then how much of my life would hinge on that decision.

A friend from the base chapel in Texas had a neighbor from Okinawa, and they knew someone who still lived there. When I arrived in Japan, I had a military sponsor ready to help me adjust, but I also had this friend, a missionary named Mei-Lee, who took me on Sundays to find a church community to call home.

When I found the church I liked, she said, "I don't go to this church normally, so I can't take you each week. But I know someone who does, and she lives in the dorm right next to yours."

Mei-Lee introduced me to a lady named Jami, a fellow Airman serving a tour overseas. Jami took me to church with her and became a good friend, encouraging me as I rededicated my life to serving God. When I started getting my life right, Jami was one of my few friends living the way I wanted to live. We spent more and more time together, started dating, got engaged during the time she had left on the island, and married a year later.

She joined me in Japan after the wedding. We stayed three more years before the Air Force sent me back to language school for Chinese-Mandarin and then came right back for another eight years.

I learned to minister to congregations through music during the years I spent in Japan. I also started my journey to becoming a "real" author, participating in writing groups and contests as well as completing a few manuscripts.

Most importantly, Jami and I started our family in Japan. All four of our children were born on Okinawa during our years of being stationed there.

I try not to spend a lot of time on questions like "What if I had done that instead of this?" With all the twists and turns of life, we can never really know the answer or how it all might have played out. How we answer is probably more about our good or bad mood in the moment than any realistic sense of what might have been.

In this case, however, I can see how much of my life and the lives around me would have completely changed. I will always be grateful for my dad's wise words, "Do your best, and let God do the rest."

— David M. Williamson —

53

Three Little Words for Success... Every Day

I have seen that in any great undertaking it is not
enough for a man to depend simply upon himself.
~Lone Man (Isna-la-wica), Teton Sioux

We've heard the words since we were children. "Make your bed" was the standard morning chore assigned to almost every kid. Was it designed to be a daily torture? An opportunity for Mom to nag? Although it took me decades to understand the power of these three words, I see that instilling this daily habit allows us to succeed at something every day... even if the balance of our waking hours goes completely downhill!

I will admit, I didn't make my bed daily as a kid, teenager or young adult. My loving parents didn't require it, as it was all they could do to get four kids dressed, fed and off to school before going to their workplaces. I was a habitual slob with a messy shared bedroom. Making my bed was something I did when my parents said, "Company is coming!" Those words sent me into a frenzy of smoothing my covers and stuffing clothes and shoes under the bed.

Deep down, I thought it was ridiculous to make a bed each morning, only to mess it up each night. What a waste of time.

As I transitioned from college student to career woman, my addiction to alcohol became more evident. Over my decades of drinking, the things in my life that I valued most — faith, husband, family, friends, our lovely home — slipped from priorities to the back burner. Alcohol had taken the reins of my life, but as a high-functioning addict, I reassured myself that because I was married, had a job and had never been arrested, my alcoholism hadn't yet exacted a serious-enough toll on my life.

Thankfully, my dear husband's oft-expressed concern about my drinking led me to go into treatment, and my journey in sober living began. It's common among newly recovering addicts who participate in 12-step programs to be assigned tasks by their sponsors, such as daily prayer, reading recovery-program literature, and calling one's sponsor. Many sponsors also suggest "Make your bed" to those they sponsor. These suggestions are designed to give daily structure to those in recovery and help them to build accountability.

Making my bed each morning allowed me to succeed at something I'd neglected my entire life. I begin the day with the satisfaction of an accomplishment, albeit a simple one. The bonus comes at day's end. Each nighttime proves that I can adopt new behaviors and beneficial habits. Pulling back the covers on my carefully made bed reminds me that change is possible, no matter how miniscule it may seem. I am capable of establishing positive new habits and personal growth, even in middle age.

I now use my brief bed-making task to practice gratitude — for my warm bed, a husband who loves me, and my life in sobriety. Of all the satisfying things that now occupy my time, making my bed first is the least I can do!

— Eve S. Rossmiller —

54

Flying Solo

*Don't be afraid if things seem difficult in the beginning.
That's only the initial impression. The important thing
is not to retreat; you have to master yourself.*
~Olga Korbut

t started out as a regular Monday morning. The alarm woke us
up. We had slept for almost eight hours.

It was time to get ready for work. Bill got out of bed first
and was heading to the shower. His body suddenly went stiff as a
board and he fell backward, hitting the hardwood floor with a thud.
I bounded to his side. He was unconscious. I could not detect any
vital signs.

I made a call to 911 and, within minutes, both fire and ambulance
teams arrived. They attempted CPR to no avail.

One of the attendants said, "I am sorry. There is nothing more
we can do." Time of death: 7:32 A.M.

Because it was a death at home, the police had to come and write
a report, and the coroner had to investigate. Cause of death: pulmonary
embolism, blood clot to the lung at age fifty-nine.

I commenced funeral arrangements. I chose a specific funeral
parlour for two reasons: It was close by, and the owner/manager was
someone I knew. I had worked for him when I was in my twenties.
At that time, Paul was a department-store executive. When his own
father died, he took over running the family funeral business.

Paul was my rock and personally assisted me through the

planning, initiation and execution of arrangements.

When his role was over, and I was in his office signing final paperwork, he said something very profound that I will never forget: "I do not normally provide advice to people, but I know you well enough to say something to you that I hope you will follow."

He said that, after his many years in the business, he saw too many women who, after the death of their husbands, became reclusive. Good friends extended invitations that they declined because they were grieving. Before long, people stopped making the effort to include them.

Paul said, "If people invite you to do things or go places, please make an effort, even if it is just to make a brief appearance. If someone invites you to lunch and it seems too overpowering, suggest getting together for coffee instead. JUST DO IT!"

I was put to the test almost immediately. The day Bill died, some friends had mailed an invitation for the wife's fiftieth birthday. We had been to a fiftieth birthday party for the husband a few years prior, and this looked like it would be a similar event. Essentially, a Saturday night at their house. A drop-in event with drinks and nibbles. Probably about 100 people.

It had only been two weeks since my husband's death. Too soon! But Paul's advice resonated in my head: Just make an appearance. Their house was only about a mile away. I could drive, have one drink, and try to stay for an hour. If I was uncomfortable, I was free to leave at any time.

What else was I going to do on a Saturday night? Probably watch something on Netflix. I kept changing my mind about going or not going. On Saturday, I decided to make the effort. I washed my hair and applied some make-up. I had purchased a beautiful and elegant black pantsuit just before my husband's untimely death. It would be perfect. But it looked like widow's clothing. I decided instead to wear a claret raw-silk pantsuit with a scarf that was claret, gold and cream.

I drove to the house and parked. I entered the house and said hello to the host. I greeted the birthday girl and had a short chat with her.

Then I headed to the bar and asked the waiter for a glass of red wine. I took a sip of the hearty Cabernet Sauvignon. It warmed my soul and was perfect for the November evening that had a chill in the air.

I looked around the room. I knew or was somewhat acquainted with about fifty percent of the people. The other half were strangers.

My husband had been a social butterfly with exceptional interpersonal skills. He could work a room better than a seasoned politician. I had been married to him for thirty years and knew him for three years before that. During that time, I was the wing person, along for the ride. Suddenly, at age fifty-three, I was flying solo.

I started to mingle. Many people graciously said they were sorry for my loss. I talked to people I knew. I was introduced to some new people and had chats with them. I even managed to have a few laughs when someone recounted a funny story.

I took my last sip of wine and looked at my watch. I had been at the party for almost ninety minutes, which was fifty percent longer than my goal. I felt like Cinderella at the ball. I bid farewell to the host and birthday girl, and then I drove home.

As I was getting ready for bed, I reflected on the evening. It had not been easy, but I did have a good time. This would be my new normal.

As other invitations were forthcoming, I sometimes pondered if I should accept, but Paul's advice kept me saying, "Yes."

A friend of mine lost her husband about five years ago, and I knew she was someone who might isolate herself from life. I passed this advice on to her, and she also abided by it.

Recently, she said she appreciated me telling her that and thanked me for the very sound advice. I told her the words of wisdom had originated from Paul, and I had simply paid it forward.

— Daryle Elizabeth Hunt —

55

Use Your Time Wisely

*Never forget the value of time. You can acquire much
in life. By comparison, time is fixed. Use it wisely.*
~Tim Fargo

"**W**hat are you doing?" my fifth-grade teacher inquired
as I hunched over the side of my desk.

"I'm packing my backpack. The bell rings in a
few minutes."

"Unpack your assignments. You still have five minutes. We work
until the clock runs out. The more you do here in class with me, the
less you have to do at home," she countered with a small smile as she
walked back to her desk. She was a very kind and sweet woman, but
I knew she meant business, too.

I petulantly pulled my math assignment back out and completed
one problem at a time as the minutes on the clock ticked away. The
bell finally rang, and I stuffed my homework in my backpack as fast
as possible and headed to my next class.

I cannot remember how many times per day she would reiterate,
"Use your time wisely." It worked. It became second nature for me to
work until the bell rang.

In middle school, I continued the practice she instilled in me. I
worked on my assignments until the bell rang. And she was right. The
more I did in class, the more time off I had at home. The more time I
had at home, the more time I had for projects and hobbies.

I continued the practice until my senior year in high school, having an entire year's worth of college classes completed before I even threw my mortarboard into the air. I used my time wisely.

I instilled that mindset in nearly every aspect of my adult life: my education, my career, and my family.

At age ten, I didn't understand. I do now. Learning how to use your time wisely also means learning what's important to you and being able to prioritize your life. It's not just a lesson in using the time you have, but in enjoying those moments, treasuring the time spent with loved ones, and living life. Truly living life.

—Patricia Ruhaak—

56

Give It Two Weeks

What it's like to be a parent? It's one of the hardest
things you'll ever do, but in exchange it teaches
you the meaning of unconditional love.
~Nicholas Sparks, The Wedding

S everal months pregnant with my first child, I found myself in a conversation with a healthcare provider about an often fraught topic for new mothers: breastfeeding. I expressed that while I hoped and planned to breastfeed my baby, I also embraced the idea that "fed is best." I had no intention of putting undue stress on myself, my baby, or my family if breastfeeding didn't work out for us.

My provider affirmed my position. Then she added, "Can I give you some personal advice? If you want to breastfeed, give it two weeks. Breastfeeding can be challenging, especially at first. But if you can make it through that initial learning curve, you often can be successful." She shrugged. "At least, that's what worked for me and a lot of people I know."

I thought about her words often in the chaotic days following my baby's birth. There were no unusual challenges, just the typical ones that go along with trying to heal from pregnancy, labor, and delivery while also realizing you have given birth to a tiny piranha who wants to eat every other second — and what she wants to eat is you!

Those four words became my lifeline.

I gritted my teeth through another painful feeding. "Give it two weeks," I grunted.

I cried in the shower. "Give it two weeks," I sobbed.

I woke up, yet again, to feed the baby. "Give it two weeks," I yawned.

Amazingly, it worked! There came a day, not very long after my daughter was born, when she and I had physically, emotionally and mentally adjusted to her presence in the outside world and to our new relationship, almost without realizing it. As my provider had predicted, we were in a much better place on Day 15 than we were on Day 1.

If I hadn't had that advice to support me through all those difficult moments, there is no doubt in my mind that I would have given up on breastfeeding and missed out on one of the parenting experiences I treasure most. Whenever I find myself in a similar conversation with a new mom, I pass on that advice. I even repeated it to myself when my second child was born.

Telling myself, "Give it two weeks," doesn't apply only to breast-feeding. So many parenting issues can be resolved by simply giving it a little time. Children go through so many different phases. Some of them can look like a crisis when viewed close-up, but many need nothing more than a little time to resolve.

Sleep regressions, irrational fears, friend drama?

Give it two weeks.

Saying, "Give it two weeks," doesn't just work with kids. It applies to most of the difficulties with change we face in life. I've passed it on to friends with and without children because it helps so much.

New job, new city, new house? Give it two weeks.

New pet, new living situation, new school? Give it two weeks.

New workout routine, new neighbors, new commute? Give it two weeks.

Of course, time can't solve all problems. But it sure can solve a lot of them. My "give it two weeks" philosophy helps me to distinguish between simple growing pains (in children and in life) and larger issues that need more attention.

As my first child gets older, I find myself passing this advice on to her. I hope that the same four words that helped me survive her baby-piranha days will help her survive the many changes she will face as she goes through life.

— Courtney McKinney-Whitaker —

A Misattributed Quote

Grandparents are a family's greatest treasure,
the founders of a loving legacy, the greatest
storytellers, the keepers of traditions
that linger on in cherished memory.
~Author Unknown

When I was eleven years old, my grandfather gave me the book *All Quiet on the Western Front* by Erich Maria Remarque. I read the book, but I think I was too young to really grasp its significance. I probably would have forgotten the book rather quickly, but my grandfather had written on the inside flap: "Success is never final, failure is never fatal; it is the courage to continue that counts." Beneath this quote, he had written a dash followed by the name Winston Churchill. I liked those words, and I repeated them every time I opened the book to read the next section.

When I finished the book and returned it to my grandfather, I asked him why he had written those words inside the book. He told me he had always liked that quote by Churchill, and he'd written it down so he wouldn't forget it. He said it was good advice to live by — not to let one success go to your head or to let one failure devastate you. He told me he believed the words were a good way to navigate the ups and downs of life, and the important thing was to always have the courage to keep trying.

I told my grandfather that I liked the quote, too — and I had memorized it.

So many times in the ensuing years those words rang out to me when I succeeded or failed at something. I would remind myself that one success was never the whole story. There was always more work that needed to be done. Conversely, when I failed at something, I could hear my grandfather saying, "Failure is never fatal. You can always get up and try again." I liked the idea that one success or one failure didn't define me. I felt it was important to keep looking at the bigger picture. When I persevered and kept trying, I found that I did gain a broader perspective and a better understanding of my individual successes and failures.

When I became a parent, I found myself repeating this advice to my young children. After one success, I reminded them not to get a "big head." Even though their accomplishment was great, bigger challenges would come. I also told them not to dwell on a loss or failure because there would be other opportunities to improve and succeed if they just kept trying. My hope was that they'd see this quote as a guide for life, and they'd learn to place both their successes and failures in context. I always tried to emphasize that the important thing was just to keep trying. I think I repeated this advice so often that it became kind of a family mantra.

Years later, when my daughter was in high school, we traveled to Westminster College in Fulton, Missouri for a summer program she was attending. I was excited to visit this college because I knew the school was the site of Sir Winston Churchill's famous "Sinews of Peace" lecture. On March 5, 1946, President Harry Truman joined Churchill in Westminster College's gymnasium for this lecture, which eventually became known as the "Iron Curtain Speech." That day, Churchill and Truman put the town of Fulton front and center on the world's stage.

Westminster College also has a museum dedicated to the life and career of Churchill, and I was excited to see it. I wanted to learn more about the man whose words had played such an integral role in my life.

Unfortunately, I was destined for disillusionment. When I spoke to one of the museum's docents, I learned that Sir Winston Churchill had never said, "Success is never final, failure is never fatal; it is the courage to continue that counts!"

I remember questioning the accuracy of this docent's knowledge, but the man said several people and various groups had examined the millions of words Churchill had spoken and written during his lifetime, and there was no record or evidence that Churchill had ever written or spoken those words. The docent did concede that many people believe Churchill made the statement, and the quote is often attributed to him, but that belief is not accurate. He called it a misattributed quote.

I asked the docent, "If it wasn't Churchill, who did say 'success is never final, failure is never fatal, and it's the courage to continue that counts'?" He said he didn't know, but it wasn't Churchill.

I left the college that day feeling confused and disappointed. I felt like I had been misleading myself and my children for years.

When we got home, my son asked me what was wrong, and I tried to explain that it was a bit of a shock to discover that something I had believed for years wasn't true.

Without missing a beat, my son said, "Does it really matter who said it? I mean, if it is good advice, it's still good advice no matter who said it. Besides, I still think the quote is a good way to live with the ups and downs of life."

I remember staring at my son and shivering. He was right, of course, but it was the words and the intonation he had used. For a second, he sounded just like my grandfather. It was a real déjà vu moment.

I told my son he was absolutely correct. The words and advice they contained were important, not the speaker.

That conversation occurred years ago, and I still don't know who originally said, "Success is never final, failure is never fatal; it is the courage to continue that counts." My grandfather passed away years before we went to Fulton, so I'll never know why he thought Churchill made the statement. I just know the quote had a profound effect on him, and it has been an important guide for me and my family dealing with the ups and downs of life. It also has taught me that good advice is good advice, no matter where it comes from.

— Billie Holladay Skelley —

The Method to a Method-Acting Director's Madness

Empathy is about standing in someone else's shoes,
feeling with his or her heart, seeing with his or her eyes.
~ Author Unknown

What? Had I heard that right? I mean, could a sane person have seriously suggested — indeed, all but insisted — that I go for three days without bathing, shaving, washing, or changing my clothes in the middle of a New York-area heat wave? But no, it was not a bad dream. I had heard it right. And the man who had just made that incredible suggestion, community-theater director Howard Lenters, was standing not three feet away from me, looking me in the eye, and awaiting my response!

This all came about in the context of a post-rehearsal discussion during which Lenters began by expressing his frustration at my apparent inability to get inside the head of my character, a starving Spanish orphan, one of the lead roles in a turn-of-the-century Spanish melodrama in which the Catholic Church figured prominently. After looking me over a good deal more thoroughly than he had during the audition, Lenters concluded, "You haven't suffered enough."

This, coming from a man who barely knew me, who indeed had never met me prior to the audition, was enough to induce a state of shock. Granted, I may not have suffered in the way my poor orphan character had — few people in modern First World countries had, after all. But I had just spent four years in a Massachusetts boarding school run by a headmaster from West Point, with its half-mile trudges through snow to the dining hall, terrible food once you got there, lack of girls, and teachers who positively got off on flunking people. That had certainly been suffering enough for most of us. In response to Lenters' words, my lower jaw dropped at least three inches, which should have answered any question he might have had as to my ability to display emotion. Jaw agape, I stood, motionless and speechless, for the better part of a minute.

"Do you know any way of learning about suffering?" he finally asked, a little more gently. Still unable to speak, I shook my head.

"I'm not sure I do, either," he said. "Still, we've got to try something." There was an ominous pause, and then came the suggestion about going without washing, bathing, or changing clothes. "That should teach you something about suffering!" he concluded, not without a certain smugness.

"Suit yourself!" I said. What I wanted to say was, "Are you crazy? Might I recommend a good psychiatrist?" But he had, after all, cast me — perhaps against his better judgment. And he was the boss. I therefore felt I owed it to him to at least try his experiment, wacky though it might be.

"See you Friday night!" he said, almost cheerfully.

"See you then," I mumbled as I left the rehearsal hall.

The next day, the temperature hit ninety degrees. By day three, it was ninety-eight degrees at noon. We were in the grips of one of New York City's infamous heat waves. (I lived in a Connecticut suburb just outside the city.) Through it all, I faithfully followed Lenters' instructions about not bathing, shaving, washing, or changing clothes. What I hadn't told him was that we had a pool in our back yard in which I swam for at least an hour each day. Without those swims, I'm sure my body odour would have been unbearable, and my fellow actors would have revolted and thrown me off the stage. As it was, the mud-caked, increasingly stiff chino pants and T-shirt looked like an outfit better suited to a criminally insane fugitive than an innocent Spanish orphan.

"I think you've suffered enough," Lenters said as I entered the rehearsal hall on Friday. "You can go back to washing, bathing and changing your clothes." A good thing, too. I was finding the filthy outfit unbearable by this time and might well have dropped out of the show rather than wear it even one more day. As if in gratitude for my deliverance, I displayed more emotion in my role than I ever had before, to Lenters' obvious approval.

Soon enough came the dress rehearsal. Facing a real audience, I managed to display plenty of emotion. For the two actual performances, I displayed even more emotion, winning a rave review from the local paper. In contrast, the actor playing the bullfighter, who had been ranting, raving and generally going way over the top during rehearsals, showed far less emotion during the actual performances and drew barely a mention in the paper.

Was there a connection between Lenters' bizarre request of me and my sudden ability to display emotion? When I took an introductory theatre course in college the following year, I immediately recognized Lenters as a disciple of Stanislavski, the Russian method-acting guru who believed that the best way to prepare for a part was to go and live that part. It seemed utter malarkey, on the face of it. Surely it was beyond ludicrous to think one could actually be another person.

But was there more to all this than met the eye? After all, the bizarre experience would stick in my memory throughout my adult life, long after saner but more conventionally expressed advice offered by professors and other mentors had been forgotten. Whatever else one could say about Lenters' approach, it had gotten my attention. I was, in fact, still thinking about this experience in my first play when, some five decades later, I tried out for my second one, the classic comedy *Harvey*, at a community theatre in Dartmouth, Nova Scotia. By this time, I recognized that Lenters had hit a raw intellectual nerve, making me obsessed with the question of how an actor engages in learning. Had I not still been obsessed with that question, I wouldn't even have considered auditioning. As it was, I did audition and was eventually cast. The role would lead to another and then eventually to eight more, plus a gig as an assistant director. In retirement, theatre has become a serious pursuit. And all from that one crazy suggestion!

Looking at it now, I suspect that Lenters may in fact have been issuing me a challenge rather than expressing any true belief in the method of Method. "All right," he may have been saying. "Here's one approach. If it doesn't work, it'll be up to you to find a better one." To this day, the most important part of any acting venture for me continues to be how I learn the role, and what, at the end, I have learned as a result of having played that role.

The lesson here may be that not all the best advice looks wise on the surface, and not all of it kicks in, like a headache remedy, within thirty minutes. Whatever advice Lenters may initially have intended, it has taken a lifetime to sink in, and it is still working. He has long been gone, but if I could have one minute with him, I'd say, "Break a leg on that celestial stage, Howard. You done pretty good despite yourself!"

— Jon Peirce —

59

Be All There

This job has been given to me to do. Therefore,
it is a gift. Therefore, it is a privilege.
~Elisabeth Elliot

'm a dreamer. I always have been. Hoping for the future and holding my breath for peaceful times to come.

I'm a thinker. I always have been. Analyzing the past. Reliving moments as if they could be changed.

After college, I wanted to travel. More than that, I wanted to live overseas. Africa was calling me. It filled my thoughts and every decision. It was why I got into the health field in the first place. But in the interest of paying student loans and being a productive member of society, I decided to get a job. The job being offered to me was in a dark hospital in a big city in Texas — hardly my Africa dream!

At first, my heart was not in it. My focus was across the ocean. But every moment is given to us for a reason. My wise mentor and big sister reminded me of a quote by Jim Elliot, one of my heroes and inspirations. Jim Elliot was a missionary in Ecuador. He was killed following his calling, following his King, following his love. He said, "Wherever you are, be all there." I had read this quote often and dreamed of being "all there" in Africa, not to working long days in a hospital in Texas.

My sister's reminder of this truth was timely. It refocused my days. It took my thoughts captive. Today is the day to "be all there." This hospital, this big city in Texas, it was my Africa.

I have lived many places since then, but I remind myself often to align those thoughts, align those dreams, for "wherever you are, be all there."

—RoChelle Crow—

60

A New Day

Hope is being able to see that there is light despite
all of the darkness.
~Desmond Tutu

While it's often thought of as a place for premature infants, the NICU is for any newborns needing intensive care. My son was full-term and the biggest baby in the hospital's NICU by far, but he was having serious breathing difficulties. He was connected to a CPAP machine and oxygen monitor and fed through a nasogastric (NG) tube.

I hated the NG tube, and my son did, too. Despite his weakened state, he had managed to rip the tube out of his nose no less than three times. The tube had to be re-inserted through his tiny nostril and down into his throat in order for me to feed him through a little milk-filled syringe that connected to the end of the tube. The lovely dreams I had of nursing my baby, rocking him while he fed, or sweetly burping him over my shoulder were dashed. Food was slowly pushed down the tube, through his nose and into his stomach, and that was it.

On the fifth day in the NICU, I protested about the NG tube, saying that I wanted to feed him with a bottle or even try to nurse him. I insisted, and the doctors agreed to let me try. My son's feedings would be closely recorded to see if he was able to get sufficient milk intake without the NG tube. After the first eighteen hours, it was determined he could not independently drink enough from a bottle, and the NG tube was reinserted.

The next morning (day six) when I came into the NICU and saw the tube in his tiny nose, I crumpled. It was a sign that he wasn't getting stronger or improving, and it made me lose hope. The doctors made their rounds and discussed new tests they wanted to try and what they had discovered so far. They still didn't know what was wrong or how to help him. He was in "survival mode," and so was I.

The CPAP machine would stay.

The oxygen monitor would stay.

And, yes, the NG tube would stay.

Seated on the plastic chair close to my son's little NICU box/bed, I started crying. The doctors were kind and tried to console me, but I couldn't stop the tears.

The situation felt so dark. We didn't have answers, we didn't have treatment, and my son was not improving. I had held on to the glimmer of hope that he could be strong enough to feed independently from a bottle, even if nursing wasn't an option at this point. Realizing he wasn't strong enough to eat on his own crushed my remaining resolve.

After a few minutes, a young nurse came and sat beside me. She put her hand gently on my shoulder. When I had contained my tears a little, she handed me a tissue and asked if I wanted to talk.

She acknowledged my fears, affirmed me as a mother, and recognized the trigger that was the NG tube. I asked again if we could take it out while knowing full well that she could not override the doctor's orders.

The nurse replied, "Not today. But remember, tomorrow is a new day."

She didn't seem much older than me, but her words were wise and hope-filled, and I held on to them. I remembered her advice and repeated it to myself multiple times a day: "Tomorrow is a new day." Today, there may be heartache, difficult tests and procedures, but tomorrow is a new day. Tomorrow has its own hope that NG tubes (or any other symbol of difficulty) cannot touch.

Parents in the NICU count every day, but we don't usually look forward to a new day with a sense of hope or expectation. The advice of this nurse completely changed my perspective away from the challenges to see the hope of tomorrow, which would always be a new day.

On day seven, the doctors disconnected my son from the CPAP machine.

On day eight, my son drank half of his milk intake orally, without the NG tube.

On day nine, he only used the NG tube once.

On day ten, the doctors approved removing the NG tube completely.

"Tomorrow" came; it just came a few days later than expected. On day fifteen, we were discharged from the hospital, and my son "graduated" from the NICU, so to speak.

What I learned from the advice of that NICU nurse was to look beyond today and its challenges and to consider tomorrow with a hope so strong that the struggles of today cannot dampen it.

After all, tomorrow is a new day.

— Ree Pashley —

My Dad, My Heart, Our Sport

Sports are a most excellent device
with which to test a man's character.
~Olaus Magnus

The first time I stepped onto a wrestling mat, I was six, but all my family members like to say I got started in wrestling the day I was born. That's because my dad used to be a wrestling coach and was pretty intense about the sport. He had coached state champions, guys he pushed and pushed to make them get to the top of the victory podium. Afterward, they all said how much they loved him. Dad stopped coaching when I turned twelve, but he never let go of his own love for the sport.

He never pressured me to win like his former wrestlers had. Maybe Dad saw I lacked their skills or mental toughness. Or maybe he blamed himself for not giving me the genetic talent one needs to be a great athlete. Either way, although he tried not to show it, I could see the hurt in his eyes when I lost. It wasn't that he was disappointed; I think he felt sorry for me.

I knew my limitations (most opponents were quicker) and my strengths (because of Dad, I knew more moves), but before I got into high school, I just wasn't serious about the sport. The brutal truth is that if you want to win at wrestling, you have to take it seriously or, as Dad would say, "You have to dedicate yourself, son. Commit to the sport."

Dad was right.

When I joined the high school varsity team as a sophomore, I committed myself and trained year-round — with Dad leading the way. He and I were together a lot. In the spring, summer, and fall, I lifted with Dad spotting me, ran with Dad timing me, and learned advanced moves from Dad to improve my technique on the mat. "You have to do more than the other guys," Dad advised me. "Practices during the season aren't enough. This is what you have to do if you want to be successful at anything."

During the season, he'd watch from the stands, and I'd join him in the bleachers to hear his critique after my matches. I listened carefully to what he had to say, and soon I began to win more matches. I placed in every tournament, even emerging as the champion in a few. The trophies and plaques glistened on my bedroom bookshelf at home. But Dad hugging me after my matches — his face beaming with pride — glistens even more brightly in my memory.

Things changed, though — literally — in a heartbeat.

At a practice during the first week of the season in my senior year, I felt my heart flutter. It stopped, started again, stopped, and then beat too rapidly before returning to a normal rate. When I got home, I told Mom, and she made an appointment with the doctor for the next day.

Dad took me to the doctor's office, and the examination revealed a heart murmur. The worst news, however, was the doctor's prognosis: I had to stop wrestling. This news devastated Dad. Nevertheless, when we drove home, Dad echoed the doctor. "Quitting wrestling is the right thing to do, Keith." The rest of the way home, we didn't talk at all. I saw again the hurt in his eyes as I sat in the passenger seat that day.

At the dinner table that evening, Dad still said nothing, worrying me. Later, I gathered the courage to confront him about the silent treatment. I stood in front of him in our family room as he sat watching the news and asked if we could talk.

"Of course, son. What is it?" He turned off the television and peered up at me.

In turn, I looked at the tops of my shoes. "I'm sorry if I've disappointed you."

He exhaled loudly and rested his hands on his knees. "What? How have you disappointed me?"

I lifted my head and met his eyes. "That I couldn't finish wrestling this season."

Dad's voice came down a decibel or two. "That's not your fault, Keith, and you didn't disappoint me."

I continued to gaze at Dad and pressed on. "Is wrestling the only thing we have in common?"

The crestfallen look on his face convinced me I had struck a nerve. Dad bowed his head. "I've been a real chump if anything I've done has made you feel that way."

We stayed quiet for a minute, both of us wondering who should speak next. I searched my brain for the right words until I found them. "I thought our only bond was wrestling."

Dad looked up at me and smiled slowly. "It was never really about wrestling, son. It was about dedication, commitment, and perseverance. The fact that you trained the way you did and competed so enthusiastically was enough for me." He finished his statement with a head nod.

I discovered I'd been holding my breath. "So, you're not disappointed or angry?"

His eyes got big. "Of course not. I've never been angry at you, and I will always love you whether you wrestle or not." Then Dad stood and hugged me, his arms enveloping me in the warmth of his body.

Wrestling has had a dramatic effect on my life. It made me healthier, more confident, and goal-oriented. I've learned to deal with losing and to appreciate winning. I'm especially thankful for the memories I have spending time with my dad on wrestling mats. He came to all my matches and encouraged me whether I won or lost. He showed me moves and taught me mental toughness. My heart may have prevented me from continuing as a competitor, but my heart is still grateful for all that Dad did to make me not only a better wrestler but also a better person.

— Keith Manos —

62

Eat the Crust First

*You cannot escape the responsibility
of tomorrow by evading it today.*
~Abraham Lincoln

n the early 1980s, I was flipping through TV channels when a perky, petite blonde with a Southern accent caught my attention. It was an infomercial, and I was soon captivated not only by her humor but her wisdom.

Her name was Rita Davenport, and she was a motivational speaker.

The product that she was promoting was a set of cassette tapes for women called "It's Time for You," and I couldn't wait to order it.

The topics covered time management, building confidence, and various other challenges that women face.

When the cassettes arrived, I listened to them over and over. Rita kept my attention, and every time I listened, I picked up something new while laughing all over again at her stories and jokes.

But she was serious about helping women, and I knew that I could share this information with the life-skills classes that I taught at the community college.

There was one bit of advice, however, that I personally needed to pay attention to. Rita shared how she never liked the crust on a piece of pie, so she would eat it first in order to enjoy the rest of her treat. (Now, I did wonder why she didn't just throw away the crust, but that was obviously not the point.)

It had nothing to do with dessert but was symbolic for tackling first any unpleasant things that we have to do in a day. I knew she was right and felt a bit uneasy about my own tendency to procrastinate. I would put off an unpleasant task, phone call or difficult project until the last minute and do easier tasks instead, as if the job I didn't want to do would go away by some miracle.

Of course, by the latter part of the afternoon, I was fatigued and found a way to put it off until the next day. Was that helpful? Of course not. It was always lingering in my mind that I "should" get it done. I once read that when we say "should," we really mean "don't want to." Listen to how many times you hear it in a week, and you will know that this is true.

And even though I felt anxiety when I would procrastinate, I couldn't stop doing it. Why was I putting myself through this?

So, I decided after listening to Rita and her pie story that I would eat the crust first from that point on. It was not easy in the beginning. Sometimes, it was downright frustrating when I looked at my to-do list and saw things I wasn't crazy about facing that day.

But I began forcing myself to eat that darn crust first, all the while hearing Rita's chirpy voice in my head encouraging me. And, as I followed her advice, I felt relieved when I tackled the job early in the day and no longer had to think about it.

This eventually became a habit for me, and forty years later, I still follow this rule most days. Sometimes, I do have outside interruptions that make me postpone something, but overall, I get the tough stuff done first.

— Claudia Irene Scott —

Pursue Your Passion

63

The Contest that Changed My Life

If you know what you want in life, don't wait for
someone else to give it to you. Go after it,
and don't let anything stand in the way.
~Tracey Lange, We Are the Brennans

To say I knew nothing about the stock market when I was twelve years old in the late 1960s is an understatement. My parents were Depression-era immigrants who likely kept my dad's factory wages under their mattress. So when my sixth-grade teacher, Mrs. Rosenblum, started off class one day by handing each of us a copy of *The New York Times* business section, I felt like I was staring at the equivalent of Egyptian hieroglyphics!

Mrs. Rosenblum (who passed away at age ninety-five a few years back) always did like to push the envelope with us. Yeah, we would privately complain to each other that she was veering too far outside the curriculum we were "supposed" to be learning. But, deep down, we kind of knew we would someday look back on her the way a retired pro athlete reflects back fondly on his or her toughest coach.

"So, class, I want you to open that newspaper I've handed you and go to the stock market tables inside. I'd like you to take your time and go through all the corporations listed, from A to Z. When your eyes hit upon the name of a company that you believe, with all your heart, is going to do exceptionally well in the future, I want you to write down the name of that company and its stock symbol."

I sure as heck was not going to read through what seemed like thousands of companies, most of which I'd never even heard of. But I did think long and hard about whether there were any consumer products or services I'd seen advertised on TV that made me say to myself, "Wow, that sounds so neat! I want THAT!" And then, out of the blue, a lightning bolt hit!

"Oh, man. What the heck's the name of that new type of television service I keep seeing all those ads for? The one they call 'cable TV' with all these new kinds of programs I can't get on my regular TV? I think it begins with a T... I got it! TelePrompTer!"

And, sure enough, I scrolled down to the Ts on the American Stock Exchange, and there it was... And it was selling for a pittance... only $2 per share! If this was going to wind up being one of Mrs. Rosenblum's "contests," then I was confident who the winner of this one would be!

Once everyone had made their stock selection, Mrs. Rosenblum announced, "So, class, remember yesterday when we were learning all about how to create graphs? Well, you're going to create a data graph of your own, beginning with the closing price of the stock you selected today. You will then chart the rise and fall of your stocks once each day for the remainder of the semester!"

"Mrs. Rosenblum, is there a prize for the winner?" my pal Michael Leitner asked (speaking on behalf of every kid in the class).

"Oh, yes." She smiled. "The winner will get a glowing reference from yours truly when he or she applies to Merrill Lynch someday to become the #1 stock analyst on Wall Street!"

I still recall the sound of the collective groan filling the classroom at her response. Couldn't we at least win an extra fifteen minutes of lunch break for a week or something? Still, I was excited!

So, let me cut right to the chase. Not only did I win Mrs. Rosenblum's contest, but I did so in a virtual landslide. TelePrompTer's stock wound up quadrupling that semester! (Note: TelePrompTer eventually became the largest cable TV provider in the U.S. and the forerunner to HBO.) Watching that stock's price chart start to resemble a rocket ship to the moon was incredibly exciting. Mrs. Rosenblum actually ended the contest early because I was so far ahead of everybody else in the class.

"Gary, I don't know what you were planning to do for your career when you got older," I recall her saying in front of all the other kids, "but I strongly suggest you consider something that involves picking stocks!"

When I got home that afternoon, I recall boldly announcing to my parents that I was planning on becoming a stock-market analyst when I grew up. I'll never forget how red my Austrian father's face turned.

"So, you vant to be a gambler and embarrass your family by losing everything vee worked so hard for?" he yelled. "You vill be a doctor. DAT's a sure ting!"

And, indeed, with all the passion of a wind-up doll on quaaludes, I ultimately did pursue the one and only route that would make my parents happy. I entered NYU's pre-med program and slogged my way through four miserable years. Between commuting back and forth every day and studying feverishly, I had little time for a social life. I was depressed as heck but didn't have enough free time to let it all sink in. Besides, my parents' world literally revolved around my brother and me, and I was terrified of letting them down.

But there was one thing that kept me somewhat sane during those awful college years... something I certainly never told my parents about. When I turned eighteen, I yanked the few thousand bucks that were sitting in the savings account they had set up for me and opened an account at a brokerage firm. And I started trading stocks... this time for real. And I did pretty well. Actually, *better* than well!

There was no earthly reason why I should have been any good at it. I had taken one economics course in high school and hated it. But there was that feeling, that thrill I had never forgotten — that time in sixth grade when I won that contest, and Mrs. Rosenblum predicted I'd become the #1 stock-market analyst on Wall Street!

Well, luckily for me, I got rejected by the four medical schools I applied to. And that summer, I found myself spending several days a week at the Brooklyn Business Library, reading and learning everything I could about the subject matter and one career path (other than maybe "mass murderer") that would upset my parents the most.

Come fall, armed with a boatload of moxie, I naively began my pursuit of a job as a Wall Street analyst. In hindsight, it was an absurd notion. But for the first time in my life, I was actually chasing *my* dream, not somebody else's version of it.

Fast forward only a few months later. I was hired by a brokerage firm as their first-ever "junior analyst." Two years later, I became Senior Growth Stock Analyst. And then, two years after that, I co-founded the firm's Corporate Finance division! Today, almost four decades later, I still happily make my living (out of my home office) doing what God clearly meant for me to do: find undervalued stocks.

I will forever be thankful to Mrs. Rosenblum for pointing me toward my ultimate career destiny and encouraging me to consider pursuing it.

"So," you may ask, "did you ever try to contact your teacher to let her know what a difference she made in your life?" In fact, I did just that!

It was probably about two decades back. Luckily, my Internet search uncovered only one "Ida Rosenblum" who fit the profile. She was living in a retirement community in Florida at the time. I took a deep breath and nervously dialed her number. Here is the conversation as I remember it:

"Hello, is this Mrs. Rosenblum? Look, you're not going to remember me in a million years, but this is one of your P.S. 209 students from about thirty years ago."

"Really? You never know. I might. What's your name?"

"Trust me. You won't remember me. I'm Gary Stein."

"Gary Stein! I remember you! You were best friends with Michael Leitner. And you were in that class with the 'girl haters club,' right?"

"WHAT? I'm just speechless, Mrs. Rosenblum! I was like the quietest kid in the whole class. I figured you'd be much more likely to remember the class clown/troublemaker type, like that kid Brooks!"

"Brooks? No, I don't recall him at all. I guess I prefer to only keep the really nice kids in my long-term memory!"

The revelations from that portion of our conversation were mind-blowing enough. But next came the coup de grâce. I told her the reason

I was calling. It was to thank her from the bottom of my heart for having created that stock market game of hers. How much it wound up changing my life and God knows how many others.

"STOCK MARKET GAME?" she responded incredulously. "I don't recall *ever* doing something like that in one of my classes!"

I described it to her in detail.

"Gary, I can honestly say that I do not recall that one at all. I must have tried it that one time and never did it again. Isn't that what you kids call a 'one-hit wonder'?"

Yes, Mrs. Rosenblum, I guess that's exactly what it was. A one-hit wonder. But for yours truly? It may very well have been the hit song of all time!

— Gary Stein —

I'm Going with You

You get the best out of others when
you give the best of yourself.
~Harvey S. Firestone

was surprised that he was even up. As I was adjusting the knot on my tie, he was suddenly there, yawning, at my bedroom door. His thick mane of hair was noticeably disheveled, and the sleepy look in his eyes told me that he probably should have just stayed in bed.

"Good morning. What are you getting all dressed up for?" my just-home-from-college twenty-year-old son, Michael, said sleepily.

"I have to go to a funeral," I answered.

"Who died?" he asked.

"A man who meant a lot to me," I told him. "A man who changed my life a long time ago."

"I guess he was pretty important to you."

"Yes," I replied. "He was."

Michael pondered my answer for a moment and then said something that caught me by surprise.

"So, if he was that important to you, then I guess that means he was kind of important to me, too."

As I stood there, stunned by what he had just said, he continued, "Hey, Dad, if he meant that much to you, then give me a few minutes. I'm going with you."

Before I could respond, Michael had gone upstairs to his bedroom to get dressed. He returned a few minutes later, and the transformation was amazing. His sleeping T-shirt and shorts had been replaced by a dark pullover sweater, Dockers pants, and real shoes instead of his favored basketball sneakers. And that thick mane of unruly hair that moments before seemed to have a mind of its own was now combed into perfect submission.

We left for the cemetery.

It was a long time ago. I was a Boy Scout on a weekend camping trip, and although I knew better, I broke a cardinal camp rule and wandered away from our site — quickly becoming lost in the woods. But, by some miracle, I found my way back just as local law enforcement, park rangers, and my troop leaders were about to set out to find me. I was otherwise unharmed, except, of course, for my pride.

Embarrassed, I abruptly quit the troop.

A few days later, one of my adult leaders came by my home to talk with me about my decision to leave scouting. He said that while what I had done was wrong, to quit would be worse. He said, "Steve-o," he always called me this, "if you stay in the troop, somehow, someday, you're going to find out that scouting will forever remain an important and influential part of your life."

By the time he left our home that night, my membership was intact — a lesson was learned.

Three years later, I became an Eagle Scout. Two years after that, I became an assistant scoutmaster serving under the very same man whose compassionate counsel had persuaded me to remain in scouting. I would one day become the scoutmaster myself and ultimately serve in various volunteer positions within the program for the next forty years.

But, as my one-time mentor had predicted, it was my ongoing membership that profoundly influenced my eventual career and my life.

While being interviewed for a patrolman's position within my community's police department, my interviewers neglected to ask me a single question concerning my interest in law enforcement. Rather, they inquired about my Eagle Scout project and my experiences as a Boy Scout leader.

I was sworn in as an officer shortly afterward.

The following summer, I married the love of my life, Karen, and a few years after that, we started our family. Michael came first, and two years later, our daughter, Tracy.

But it was my service as a scoutmaster that contributed to my being selected as a detective assigned to the department's Youth Bureau. This new position required my participation in countless speaking engagements, which necessitated the need to craft relevant speeches that were both entertaining as well as informative. When one such engagement resulted in a noticeable emotional response from my audience, my prepared speech became the basis for my first-ever published piece. And, just like that, a newly minted freelance writer was born!

So, you see, my career, my marriage, my family life and, later, my writing successes were all the direct descendants of a membership decision that was decided during my more formative years.

I now needed to share this information with someone special.

Not long after retiring from the department, I visited with my one-time scoutmaster — now in his mid-eighties. That night, as we reminisced, I reminded him of things that he'd taught me — of lessons learned, and about the time when his astute advice convinced me that it was a far better decision to remain a Scout than not. I reminded him that, as he had predicted, scouting, in one way or another, has remained an influential part of my life.

But suddenly there was something else that I needed to say — something else that I needed him to hear. So, I sat down on the chair next to him and began.

"How different my life might have been had you not talked me out of quitting the troop," I told him. "You changed my life, more than I can ever say, and for this, I will always be grateful."

And it was true. The path on which my life would eventually travel was a direct result of his counsel — Eagle Scout, scoutmaster, police officer, husband, father, detective, writer.

I stood up and extended my hand, the good Scout — anticipating that we'd share the official handshake. Instead, he slowly rose from his chair and hugged me as he softly whispered, "Thank you, Steve-o."

We may never know the lives we've touched until, if we are lucky one day, we do. My old scoutmaster, after so many years, finally knew.

It was the only time that I ever saw him cry.

As we gathered graveside and my troop leader was laid to rest, I thought about my earlier conversation with Michael. "So, if he was that important to you, then I guess that means he was kind of important to me, too."

I also remembered a prediction made years before: *Scouting will forever remain an important and influential part of your life.* Of course, he was right — the proof of which was standing next to me and wearing a dark sweater, Dockers, and real shoes — my son Michael, a direct descendant of a membership decision decided during my more formative years and of whom I couldn't be any prouder.

It seems that as we were saying goodbye to him, my former scoutmaster, Mr. Bradshaw, had taught me one final lesson.

— Stephen Rusiniak —

65

Keep Showing Up

Believe you can, and you're halfway there.
~Theodore Roosevelt

started running competitively almost as soon as I could walk. I was three years old when I toed the line of my first official race. My mom and both of my siblings were runners, so the sport was built into my life from the beginning.

When I was young, running always represented freedom and joy. I ran because it made me feel powerful. This pure, concentrated love of the sport gave me wings that carried me through even the toughest practices and races. However, as I got older, the pressure started to creep in. My dedication to running had yielded results. I was winning, but I became so self-critical that I lost sight of my real purpose as a runner: to have fun. The pre-race hours that had previously been filled with gleeful anticipation became long stretches of overwhelming anxiety. I even began to dread hard workouts, knowing I would be disappointed if I didn't achieve my goals.

Though the pressure I put on myself was difficult to endure, I still loved running at my core. I continued to compete on the varsity cross-country and track teams in high school and was a seven-time state qualifier heading into my senior track season. If the season went as planned, I would finish my high school career with a perfect eight.

That spring, I trained harder than I ever have, balancing grueling workouts with college applications, schoolwork and extracurriculars. By mid-May, I was exhausted and overwhelmed. Then, I felt a twinge in my left calf. In the days leading up to the regional meet, I tried to stretch and rest the pain away, but nothing seemed to help. To continue my season, I needed to finish my 1,600-meter race in the top two. My only choice was to get to the line and see what I could do.

In the first chaotic moments after the gun went off, I thought I might have a shot. I sprinted off the line and fought for a position in lane one. After the first lap, I fell from first to second place. As the pain in my leg worsened, I dropped to third, then fourth. I fought against the pain and tried to focus on catching the girls in front of me, but I was only losing ground. As I passed my mom on the sidelines, she mouthed, "You can stop." Her words went straight to my heart. In ten years of competitive running, I had never dropped out of a race. But I had also never had an injury like this. In a split-second decision, I stepped off the track and into the grass, effectively ending my season. I would never run another high-school track race.

The rest of the week passed in a blur of hugs, tears, ice cream and crutches. I wish I could say that things got better immediately, but that's not quite the truth. Instead of preparing for my first college season of cross-country, my summer was spent in physical therapy. I took months off from running — missing out on road races and quality time with my family. When I was finally able to run again, I was out of shape and couldn't keep up with my new college team. The subsequent three years brought more injuries and more time on the sidelines.

But one sentence changed everything for me. On March 5, 2018, elite long-distance runner Desiree Linden tweeted: "Every day, I make the choice to show up and see what I've got, and to try and be better. My advice: Keep showing up." A month later, she won the Boston Marathon.

With just a few words, Desiree accomplished what no other motivational quote could: She cut to the core of running and reminded me how simple it really is. I realized I didn't have to be perfect every day. I just had to show up and give what I had. Consistency, passion, and a healthy dose of stubbornness would be the key to my success.

Now I'm twenty-three years old, and high school and college are behind me. I remember the friends I made and the challenges I overcame, but the disappointments don't sting like they used to. I still run every day and have completed four marathons. Joy and gratitude are the center of my practice. I feel like a kid again. Injuries are never fun, but I have learned to take better care of my body and be grateful for what it can do — whether I'm winning races or taking a casual stroll down the block. Thanks to Des, I can always return to the calming belief that things will go my way if I just keep showing up.

— Sophie Bolich —

66

A Lesson in Staying Where You Are

Start where you·are. Use what you have.
Do what you can.
~Arthur Ashe

I sat there at a loss for words. I'd just been told that I wasn't selected for any of the four available training officer spots. Despite my positive attitude and hard work, I had been passed over. I was told I needed more experience, ironically, for a position that I was seeking *in order* to gain more experience.

"Are you okay with this, Sam? Do you have any questions for us?"

The training coordinator prodded me with a slightly worried look on his face as he scanned mine for any sign of a reaction. I opened my mouth to say something after a lengthy pause.

"Um… no questions. I understand. Thanks for considering me at least."

"We could only pick four people, and you really were pretty high up on our list. Please don't hesitate to apply again whenever we open up some spots. Okay?"

I muttered my agreement and left the room, feeling a mix of emotions. I was shocked, disappointed, frustrated, and a little bit angry. I went about the remainder of my shift feeling regretful that I had even put myself out there.

The next day, I was scouring listings on Indeed.com for jobs within ten miles of my zip code. I was not about to stay at a place where my talents were not appreciated. I had been employed with my agency since July 2015 as an emergency telecommunicator. Being a police and fire dispatcher wasn't just something that paid my rent bill or gave me the means to order Thai food at least twice a month. I felt it was my life's calling and purpose!

This rejection felt like the biggest slap in my face, and I wanted to make the biggest, loudest statement that I could about how I truly felt. To me, quitting was the answer. I was about to forfeit the years of learning and sacrificing that got me where I was when my mother intervened.

"It's one thing to leave a job on your own terms; it's another thing to leave because you'd rather give up than persevere," my mom told me one morning over breakfast after I admitted my plans to find new employment. "God put you here, and when He's ready for you to move on, He'll open a new door for you."

I decided not to quit. I might not have gotten the promotion I wanted, but I could still achieve what I was after. I could find a way to combine my passion for the job with my passion for teaching and training others, while gaining the experience that I wanted to have on my resume. I took my mother's advice to heart and stayed put. In the year 2020, amid the racial tensions of a world racked with violence and political division, I was inspired to write a guest blog titled, "Bigger Than the Bias: Being a Person of Color in Public Safety." In this post, I shared my viewpoints on the necessity of conversations about police brutality, why we shouldn't defund the police, and the conflict of being a Black 911 dispatcher who supports law and order but also believes in protesting as a means of getting a message across.

That same year, I would pen an op-ed for *The Atlanta Journal-Constitution* on the Black Lives Matter movement being an overdue wakeup call in a world where systemic racial inequality is still the reality. In 2021, the next opportunity that would come my way was a chance to present a sixty-minute Crowdcast session on "empathy and kindness in public safety" live before a virtual audience of hundreds. I pitched my presentation, "10 Things Your 911 Caller Wishes You

Understood," and I was accepted despite having no public-speaking experience. That session opened up the door for me to present before other live audiences and eventually in-person on increasingly larger stages. It also led to me appearing on several podcasts where I was able to educate and speak to other dispatchers on topics like overcoming bias in the workplace and restoring kindness to the forefront of all that we do.

Applications did open up again for training officers at my agency. In the room when I interviewed a second time, I sat opposite that same training coordinator, a lot less shaky and far more certain of myself this go-around.

"What experience do you have in training, and how have you prepared yourself for this position?"

"Well, to be honest, when I was turned down over a year ago, I realized that I didn't need the new title, or the different uniform shirt, or the specialty pay to prove that I really do care about teaching other dispatchers. I decided to start with what I had, right where I was in this place in life…"

I handed my new resume to my two interviewers. It listed exactly how I had kept myself busy that year — every workshop or virtual conference I had taught at, every podcast I had appeared on to discuss topics important to our field, and the titles of every publication I had authored as a contributor to a couple of esteemed journals.

"This is how I've prepared myself for this role with the training division. And it has honestly been fun proving my worthiness to me."

I was called back for a follow-up two weeks later where I was told that I was "easily the most qualified candidate to have applied." The job was mine. A year after being turned down for that promotion, I got the position I wanted. A year after I almost rage-quit purely out of spite. In that time, I'd shown I had the mental aptitude, the emotional capacity, and the chops to train others. I had put feet to my passion and had a resume's worth of speaking engagements and workshops to show for it. Last year, I was selected to speak at the two largest annual conferences for public safety telecommunicators in the country: APCO and NENA. I learned a lesson in staying exactly where I was and making the best out of what was right in front of me, and my efforts paid off. If not for my mother's advice, I'd never have reinvented myself.

— Samantha Hawkins —

67

The Words I Needed to Hear

And you ask, "What if I fall?" Oh,
but my darling, what if you fly?
~Erin Hanson

I n second grade, while other kids played outside at recess, I stayed behind at my desk and created books from construction paper. Using the limited vocabulary of an eight-year-old, I wrote stories and dreamed of one day becoming an author. My second-grade teacher urged my parents to nurture this desire, but they didn't take my juvenile aspiration seriously.

Through adulthood, the desire to write remained. The dream never died but there were more certain ways to generate income, so I was steered in different directions. None of the jobs I held afforded me the opportunity to write, and raising two daughters gave me little free time to pursue becoming an author. However, I held onto the dream that had flickered in me as a child. I co-authored a local history book and wrote some of the curriculum for our elementary school's puppet ministry, but I wanted to know my work was good enough that someone would pay for it. It wasn't about the monetary compensation; it was more about the emotional reward it would bring if someone said, "Your story is good enough for us to pay you to allow us to publish it."

At the age of fifty-eight, after working as a Realtor for several years, I escrowed my real-estate license. I continued to manage the office of my husband's construction company, but I was looking for something that would fill the void of our now empty nest. I wanted a job that wasn't stressful and didn't require a lot of time. Writing stories and sharing them on social media filled some of that void, and the stories garnered quite a few likes, but it never crossed my mind as I approached my senior years that writing could be a career for me.

The January after escrowing my license, I posted on social media that I was looking for part-time work. I told my Internet friends that I was searching for something relaxing, such as driving a school van, babysitting, or working retail. My solicitation for suggestions didn't generate much feedback.

Shortly after my failed work-wanted post, a friend from high school passed away. Entering the funeral home for her visitation, I immediately spotted another individual from school who was also my friend on social media. We hadn't seen each other in several years, so I walked over to greet her. Anticipating that her first words would consist of how long it had been since we'd seen each other, I was shocked at what she blurted out. "You don't want to drive a school van, or babysit, or work in a store; you want to write. You *need* to write."

She had been reading the stories I shared on social media and had always commented with encouraging words. But no one had ever spoken these words to me. I had never even spoken these words out loud to myself. Hearing someone verbally solidify my desire to write was foreign to me, but those simple words she uttered kindled a flame that had only been a flicker for a long time.

Thinking about our recently departed classmate, I wondered how many of her dreams were left unfulfilled when she departed this Earth. Deep inside, I knew I still wanted to be an author. I wanted to follow my friend's advice. I wanted to write. I *needed* to write.

I went home that day and composed a story about an event that was very special to me. After editing my words for what seemed like a million times, I got the courage to submit it to a magazine I had subscribed to for years. I even got brave enough to write several stories and send them to other publications.

Sadly, a year passed, and I didn't hear anything back. I was convinced my dream would never be fulfilled, and I was foolish to think otherwise.

Then it happened! There in my e-mail inbox was an offer from the magazine I had sent my first story to. I couldn't believe it! Finally, there was a contract for my review, and someone was willing to pay me for the use of my story. Imagine my excitement when, a couple of days later, another offer arrived by e-mail from a major book company! I truly felt as giddy as an eight-year-old girl by the end of the week.

Since that time, I have had the honor and privilege of being featured in several publications. My hometown newspaper even shared the story of my path to becoming an author in a front-page feature last year, and my desire to write has grown even stronger now that I've seen my words in print.

It's hard to believe that a few simple words of advice and encouragement on an otherwise sorrowful day would lead me to achieving what I'd longed for since I was a kid. I am now comfortable referring to myself as an author. While I wish someone would have given me advice to pursue my dream many years ago, I'm thankful I won't leave this Earth with that dream locked deep inside me — a dream that started long ago in an elementary-school classroom with some construction paper and a yellow pencil.

— Tamara Bell —

68

A Woman Walks into a Pub

*Working hard for something we don't care about
is called stress. Working hard for something
we love is called passion.*
~Author Unknown

The day I moved into the coed dorm in my junior year was a baptism by fire. The movie *Animal House* had been released that summer, and as I entered the lobby, struggling with an armful of bags and boxes, a mostly naked guy slid across the tiled floor with a beer in hand, screaming "Toga!" I stood frozen with a dumbfounded expression, questioning my decision to transfer to this prestigious college.

I was a fish out of water, a transparent minnow among 61,000 students. I had previously attended two small colleges near home so I could commute and help my family with daily cooking, chores, and caring for my much younger brother. My mom confessed she'd be lost without me as she lacked domestic skills and was more adept at running her business. She aspired for me to have a respectable career in medicine. My talents for writing, performing arts, languages, and public speaking were deemed impractical; they would not lead to financial security.

I willingly conceded and became a pre-med major, but I struggled with the arduous biology and organic chemistry classes. No matter how hard I studied, it seemed impossible to memorize the chemical formulas and scientific data. I would read every chapter into a tape recorder and hit Play, listening over and over again, and praying it would sink in. I relied on short-term memory during exams to maintain my academic standing.

I was raised in a strict Cuban household in which I was chaperoned until I was eighteen. There were no sleepovers or teen parties. I was not prepared for the free-spirited, social experience of higher education. It took several months before I made my way to one of the college pubs where students mingled, played pool, and exchanged woes about sleepless nights and roommate dilemmas.

I was sitting alone at the bar, entertained by the characters and flirtations around me, when I felt a tap on my shoulder. A tall, cheery brunette with wavy, shoulder-length hair sat beside me. She recognized I was a new student and wanted to welcome me. We had an instant rapport and began laughing and exchanging our experiences as if we were two lifelong friends. We shared a love for foreign languages, and she invited me to meet her roommates in the French quadrant, where they hosted popular block parties.

"What's your major?" she asked.

"Pre-med," I responded.

"No! No! No! That's not you!" she exclaimed.

Her response caught me off-guard and intrigued me. How could someone who had met me minutes ago form such an adamant conclusion? Yet, her curious statement reinforced what I had long felt to be true. With trepidation, I asked what major she thought suited me.

"Communications. You should definitely be a Communications major. I'm going to set up an appointment for you to meet Dr. K, the head of the department," she affirmed.

I had no idea what that major involved. She explained the industry, and I instantly knew I had to pursue it. Journalism. Human behavior. Public speaking. Mass media. No counselor or teacher had ever advised me to consider this path. The advertising, marketing, and communications fields were predominantly a man's world.

Walking into Dr. K's office, I saw an attractive, smartly dressed woman with a confident smile, blue eyes, and a frosted bob hairstyle sitting behind an executive desk. I instantly felt comfortable in the plush leather chair, and, minutes later, she urged me to switch majors.

"With only three semesters left until you graduate, you will have to get special permission from the dean to take twenty-two credits. You'll need a couple of internships and two jobs in the field. The pre-med classes you've already taken will be counted as electives. You'll take beginner and advanced courses at the same time, but you'll figure it out," she advised.

I quickly calculated my schedule and realized I'd sleep four to five hours a night. But I could do this. I secured three part-time jobs as an assistant in a public-relations department, a telemarketer in a research firm, and a Spanish tutor (to cover bills) at 1:00 A.M. in my apartment. I interned as a bilingual research assistant for a public television program and conducted grassroots research for a company. Days fused into nights, and I loved every moment.

Switching my major was an intensive process, but I did well in all the classes and became an honors student. I never needed to use that tape recorder again. Dr. K recognized my eagerness to learn and took me under her wing. I became her right-hand person at marketing conferences, sleeping on her apartment couch the nights before her presentations to help collate the training binders. I watched in awe as she took command, coaching hundreds of Fortune 500 workers on teamwork and effective management skills.

Dr. K taught my Intro to Communications class, where I met a young man who, years later, I would marry. As I got to know him, I was shocked to learn that the woman I had met in the pub was his intramural softball scorekeeper. A couple of years after graduating college, we married, and the friends I made in my Communications classes, along with Dr. K, served as my bridesmaids.

Two weeks after our wedding, my husband and I founded an advertising and marketing agency that has flourished for more than forty years. I am a volunteer mentor for entrepreneurial middle- and high-school students, guiding them to discover their career and business aspirations.

I believe that every person who crosses our path has a purpose in the tapestry of our lives. By exploring the advice of a woman who walked into a pub, I fulfilled my calling and am guiding others to follow their hearts.

—Barbara Espinosa Occhino—

69

You Are a Writer

*To succeed, you have to believe in something with
such passion that it becomes a reality.*
~Anita Roddick

I won a full scholarship to the University of Virginia, but near the
end of my first year, I had to drop courses to undergo surgery
to replace the lower femur of my right leg. The osteomyelitis, if
malignant, would have meant the loss of the leg and probably
death within six months due to the cancer's metastasis.

The first surgery was a biopsy that was complicated by a hemor-
rhage. UVA allowed me to drop courses, and I was carried up and
down steps to salvage other classes by the Sigma Nu fraternity. I had
visions of becoming the UVA football team punter, and the Sigma Nu
jocks had me on their rush list, hence their interest in my welfare.

After my final exams, I entered the hospital again for the femur-
repair surgery. The postoperative pain was severe. I remained in the
hospital for nearly a month and began my rehabilitation therapy there.
My poor leg had shriveled into a stick.

I began my second year at Virginia with an undiagnosed severe
case of mononucleosis. Many years later, when my enlarged spleen
was discovered, the condition was traced to this period. The illness
proved to have significant ramifications for my life. The fact that I
was not a quitter, which had won me team captaincies in football and
basketball, now worked against me as I sleepwalked my way through
a very difficult academic year. I was not able to attend enough of my

8:00 A.M. French classes to pass, but the career-changing obstacle was the two semesters of organic chemistry. I got a D the first semester and foolishly took the second semester despite the professor's warning. I got an F. The failures that year destroyed my grade-point average, and I lost my scholarship.

By the end of the second semester of my second year, despite my academic losses, I was recovering from the doldrums of mononucleosis. Fatalists might conclude from the bone disease and the mono that I was being pushed away from medicine, but after my experiences with orthopedic surgeons, I thought that I might want to be one.

Then the path forked. I went unknowingly into a new direction.

The term paper due in my American literature course was to be written from a list of subjects provided by the professor. I was not interested in any of them, so I approached the professor with an alternative idea. For me, *The Sun Also Rises* by Ernest Hemingway needed a better concluding chapter, which I proposed to write as my term-paper submission. My suggestion amused him as he explained the requirements of such an attempt. First, the added chapter would have to conform to Hemingway's style and structure. Second, it would have to satisfy the denouement of the novel's plot. Third, all the characters, especially their dialogues, must convey their essence as established by Hemingway. I agreed. Then, he told me the consequences of my audacity. If I pulled off the hat-trick concluding chapter, I would be rewarded with an A. If not, I would get an F. There was no middle ground.

When the graded papers were returned on the last day of class, my professor, Rex Worthington, handed me my A and said that we should have a chat. At a restaurant off campus, he told me that I was the first potential literary artist that he'd ever had in his classes. He had written a much-praised first novel in graduate school, but choices and family circumstances had prevented his continuation as a novelist. He wanted me to be aware of the challenges and obstacles ahead for anyone who pursued the literary arts. I told him that I still intended to go to medical school, but I was deeply impressed by his candor and sincerity.

I did not register for organic chemistry the next year but took a two-semester course on the novel taught by the brilliant Robert Scholes. I found myself drifting into the English department although my major was still psychology.

If Rex Worthington had not told me that I was a writer, and I had not failed organic chemistry and been shown the power of the novel by Robert Scholes, I never would have sought an interview to join UVA's first creative-writing class to be taught by George Garrett. I entered his office for my fifteen minutes of interaction; somehow, we connected on the fact that we had both been boxers, and we began to swap fight stories. Then, there was a knock at the door, and the next student was waiting. I turned at the door and realized that George and I had not talked about my writing, nor had I shown him any samples.

"Am I in?" I asked.

"Are you kidding?" he answered with a laugh.

George Garrett, a significant literary artist and the devoted mentor to a legion of writers like me, became the pivotal character in the direction of my subsequent life. And, in his unique unconventional class, I made lasting friends for life — Henry Taylor, Pulitzer Prize Winner for Poetry in 1986; Kelly Cherry, celebrated poet, novelist, and critic; and Bob Friedman, who would later publish many of my books. George also introduced us to the literary luminaries that appeared at UVA. William Faulkner was the writer-in-residence, and George gave us access to him at informal coffee breaks. We also met Robert Frost in the last year of his life, among others.

At the end of my graduation year I served as the publisher for an anthology of creative writing from Virginia. George edited the book and wrote the foreword, and Pulitzer Poet Richard Wilbur wrote the afterword. The slim volume contained the work of both students and faculty and is now a landmark collector's item in the history of UVA's development as a writing center.

The advice that Rex Worthington and George Garrett gave me — that I had a literary future — survived a post-graduate year in Scandinavia and two years in the Vietnam War-torn Army. I spent the next thirty years editing and writing feature stories for magazines. My writing was praised, but it didn't fulfill any literary promise. Finally, thirty-three years after Professor Worthington forecasted my talent, the first of five novels in the Booker Series was published in 1997. It was the first novel in the new genre labeled Visionary Fiction. I was then recognized as a pioneer in that field and went on to publish more than twenty books and write the poetic libretto for a classical music oratorio that premiered in France in 2019.

I may not have won a Pulitzer Prize, but I did fulfill what two wise counselors forecast for me — even if I was fifty-six before my first novel appeared.

— Monty Joynes —

70

Think of Everything as an Adventure

Attitude is the difference between
an ordeal and an adventure.
~Bob Bitchin

I f you're going to get lost anywhere in the world, then it's probably best to get lost with someone you love. Take it from me, I know from experience. My mother and I have been traveling companions ever since my father died forty-one years ago. That's when we started to explore the world together.

With travel guide in hand — or, these days, our smartphones — we're constantly seeking out things to see and places to go that are off the beaten path. We've never gone in for beach vacations, soaking up the sun and sipping piña coladas. Sometimes I think it might be in our best interests if we did, though, as wandering forgotten paths and back roads can often lead to trouble.

Like that time in Italy when we drifted from a tour of the Duomo Cathedral in Milan and decided to head for the top floor of the immense, architectural behemoth in order to get a bird's-eye view of the city. Being Italian-language illiterates, we must've read the signs wrong. We somehow wound up roving the perimeter of the Duomo roof, a million steps pitched as steep as a slalom ramp with no handrails. Add our shared fear of heights to the open-air mix, and the concept of "bird's eye" took on a whole new meaning!

In France, Mom and I unwittingly took our lives in our hands when we hailed a Paris taxicab, and the driver proceeded to speed like a bat out of hell through the city streets, taking us to the Louvre practically via Belgium, with a fare to match.

In San Francisco, Mom's hat blew off her head, and I foolishly chased after it as it tumbled down Filbert Street, considered one of the steepest navigable roads in the Western Hemisphere. I retrieved the hat but got on the wrong streetcar back to the hotel.

On safari in Kenya, we forced our driver to pull over on the side of a dirt road to make an informal pit stop. The two of us squatted behind some acacia trees and did our business, not realizing that a 2,000-pound African Buffalo was bearing down on us from the other side of the brush.

There was the detour-trip that Mom and I took through the Midwest, and how the power window of our rental car broke and we had to drive with it open for two hundred miles — through a sub-zero blizzard. Once, a faulty GPS led us down country roads into the deep South amid houses surrounded by razor wire and homeowners bearing shotguns. And we'll never forget a windswept evening when we boarded a four-seat prop plane in Skagway, Alaska, only to realize that our pilot was making his maiden solo flight over the glaciers.

But it was a waitress, a stranger who served us a memorable, extra-cheesy, deep-dish pizza on a hot summer day in Chicago, who set us straight — not only about the Windy City but also about life. A simple turn of a phrase she uttered has stayed with us for more than two decades.

After we polished off that delicious pizza, she brought our check. When she spied us struggling with a map of downtown, trying to chart our itinerary via the "L" train, she pulled up a chair at our table and generously routed our course. Before she left us, she said, "Now, don't you two worry — you'll get to where you're supposed to be. And, if you get lost, don't panic. Just think of it as an adventure!"

Her directions proved right on target — in more ways than one. She might've crossed our paths for only a brief moment in time, passing in and out of our lives as fast as the "L" train, but the directions of her off-the-cuff wisdom have stayed with us for more than twenty years. Whenever Mom and I find ourselves lost in this life — be it exploring unfamiliar corners of the world or even facing discouragements, big and small, that creep into daily living — we look at each other, smile, and resurrect that wise waitress and her motto all over again: Think of everything as an adventure!

— Kathleen Gerard —

71

Breathing Belief into Those Who Doubt

*If you doubted your fears instead of doubting your
dreams, imagine how much in life you'd accomplish.*
~Joel Brown

"The dream begins with a teacher who believes in you, who tugs and pushes and leads you to the next plateau, sometimes poking you with a sharp stick called 'truth'." These words were spoken by legendary news anchor Dan Rather and they rang very true for me.

From the time when my neophyte poetry efforts were published in the junior-high-school yearbook, I wanted to write. As opposed to most of my school friends, I loved essay questions on exams and lengthy term-paper assignments — anything that allowed me to write to my heart's content. To this day, the prospect of writing — be it an entire book, a magazine article or a three-line blurb for a book cover — is to me like a child being given room to run outdoors.

Our high school began with tenth grade. When I started, I joined the newspaper staff as a novice sophomore amidst a sea of sophisticated seniors. Our journalism advisor was Gene Genisauski (or Mr. G, as he was affectionately known by his students). As a teacher, Mr. G had an extraordinary gift for reaching his students. He commanded the respect that all teachers earn and certainly deserve — but, at the same time, he was always approachable and related to his students in such a way that it felt as though we were speaking with a trusted friend rather than someone who determined our grades. Most important, Mr. G possessed both the ability and the desire to breathe belief into students who may have not believed in themselves — including me.

In what I had believed to be highly questionable wisdom, Mr. G appointed me editorial editor. Sophomores were simply not granted that level of responsibility or prestige; in fact, sophomores were not even supposed to be on the newspaper staff at all. And who was this newly crowned editorial pipsqueak surrounded by? The aforementioned seniors. Not just any seniors, mind you — the student-body president, the captain of the basketball team, academic overachievers abundant, and the bane of my existence at the time... the co-editors-in-chief. (With brilliant minds, they went on to careers as a well-respected orthopedic surgeon and a prominent attorney.)

However, Mr. G never once cared about my standing as a sophomore, nor did he compare me to the rest of the student staff. Instead, he focused on raw talent that I did not yet see and gumption that I had not yet discovered.

When the inevitable criticism and merciless teasing from other staff members finally became too much, I did what any self-respecting fifteen-year-old would do: I attempted to give up my editor position. Mr. G refused. I naturally protested; however, as Mr. Rather stated so beautifully, Mr. G "tugged and pushed." He insisted and encouraged. He breathed that belief into me when I refused to believe in myself.

When all my previous arguments for resigning proved to be for naught, I played what I thought to be my "ace in the hole" by reminding him yet again of my status (or lack thereof) as a sophomore. Mr. G then replied, "All you are is younger. You are NOT less talented. You are NOT less capable. You are younger. That's all. So, you don't get to quit. You don't get to give up. You're going to show them what you've got instead."

Left with no alternative, I showed them.

"Showing them" did not exactly transform my life overnight. I still had lively arguments with the aforesaid editors-in-chief, and the teasing and criticism continued. However, in his refusal to accept my resignation, Mr. G's words also compelled me to stand up for myself, find my voice and make myself heard — something we are all called upon to do throughout our lives.

When I began to pursue a writing career years later, Mr. G's wise advice and direction returned with a loud echo. On the journey to becoming a published author I faced rejection, naysayers, general negativity and what some might consider insurmountable obstacles. Did I experience moments of discouragement? Absolutely, particularly upon receiving comments like: "You're writing about what? That's so depressing." (My specialty is loss, grief and bereavement.) "Who's going to listen to you when no one knows who you are?" And, a personal favorite, "You'll never make it in this business."

With each negative comment or rejection, Mr. G's words echoed inside my head once again: "You don't get to give up. You're going to show them what you've got instead."

So I did.

Today, I am blessed to be a published author with several bestselling books to my credit and a career that changed the entire trajectory of my life and the lives of my family. How wonderful it was to be able to express my overwhelming gratitude to Mr. G — whose advice literally put me on the path that I walk all these years later — by including a dedicated paragraph to him in the Acknowledgments of my first book.

"The dream begins with a teacher who believes in you..."

It did indeed. And because of Mr. G's advice to a fifteen-year-old trying to find her way, the dream continues to this day.

— Carole Brody Fleet —

Chapter
9

Put Things in Perspective

72

Reality

*Solitude is where I place my chaos to rest
and awaken my inner peace.*
~Nikki Rowe

During my high school and college years, the expectations of my parents, teachers and professors kept me on track, focused primarily on classes, homework assignments, and part-time work. But when college ended — leaving me in charge of my own life — I had a real problem with planning and follow-through. I'd always been an aggressively motivated student. But now that the "assignments" were largely mine to determine, I was lost. I would wake up filled with plans for the day only to discover that I accomplished very little on my list. I felt overwhelmed and discouraged.

I whined way too much to my first husband — who, in my mind, always seemed to plan and execute his own complicated schedule and goals with incredible energy, grace, and effectiveness. On more than one occasion, I'm sure he just wanted to shout: "Oh, grow up and stop griping!" But I was struggling to the point of depression over what I viewed as my own personal failure to launch.

Early one morning, when I was already anticipating the failure of that day's plans, my husband sat me down, looked me straight in the eyes, and said, "Wendy, you've got to understand something. The mind can always think of a hundred more ideas and plans for a day than the body could ever accomplish in twenty-four hours."

It was such a simple, logical statement. Yet, for me, it was radical.

Earth-shattering. I instantly knew it was true — and exactly what I needed to incorporate into my life. I can't say that things changed immediately, but those words provided a starting point. My husband's advice offered me a far healthier perspective from which to address my foundering self-confidence and near-crippling insecurities.

My first marriage didn't last, but my first husband's words have endured. Whenever I feel frustrated or worn out by my endlessly looping mind, I remind myself of the brain's immense power — and the body's inability to keep up with it. Over the years, when my kids and grandkids have expressed similar frustrations, I've attempted to offer them the same speed-of-thought vs. reality-of-action advice. If the message resonates with them, as it did with me, I hope that they, too, will eventually come to set kinder, more realistic day-to-day goals for themselves rather than berating themselves for "things left undone."

Two simple sentences helped to ground me forty-five years ago, and those words of wisdom continue to guide me today.

— Wendy Hobday Haugh —

73

A Hundred Years from Now

There are things known, and there are things unknown,
and in-between are the doors of perception.
~Aldous Huxley

Grandpa used to ask, "Will it matter a hundred years from now?" It was his way of calming me down when I was upset about something that most likely I would forget about by the next day. And, of course, the answer was always "no." Grandpa was a very wise man.

He wasn't my grandpa by blood or even by marriage. But the moment I met him, I adopted him as my own. He was ninety-two at the time, and he used to tell me, "You can't do things at ninety-two that you can do at seventy!" I was in my forties at the time, and I loved the perspective on aging that he gave me.

At ninety-two, Grandpa was still driving himself wherever he wanted to go, mowing his own yard (and his neighbors' too), and greeting every member of the congregation at church on Sunday. He cooked dinner every night except Monday. On Mondays, he picked up a pizza because it was on sale. He loved watching Thunder basketball. We even went to see a game on Christmas Day one year! He loved *Bonanza*, *Andy Griffith*, and *The Beverly Hillbillies*. One time, he got really flustered when I walked in and caught him watching women's wrestling.

And then there was the day of "the race." His grandson Chris and I had purchased two retired police patrol cars from an online surplus auction. They were located about a hundred miles away, and we all loaded into Grandpa's car to pick them up.

On the way home, Chris and I decided to see what our new cars were made of. We were flying down the highway at over ninety miles an hour, and Grandpa was right behind us! When we got home, he hopped out of his car with a spring in his step, and his eyes lit up like a teenager. He excitedly proclaimed, "My old Buick's still got some spunk in her!" And so do you, Grandpa, so do you.

I learned so much from that man—some of it from talking to him and listening to what he had to say, but most of it from watching him and the way he handled life. And I can still hear him asking, "Will it matter a hundred years from now?" The answer is still always "no."

It took me over ten years to understand how deep that question really goes. Like a broad-spectrum antibiotic, it can cure a lot of what ails you, even if the exact source of infection cannot be identified.

I was going through an extremely difficult period. Both my professional and personal lives were in shambles. I was devastated on every level. My dreams were gone, and I was struggling to forge a new path without having much of an idea what direction I should take. Although I had a list of amazing accomplishments, nobody cared about that anymore. They only cared about what they thought I had done wrong. It was a battle that couldn't be fought, let alone won.

One day through the darkness, I heard Grandpa's voice asking, "Will it matter a hundred years from now?" And, for the first time, I acknowledged that it wouldn't. I am not going to show up in any history books. Neither my virtues nor my flaws will ever be written about in any volume that will be studied by future generations.

Someone told me, "You really aren't that important," which sounds like a bad thing, but on the particular subject we were discussing, it was a very good thing. I was a blip on the radar, but radars change quickly. Storms form, rage, and subside, and new storms come to take their place. I was not experiencing a Hurricane Katrina—just a spin-up tornado that wreaks havoc and then is gone. True, I would be picking up the pieces for a while, and my life would never be the same, but life is not meant to stay the same.

During his lifetime, Grandpa had two full careers—as a car salesman and then as an undertaker—and that was after serving his country in the Army during World War II. But you won't find him in the history books either.

Grandpa said that he never made a difference in the world, but he always tried to make a difference in someone's day. He made sure they got a good car. He treated every grieving family with caring and respect. In his later years, he would come home from church smiling and say, "I sure do feel good after shaking all those good Baptists' hands." And I know they felt good after shaking his hand as well.

Grandpa believed that if you brighten someone's day, they might brighten someone else's day, who might then brighten someone else's day. Grandpa believed in ripples.

It's possible that one of those ripples he started went on to touch someone who did do something that will matter a hundred years from now. It's also possible that some of the good things I have done will ripple out to make a lasting difference. I hope so. But, either way, my name won't be attached to it, not even as a footnote.

Will it matter a hundred years from now? Even Hurricane Katrina will be nothing but something people read about and try briefly to imagine. We already live in a world where a whole generation doesn't remember life before 9/11. They have never flown without taking their shoes off at the airport! And Covid? We still don't know where that road is going, but most likely there will come a time when nobody remembers what life was like in 2019.

World-changing events fade into "the new norm" and then into "life as we know it." Life-changing events have a much smaller circle. Personal tragedies, no matter how devastating, rarely escape their bubble.

I weathered my storm by remembering it was *my* storm. I held on tight to the knowledge that I did not have to change the world; I only had to change *my* world. My little blip on the radar... which certainly would not matter a hundred years from now.

—Linda Sabourin—

74

Time Travel

The trick is to enjoy life. Don't wish away your days,
waiting for better ones ahead.
~Marjorie Pay Hinckley

'm directing twenty-two little bodies to the buses for dismissal. It's like herding cats, but it's a skill I quickly mastered when I became a kindergarten teacher.

After the children are carefully led to their spots, I begin walking back toward the school building. As I pass a coworker, I say, "Ugh, I wish it was Friday." It's only Tuesday, and I'm already dreaming of the weekend. Less chaos. Less responsibility. Less work.

She glances up with a gentle smile and says, "Nothing like wishing your life away." Her words are so powerful that I'm speechless. I'm not even sure if she realizes their impact as she holds the door open, and we both step inside.

We don't say a word walking back to our individual classrooms. I'm still mesmerized by her words: "Nothing like wishing your life away."

She's so right. I've literally made a statement wishing a couple of days would just evaporate. And when I said it, I meant it. I wanted the week to hurry to the weekend. But now, after hearing six simple words, I'm regretting my desire to speed up time, to erase or move past the events and moments that would happen in those days. What would those days bring that I'd be missing out on?

I don't want to wish my life away.

I needed this reminder, and I appreciate that it came from a colleague whom I admire and trust. She most likely doesn't know that I'm still here at work, sitting behind my desk, reflecting on her inspiration. I know that when I get up from this chair, there will still be endless to-dos and overwhelming responsibilities, both at work and at home, but I also know that I want them.

I want this life, both the easy and the trying parts. I want this job, both the rewarding moments and the unsuccessful ones. I want the todays and the tomorrows just as much as I want the weekends and the holidays. I don't want to wish my life away, not one moment of it. And who knows how long I've been wishing just that — for the week to hurry, for the weekend to come, for the month to end and summer arrive, for the days to hurry to get to the night, for pieces of my life to evaporate into thin air.

"Nothing like wishing your life away." Those six words changed my perspective and also my wishes.

I no longer wish for days to hurry or to time travel to dates and moments in the future. I no longer wish my life away.

— Chelsea Ohlemiller —

75

The Best of Me

*Doing your best can be exhausting enough without
doing everyone else's best while you're at it.*
~Sarah Knight, You Do You

I pushed open the door to my home, my shoulders sagging and my eyes bleary. I had pulled another all-nighter and then spent a full day at the office. And now I had twenty minutes before my three energetic girls would come bounding through the door, full of stories, requests and homework demands that would keep me on my toes until their bedtime. And, in those twenty minutes, I had to straighten up the breakfast mess still on the table, return several phone calls, and cook a nourishing dinner.

I felt a tension headache coming on.

P-day, as I liked to call the day that the local newspaper at which I was editor went to print, was always like this. No sleep, no food, lots of caffeine, and very little patience and stamina left over for my children.

And if I was truly honest with myself, it wasn't only P-day. Mine was a demanding job. Our paper was a small operation, which meant a lot of work on my shoulders. I wrote several columns, edited several others, and pulled yet others together. I spent my days at the office, my nights at my home computer and, somewhere in-between, parented my four adorable children and ran our busy household. My long-suffering husband was my equal partner in those last two departments, but my children still needed a present mother. I felt like I was investing so much time and energy in my work that it was hard to muster up the enthusiasm for my children.

"Mommy! Mommy! You're never going to believe what happened in school today!" There they were. My twenty minutes were up, and I had barely gotten started on dinner.

I put on my best cheerful voice as I greeted them, hoping they wouldn't discern the effort it took to inject cheer into my greeting.

My six-year-old launched into a long-winded story about frogs, the playground and her best friend Sara. I tried to keep track, really I did, but my eyes kept glazing over as I stirred a pot of noodles with one hand.

"Oh wow, that's wonderful, sweetheart," I interjected at what I hoped was the appropriate moment.

And so the evening wore on in a blur of dinner and homework, bickering and bath time. I nodded off on the couch three times in the middle of homework, much to my oldest daughter's indignation. And I absentmindedly responded, "Yes, sure," when my four-year-old asked me how many miles away we were from the sun. I think I did okay otherwise, although I don't remember all the details on account of my extreme exhaustion. I tried to give my all to my children, but after the day that I had had at work, I'm afraid my all wasn't all that much.

I breathed a sigh of relief when I finally ushered the last one successfully into bed. My parenting duties dispensed with, I was back at the computer. Thankfully, I had no urgent deadlines for the following day, so I knew I could work for just a couple of hours before heading to bed myself.

I opened my e-mails to find a message from my colleague containing the quote of the week selected for the following week's issue.

"Quote of the Week" was a fairly new column in our paper, and one of my favorites. I am a quote junkie and have many of those pithy sayings hanging on the walls of our home. While I wasn't charged with searching for and selecting the quote each week, I had to give the go-ahead before it was sent to the designer for layout.

I opened the e-mail and read the quote, recoiling as if I had been physically hit. This one resonated with me way too well.

The quote read: "Our children deserve the best of us, not the rest of us."

Images of my day, and then of the past weeks, months and years, flashed through my mind. Showing up at work with the enthusiasm of a new day but coming home weary and spent. Zipping through the bedtime routine so that I could get back to work. Attacking my deadlines with relish and bath time with dread.

I realized how much I had been investing in my work and how little I had left for my children. This quote described everything that was wrong with my priorities, with my work-life balance, in a few simple words. I had been putting my best self into my work and giving my family my stale leftovers.

I shut down my computer and went to the living room, where my husband had just sat down with his evening coffee. We had a lot to discuss.

The following day, I mustered up every bit of courage that I had within me and approached my bosses for a chat.

We spoke for a while, working out a way to simplify my job and shift some of the burden of my responsibilities so that I could come home earlier and have some emotional reserves left for the most important people in my life.

The shift was transformational. I noticed the difference in myself, but also in my family.

They smiled more and acted out less. The more family time we had together, the more grounded and settled they became. The deeper the eye contact we shared, the more meaningful our relationships became. And you know how hard it is to make any kind of meaningful eye contact when your eyes are half closed!

Over the years, I've shifted my work life even more as the family needs have shifted. I now work only from home on a freelance basis so that I can take on work as family life allows it.

I've learned to fill my life with family and let work fall into the empty spaces, instead of vice versa. Financially, things are tighter, but we've always had enough to live on. And, even more importantly, we have a life that is rich because it is filled with the most valuable people.

That brings me to another of my favorite quotes: "If you want to feel wealthy, count the things you have that money can't buy."

By learning to give my children the best of me instead of the rest of me, I have indeed become wealthy beyond measure!

— Devora Adams —

76

The Time Will Pass Anyway

People with goals succeed because
they know where they're going.
~Earl Nightingale

"This is so frustrating!" I grumbled over the phone to my friend. "I've been counting calories for two weeks, and I've only lost one pound."

As a habitual dieter, I was used to a more impressive start to any new diet. This time, I'd focused on counting calories but with fewer restrictions on what I was eating. The slow progress of losing weight at a healthier speed was demoralizing, and I'd taken to venting my frustrations to my friend, Patricia.

"You're tracking everything you're eating, right?" she asked, free of any judgment in her tone.

"I am," I replied, "and my doctor told me to expect to lose two to four pounds a month, but I just thought it would be faster. At this rate, it's going to take me two years to lose this weight!"

I flopped onto my couch with a sigh, frustrated that my goal was so far out when previous diets could knock fifteen pounds off in a month or two.

Patricia paused on the other end of the phone, letting my frustration settle before finally responding, "The time will pass either way. It's not like your life will be on hold until you reach your goal weight. It'll just happen, and as long as you keep tracking what you eat, you'll lose weight along the way."

In that moment, something in my brain clicked. Not only was she right, but she made me realize that the whole point of tracking my food and reducing my calorie intake was to build a new normal way of eating. I don't recall the details of the rest of our conversation, as I'm sure we veered off weight and onto the latest episodes of our favorite shows, but her advice changed the course of my relationship with food and goals permanently.

While it's true that fad diets work in that they result in enough of a calorie deficit for a person to lose weight, they don't tend to work long-term because they aren't sustainable. Either you're just not eating enough, or you aren't getting enough variety. Eventually, you stop being on the diet and go back to how you ate before. This leads to gaining weight, which might lead to a new diet, and the pattern repeats itself. I was carrying around 100 pounds more than I wanted to, and my doctor suggested tracking what I was eating and counting calories with a daily goal of staying a few hundred calories below my total daily energy expenditure. Basically, if I wanted to lose the extra fat, I needed to consume fewer calories every day so my storage was used instead. The most sustainable way to do this is with small reductions in what you eat and to do so every day. Or, at least, most days. My favorite food will always be a brownie sundae, but rather than excluding it from my life, it's turned into a food I have occasionally instead of every week.

Patricia's advice was to stop rushing the process and just live my life. "The time will pass anyway" became a mantra that ultimately helped me lose more than 100 pounds over two years. It did so much more than help with my weight-loss goal, though. I began to apply it to every goal I had, especially if I felt like something would take too long.

I can control a lot of things in my life, but time is not one of them. The time will pass anyway, so why not take another small step each day toward what I want in the meantime?

— Charlie Morrow —

77

Roadblocks

You don't realize it at the time, but some of life's
roadblocks, detours, and rejections
are answered prayers.
~Steve Maraboli

One evening I was running late for a meeting, and I passed a friend in the hallway. My friend asked the obligatory question, "How are you doing?" But, rather than give the expected response, "Good, how about you?" I decided to unload my frustration with traffic, people who can't put down their cellphones at traffic lights, poor visibility in the rain, tailgaters, and everything else about my stressful commute.

Instead of empathy, my friend asked a thought-provoking question: "How do you know if God, the powers of fate, or your guardian angel didn't create those roadblocks?" The inference was that I might have been spared something much worse than being late to a meeting. My immediate reaction was to laugh and walk on, but later I began to unpack what he had asked. Over the next few days, the more I thought about his haunting question, the more wisdom I was able to see in it.

I thought about family experiences and things that have happened to me, and the seed he had planted started to grow. I remembered an uncle who was late for a flight, and the flight he had missed went down. I remembered my dad telling me about events that helped him avoid several brushes with death. I recalled my grandmother telling me that she had stopped working near her kitchen window to answer the phone just before a bullet came through it (from a neighbor shooting walnuts out of a tree).

I remembered other times when delays kept me from accidents on the same roads I was traveling on. The most memorable example was a white-out snowstorm. We were forced to take a slower route, which was very frustrating. Later, we heard that a family of four, just like ours, was killed by a truck on the highway we had planned on taking. As these and other memories came to mind, I asked my wife if she could remember anything similar. She shared a few and then said, "Thank God for unanswered prayers" from the Garth Brooks song.

I asked what she meant, and she said that it can be easy to be so focused on an outcome and being on schedule that better possibilities are not considered. We can be determined to make it to a meeting on time, to find a better job, to have relationships or events happen as we imagine, and we don't see other or even better options. When things don't happen as expected, or we are delayed in traffic, it's easy to get stressed, angry, rude, and ungrateful. Ungrateful for what might have been great effort on the part of some person or some power to spare us from ourselves or some unforeseen tragedy. Ungrateful for a better outcome than we had hoped for.

She went on to give examples of times she felt disappointed when job searches did not work out, only to be offered jobs that were much better. Had her plans and prayers been answered the way she had wanted, her day, her career, her life might have been much different. Like the lyrics to Garth's song say: "Some of God's greatest gifts are all too often unanswered prayers."

The more I thought about my sometimes emotional reaction to disappointments, the more I realized that the people I admire most in life have the ability to roll with the punches. These people don't get upset nearly as often as the rest of the world. They maintain positive energy and demonstrate grace under pressure. This doesn't come naturally. This comes from a belief that there is always a reason and someone is looking out for their better good. I want to be more like that. My little slice of the world would improve if I could pull that off.

Ever since my friend gave me his advice in the form of a question,

I have become a bit more mellow. I have lost weight, my blood pressure has gone down, and I feel less stress. I think the mindset that someone is looking out for my best interests has been very positive. It may or may not be happening every moment of every day, but keeping my friend's question in mind puts me more at ease and has improved my life.

— Thomas Brooks —

A Glimmer of Hope

Heavy hearts, like heavy clouds in the sky, are best
relieved by the letting out of a little water.
~Antoine de Rivarol

I met Kimmie when we were in high school. She was a freshman; I was a junior. I was known to be a math whiz, and someone recommended me to tutor her in geometry. Afternoons after school, Kimmie would come to my house to study. We'd sit at the kitchen counter, share snacks, and sometimes actually do some math.

When the school year ended, Kimmie passed geometry, and she kept coming over. I was the youngest of five, and she was like the little sister I'd always wanted.

My new best friend was like a member of the family. While hanging out at the house, Kimmie naturally got to know my older brother, James. He was charming, funny, handsome and kind. It was no secret that she had a huge crush on him. She fell for him and he for her. They dated for several years before he asked her to marry him. It was the happiest day of her life.

Several weeks later, over a pitcher of margaritas for courage, I urged her not to marry him — for her sake, not his. James was schizophrenic, and although his mental illness was managed with medications, it was unpredictable and chronic. It was not going to go away. Life wouldn't be easy. Kimmie took no offense. She said she understood but that she loved him as he was. Of course, she would marry him.

Their marriage was rocky for sure, but they loved each other.

They were one of those couples who wore matching costumes on Halloween. They had friends over for barbecues in the summer. They laughed a lot. He'd been James to us his whole life, but we started referring to them as Jimmy and Kimmie. They had a son and named him after his dad.

James's mental illness was difficult to keep in check. It was predictably unpredictable, and he periodically ended up hospitalized. Eventually, the stress of marriage become too much for both of them, and they divorced.

Kimmie was the best single mother ever. She was always on the side of the field for her son's soccer games. The neighborhood kids gathered at their house for snacks after school like we had done as teenagers. All the kids called her Mom.

We were devastated when Kimmie developed an aggressive cancer. She was fortunate to get enrolled in a clinical trial. After two years of extensive treatments, Kimmie was one of only a few left standing from their original clinical tribe of sixteen.

Chemotherapy and radiation protocols saved her life but not without a cost. For the rest of her life, she was in constant pain from numerous complications and required continuous medical interventions. But no one would ever have known.

She took her son surfing and skiing, and taught him to cook gourmet meals. She lived to see him graduate from high school and then college. Before she died, she made sure he knew her Italian grandmother's secret recipe for lasagna. She provided a level of stability and unconditional love that helped him to become the outstanding man he is today.

I followed my boyfriend, the man of my dreams, to another city. That relationship ended badly. I felt like a failure and returned home lost and brokenhearted, sharing my grief with Kimmie, the one person on the planet I knew I could turn to.

As I lay on the couch crying, she said, "Jude, we all do stupid stuff and always will. We're human, and it's okay. You shouldn't regret what you do for love." She told me to wallow for as long as I had to, but this pain wouldn't last forever and my life would get back on track.

Although she didn't say it, I knew she was referring to that night years ago when I urged her not to marry my brother. She got to marry her childhood sweetheart and raise a son she loved beyond measure. She had no regrets. She hoped I could live as fully as well.

As I tried my best to absorb her words, she said one more thing. "When you finally give in to your feelings, and you cry, really cry, like you're doing right now, it means you're on the verge of a solution. While you're sobbing, somewhere in the back of your mind you're working on the cure. Trust me. I know."

As for letting go of regrets, I haven't quite mastered that. One I definitely have—that Kimmie and I didn't have more time together. I will always miss my best friend and sister-in-law, whose sage advice I never forget. Wife and mother extraordinaire, she was the most unconditionally loving and non-judgmental woman I've ever known and the sister I never had.

And, whenever I get down, I remember Kimmie's words. Her advice has served me and continues to give me comfort. Whenever I have a problem, and I cry, really cry, I always have a glimmer of hope and trust that a solution is on its way.

—Judith Shapiro—

Look at the Fish

Calmness is the cradle of power.
~Josiah Gilbert Holland

My windshield has heard some pretty ill-tempered talk from me. "I'm driving here. Stay on your own side of the road.... You want to tailgate me? Watch how slowly I can drive.... Hey, your turn signal isn't optional equipment...."

However, when I began my career as a pastor, with a "Clergy" sticker on the bumper, I had to morph my verbiage to meet expectations. "Oh, yeah? Well, bless you" became my standard response.

Then I became a Navy chaplain and headed to Iraq with the Marine Corps. A combat arena can bring out the worst in a frustrated and tired person, like what happens during a commute. But, unlike a commute, that ever-vigilant environment goes on for months, keeping stress hormones raging until they become a person's new normal. I didn't know how profoundly it had affected me until I returned home and tried to drive as if nothing had changed.

To say my edginess had been honed razor-sharp is an understatement. What used to be an almost comic monologue became pure road rage. I thought my alarming behavior would pass, but it didn't.

Thinking a vacation might help, my husband and I headed to Cancun, Mexico. Since Ken is a diver, we planned for him to dive each day while I sat by the pool and read. On the first morning of our vacation, I grabbed a novel, found a shady spot, and settled in to read. Then I noticed Ken standing at the foot of the lounger.

"Your dive lesson begins in ten minutes."

"But I…"

"No buts. I paid for your lesson. You're taking it. It's only in the pool."

I followed him. Being underwater without the need to surface was strangely peaceful. All I could hear was the rhythmic bubbling of the regulator as I slowly inhaled and exhaled. For the first time in a long time, I felt calm.

After the lesson, Ken was waiting for me. "How was it?"

"Better than I expected…" He stopped me mid-sentence.

"Good. Your first open-water dive starts in forty-five minutes."

"But I…"

"No buts."

My instructor's name was Manuel. I could tell he expected me to follow his directions to ensure a safe diving experience, and I was grateful. Before we got into the boat, he reviewed what I needed to know about gear, gauges, and getting to the ocean floor. As the small boat headed out to the reef, Manuel gave me one last instruction.

"Since we cannot talk underwater, we'll have to rely on hand signals. Thumbs up means you need to surface immediately. Hopefully, you won't need that." Forming a circle with his right thumb and forefinger, he said, "This is the okay sign. Periodically, I will ask if you're okay. Before you answer with the same sign, I want you to do three things. First, check your air gauge to make sure you are not running out of what you need to keep you alive. Second, check your equipment to see if anything is amiss. And, third, look for potential danger, like a speedboat, torpedo or shark."

"There could be sharks?"

"It's the ocean."

"What if I see one?"

"Try not to annoy it. Let's go over this again. I give you the okay sign. What do you do?"

"Check for the immediate threat of lack of oxygen. Then check for the pending threat of equipment malfunction. Last, check for a potential threat like a shark. Shouldn't I check for the shark first?"

"You won't get away from it if you don't have air. And if all those threats of yours are, how do you say, 'neutralized,' then what?"

"I return the okay sign, not the thumbs up, right?"

"Right."

When we got to the drop spot, I fell backwards out of the boat, letting my heavy air tank lead the way. Then I followed Manuel down a rope to the ocean floor.

Immediately, curious fish surrounded us. Iridescent, spiny, blue, pink, silver, even striped fish. Fish blowing sand off the sea floor, hiding behind coral, slipping past my face mask. Fish everywhere! With Manuel leading the way, we swam in, under and around the reef.

Then, a large eel slipped out of its hole. I stopped dead. Eels look like thick snakes. I'm not a fan of snakes. Perhaps other dangerous creatures lurked nearby. I was in an environment I didn't understand, with a person I didn't know, using unfamiliar equipment. I froze.

Manuel caught the panic in my eyes. He gave me the okay sign. When I didn't respond, he pointed to my air gauge. I had lots of air left. I felt my gear. Everything was in place and functioning. No torpedoes or speedboats headed our way. Fish swam around us with no sense of urgency. Everything was as it should be. I gave Manuel the okay sign. But my eyes, wide and staring, betrayed me.

Manuel signaled again. I did a second inventory and then signaled back. Manuel pointed his fore and middle finger at his eyes and then turned his wrist to point away. We hadn't covered this sign, but I knew it meant "look." Then he put his palms together and wiggled them to tell me to look at the fish.

In my panic, I had forgotten to do that. As we continued our dive, I tried to regain the fascination I'd had when we first descended, but it was impossible.

Back in the boat, Manuel pulled me aside. "Diving is about wonder and beauty. It's an opportunity to relax and enjoy the environment. It's not an exercise in controlling panic. You need to dive more."

On that trip, I did seven open-water dives and two cave dives. I got more familiar with the equipment and ever more fascinated with the diversity of life on the reef. Again and again, Manuel gave me the okay sign until I could do the three checks automatically.

Do I have what I need to sustain life where I am? (Oxygen.) Is what I rely on functioning? (Gear.) Is there a potential problem I can foresee? (An anchor dropping on my head.) If all is well, then look at the fish. Just look at the fish. Appreciate them for all they are. That is why we are here.

On my first day back to work after vacation, I again had to face the horrific commute that had become so unbearable. And wouldn't you know it? A driver cut me off.

Automatically, I took a deep breath, noted my car was still functioning, and the surrounding drivers posed no additional threat. "The trees are already budding. I love those pale green leaves. Looks like spring has arrived," I told my windshield.

Without thinking, I'd done the check and moved on to appreciating the world around me, a world sometimes in need of laughable, somewhat grouchy commentary, but never more rage.

— Laura Jane Bender —

80

Save Yourself

I attract what I am. Life will have vasty barren places
until I cover my own desert with green.
~Muriel Strode

I was in my early twenties when I met my husband. I was confident and educated, and I had a full-time job. I had goals and dreams, and absolutely no intention of allowing anyone to stand in the way of my plans. It's amazing how empowering youth is — believing yourself to be brilliant in the ways of the world. Ignorance really is bliss.

I knew him from high school, but we had lost touch over the years, and I had no idea what he had been doing with his life. He shared very little — some ups and downs and a bad break-up. He didn't drink or use drugs. He told me he had learned that it was better for him to abstain, but he didn't elaborate. Some shared high-school memories were enough for him to become part of my life almost instantly.

I told myself that this could be fate. I was a hopeless romantic, and this scenario was pulled right from the pages of countless romance novels. I could feel darkness around him at times, but there was also an easy smile, and a love of animals, children and being outdoors. I told myself that everyone has a past, and the present was what mattered. I jumped into our relationship with my heart wide open and my eyes closed.

We weren't together very long when our talk turned to children. He claimed to love them. Everywhere we went, children seemed drawn to him, and he was at ease with them. I convinced myself that this was yet another reason why fate had brought us together. Soon after, I was pregnant with our first child.

It was then that I could see the darkness taking more of a hold. He started to buy beer, and when I asked about it, he acted like I was being ridiculous. And I felt I was. Can't a man enjoy a beer after a hard day of work? His job was seasonal. As the leaves changed on the trees, so did his moods — gradually, from bright and sunny to darker, more mysterious shades. Just like looking out the window each autumn morning, I never knew exactly what would be waiting for me.

That winter was difficult. We struggled financially, and he became more and more distant. I always had the feeling he was hiding something. It wasn't that he was lying. It was what he wasn't saying. More and more, I smelled alcohol on his breath, and the pile of empties started to take up space like a flashing neon sign warning of danger ahead.

Then, the weather changed, and so did he. His smile returned, and he started to laugh again. The empties disappeared. We welcomed our first child, and my heart swelled with joy and hope. I was certain that those dark months had been just a small detour off our path to happiness. The stress of life had gotten to him. Things would be fine now.

Life went on, and we added another child. But life is never simple or easy, and we faced challenge after challenge. I struggled to hang on as he lost his grip on sobriety over and over again. The bad days outnumbered the good. I begged, pleaded, bargained and cried. I threatened, made deals and watched every single promise get broken by a man I no longer recognized. I was hurt, scared and unable to fully accept or understand what was happening to our marriage and family.

Addiction is like a landslide. As it picks up speed, it destroys everything in its path. It can't be outrun. And no one is safe from the destruction and despair it leaves behind. One night, the landslide caught up with me. It was a bitterly cold night in the dead of winter, and as beer bottles smashed around me, narrowly missing my head, something inside me finally screamed at me to run. I knew in that moment that if I didn't take our children and go, the landslide would finally pull us under and consume us completely.

After we left, the promises came hard and fast. If we came home, he would see a therapist. He would attend Alcoholics Anonymous meetings. He promised he would change. He would get help. I had heard all these things before. They had become the broken record of the soundtrack of our lives. But no one gets married because they want the marriage to end. No one starts a family with the intention of tearing it apart. I began to falter. I began to think… maybe. Maybe, this time, things would be different.

I told a good friend that I was thinking of going back to him. She made me promise I would do one thing first: meet with her dad. Her dad was a recovering alcoholic. He ran AA meetings and sponsored many men trying to become and stay sober. I told her I would, and a meeting time was set.

I didn't know what to expect when we met. In my heart, I had already decided to go home and give my husband another chance. But, as he spoke, all of that changed. He explained to me that nothing I could do would ever stop my husband from drinking. He explained that alcoholics have to want to quit and decide for themselves that they want to quit, and no one else can make that decision for them. He said that most have to reach rock bottom before they come to that realization. I told him my husband had hit rock bottom. He had lost his wife and children. He told me that might not be enough. Sometimes, rock bottom was prison, or even death.

The advice he gave me was to take my children and walk away. He told me I would lose myself by trying to save someone who wasn't ready to save himself. As his words hit home, I realized that, for a long time, I had already lost myself.

I took his advice. We didn't go back. My husband, now my ex, never did seek help or make any changes. He destroyed any chance at a relationship with his children.

And, thanks to the advice of a man I hardly knew, I was able to move on and give those children a healthy and truly happy life. I found myself again. We escaped the landslide. His advice didn't just change my life; it saved it.

— Jesica Ryzynski —

81

The Blessing of Work

The art of life lies in a constant readjustment
to our surroundings.
~Kakuzō Okakura, The Book of Tea

"**Y**ou should take all of them," my mother-in-law said. It was 2001, and we were looking at my kitchen counter full of teacups and saucers, part of our Denby Imperial Blue dishes set. My husband and I had registered for the dishes before our wedding in 1994. They were beautiful and my favorite colors — crisp white and bright blue.

"I don't know. I can't imagine I will use the cups and saucers much." A wave of grief and fear overwhelmed me. My husband and I were packing up our Ohio house to move to Oregon for his new job — a great job that would make use of his newly earned Ph.D. and pay him enough that I could stay home with our one- and two-year-old children. It was a gift of time with our precious son and daughter. But I was scared, at thirty-five, to leave the only state I'd ever lived in, leave my friends and family behind, and be without a job and have my role be "stay-at-home mom."

My shoulders slumped, and my tears welled up. I hung my head and looked at the dishes, bright-colored towels, and collection of quirky flower vases, some of which I'd had since high school. My whole life, my memories and experiences, were laid out on the counter.

My mother-in-law started wrapping the teacups and saucers in newspaper. Her fingers smoothed over the newsprint, which smudged her hands. "You can do this," she said, continuing to pack. "Listen to me. You get up. You get dressed. You pack four lunches, and you take the kids to school (what we called day care — it was at a university after all), and you work hard every single day. Even when you're not working at your job, at night or on the weekend, you're still working, just at something else. And this move, this will just be a different kind of work, and you can do it."

It might have been the most I'd heard her talk all day, at least to me. She looked taller for a second. She seemed louder, like maybe she was saying something that mattered. I stretched my sweatshirt sleeve over to wipe my face. She picked up a box of tissues and waved it at me, while her other hand continued to work on the packing. I felt a quick twinge of guilt. She was the one doing all the work at the moment, while I sulked in my fear and worry.

I loved my job at the attorney general's office. I loved my friends, the neighborhood, our church, and all aspects of my life. I had lived in Columbus since I started college at eighteen, and it was the perfect city, I thought. There was something for everyone, and everything for me. I had already figured out where I wanted our kids to attend elementary school and where I hoped we would live one day when we could afford it. I had favorite places to buy groceries, have picnics, and go for walks. We had plans to adopt a dog once the kids were older, and our parents came to visit monthly and stayed a weekend or longer.

I dried my face and pushed up my sleeves. I started packing the plates, and my mother-in-law interrupted my placing of them in the boxes. "If you set them in this way, up and down, they're less likely to break in the move. If you stack them flat, like you do in the cupboard, even if they're padded with all this newspaper, they bear the weight of everything and might crack while they're traveling." She did know something about moving. She had moved with her husband and four kids many times for her husband's job. But she didn't have a career, and she didn't have a bunch of friends and plans like I did.

"You know," she continued, "you're fortunate in that you like to work." My neck bristled with anger. "It's a blessing."

I was annoyed by her comment — fortunate that I like to work?

I mean, I like a paycheck. I like taking care of myself and my family. I like doing things and using my education. I started heating up in my gray Ohio State sweatshirt, feeling far removed from the teary-eyed dishrag I'd been just a few minutes before.

Then, she was looking right at me. Her pale blue eyes opened wide as she told me, "Not everyone likes to work. Some people are afraid of it or don't know how. Or maybe no one ever showed them how enjoyable and satisfying it can be. I don't just mean working at an office or a desk or something." She seemed to think I just sat at a desk all day. This bothered me, too, but I kept listening as I packed the plates on their sides.

"This move will be work, and when you get to Oregon, it will be work. But you know how to work, and you like it. You know how to stay busy, and you like being occupied. You're not afraid of it, and you figure things out. It's a blessing, your enjoyment of work. You're smart, I've always known that, and you're happy. You will get there, and you will work, and this will be a good move for you. For your family."

I listened and accepted her hug when she came over and crushed me into her tiny frame. I inhaled her warm embrace, her Oil of Olay-scented kindness. I almost felt a little tipsy as I thought about her admiration or, at least, fondness for me that afternoon. She believed in me. She had faith in me. My mother-in-law, with whom I had an admittedly complex relationship (aren't they all, at least at times?), was rooting for me.

And... she was right. I got there. We got there. To Oregon. And I worked. I worked at setting up the household and finding the local library and swim center for the kids. We made friends and found our lives. It was work, but I like work. I was fortunate in that I appreciated the blessing of work. And I still do.

— Jennifer Priest Mitchell —

Reach Out and Connect

82

The Longest Hug

One of the best feelings in the world is when you hug
someone you love, and they hug you back even tighter.
~Author Unknown

I shifted uncomfortably in a metal folding chair as the women's leader spoke to the young moms gathered at church on a sunny Friday morning.

"Do you hug your children?" The slim, brunette woman standing before the fireplace scanned the audience of attentive moms, who were all nodding. "I'm sure you do, but do you hug them long enough?"

She meant to encourage us with those words. However, eager to be a good mother, I felt like a failure.

As sunlight streamed through the windows of the cozy fireside room, Pam smiled and continued. "You might have a child who wants lots of hugs or one who needs longer hugs." She crossed her arms over her chest and squeezed her shoulders with her open hands. "Why don't you try staying in the hug until your child breaks it off?"

At ten years old, my fun-loving yet reserved son, Robby, often asked for hugs. But I shied away from lingering touches because I didn't receive a lot of physical affection growing up. I wanted a quick hug to be enough for him.

The older, experienced woman continued her lecture, and my thoughts drifted to my childhood. As missionary teachers in a rural Nigerian village, my parents raised my four siblings and me in that beautiful country among its wonderful people.

However, at age six, my parents sent me to an international boarding school four hundred miles from home. Dorm mothers didn't give many hugs. Instead, a hurried kiss on the head served for a bedtime ritual.

Soon after I arrived for first grade, I fell on the playground and skinned my knee. I limped to the nurse's office where I plopped down on a wooden bench with seven other kids in the waiting room. When it was my turn, the school nurse roughly cleaned the wound, slapped on a bandage, and sent me on my way. I bit my lip and fled to my room where I threw myself on the bed. In that silent, lonely dorm room, I sobbed rivers of tears into my pillow. All I wanted was my mother to hold me. Nobody consoled me, so over time I buried my need for comfort and affection and learned to take care of myself.

That independence served me well when I married Chris and we raised three children. As a pilot, my husband flew away for half of each month, leaving me to parent alone.

At each goodbye, I blocked out my grief and focused on the day's duties. Brusque and organized, I looked competent, driving three kids to their classes, practices, and games on my own. However, by cutting off my emotions, I unintentionally lost the ability to be a cheerful mom.

Pam's voice drew me to the present as she sent us into our small-group discussions. With only four other moms, I felt comfortable sharing, but I also wanted to defend myself. "I'm worried my son's love tank gets only partly filled each day. But at least he doesn't live at a boarding school."

One of them patted my hand. "You're doing a fine job. I've seen you hug him plenty of times."

That afternoon, when Robby walked in the door after school, he tossed his backpack on the couch and then sauntered into the kitchen. "What's for snack?"

I stepped toward him. "Could I give you a hug first?"

"Sure, Mom!"

In front of the fridge, we stood with our arms around each other. I was determined not to break first.

After what seemed like an eternity but was probably just two minutes, he sighed. "I'm looking forward to Christmas."

I chuckled over the top of his blond head and pulled him closer.

After that day in the kitchen, I realized the significant comfort these hugs brought to him. They became a daily habit — one that we kept even through Robby's teenage years.

Now in his twenties, my lanky son lives at home while job hunting. Over the past two years, he walked through some deep valleys. Sheltering at home in 2020 for Covid-19 restrictions brought anxiety and depression for him. I'm so glad we'd already made healing hugs part of our daily routine.

On the days when Dad is home, he joins in, and we bask in the warmth of a group hug. Our now-happy son says, "This is the best part of my day!"

It's the best part of my day, too. The habit that began as a way to connect with Robby has brought me healing. Sandwiched between my son and my husband, I feel wrapped in a warm cocoon.

The long family hugs make up for the comforting cuddles I missed in my childhood. I'm always the last to let go.

— Debbie Jones Warren —

Go with the Flow

A wave is no less free because
the current helps it along.
~Marty Rubin

t is as important for us to receive as it is to give. There is a natural flow to receiving and giving. I once read this advice from a woman, Anita Moorjani, who wrote a book about her near-death experience. The phenomenon of dying and then returning a changed person captivated me. I was fascinated by the pearls of wisdom coming straight from the heavens.

This natural flow sounded easy. Just start by taking something that is offered, and things will begin to move in harmonious ways. Well, not so for me. I found it fairly easy to block this flow. Refusing help was something that came naturally to me. When my husband had a heart attack and was hospitalized, everyone extended a hand to try and help. Family and friends offered their assistance with groceries or dinners. Some even offered to sit and pray with me or just hold my hand. I was stunned at the willingness of others to give of themselves.

At this time, my son was in the process of relocating for his job and was working virtually from our house. I found it easy to accept his help since it was not out of the ordinary for him to walk the dog or run an errand for me. But he had to be on the clock working most of the time and was limited in what he could do for me.

Coming back from the grocery store on my way home from a long day at the hospital, I mentioned to my son how people had offered to bring us dinner, but I had refused. He got somewhat upset with me, saying, "Mom, you need to be more like me: a bit of a freegan."

I asked, "What's a freegan?"

"Technically, it's someone who helps the environment by retrieving or using discarded foods. But my version involves accepting food, especially meat, when someone offers to buy or make it for me," he quipped. As I laughed at his personal philosophy, I also heard a whisper: "People want to help, and you need to allow it."

I decided to listen and give this receiving thing a try. I called one of the friends who wanted to bring us dinner. I asked her to bring over a pizza the next day. (I needed to start with baby steps and figured picking up a pizza was the easiest for her.) The next day, when we had a torrential rainstorm at dinnertime, I started to regret my decision. My friend called to say she had the pizza but was still at the restaurant. She was waiting for the rain to slow down a bit so she could get to the car without drenching the pizza box. I apologized because I knew I was causing a real inconvenience — just one of the many reasons I didn't accept help from others.

When the pizza arrived, I thanked her profusely, and then my son and I attacked the box. As I bit into the hot, cheesy dough, I had an aha moment. Yes, I felt bad for putting her through this inconvenience, but if I had to try and keep myself and a pizza dry after spending the day with my hospitalized husband, then I would have lost it. I didn't have any spare energy for anything else, especially creating a creature comfort for myself. I was wiped out from going back and forth and being the strong, positive cheerleader for everyone in my family. That bite of pizza felt like comfort, and comfort was exactly what I needed.

I was so grateful in that moment that I realized I needed to say yes to all the others who offered their help with meals.

After eleven days, my husband was finally able to come home, and I started to fall back into my old habit of resisting help. I started thinking about all the ways I needed to repay people.

The next day, I got a text from a friend whom I hadn't heard from in over a year. She'd found the meditation CDs I had lent her and wondered if I wanted them back. I could not text back fast enough.

"Yes!" My family could use any and all introspection, reflection, and quiet time. I arranged to pick them up at her office.

This friend owns and operates her own potpourri company. After some time catching up, she asked, "Would you like some potpourri?"

"Why, yes, I think I would."

She picked up a case and said, "Here, it's an old line, and I have so much of it that you're actually doing me a favor by taking it." I looked into the box and saw fifteen bags. Jackpot!

Driving home with the smell of spiced orange and bergamot filling the inside of my car, I paused and gave thanks. I laughed to myself as I thought: *I don't care if my friends want potpourri. I don't care if my friends even like potpourri. But the Universe has given me potpourri, and that is what they are receiving. I am amazed at this divinely orchestrated dance of giving and receiving.*

—Jill Guerin—

Go Help Someone Else

*Gratitude and love are always multiplied when you
give freely. It is an infinite source of contentment
and prosperous energy.*
~Jim Fargiano, The Spoken Words of Spirit

t was 2009, and I was lying on the bathroom floor, curled into the fetal position with tears streaming down my face. Six months earlier, I had been sitting at my desk, minding my own business when the phone rang.

"I'm in big trouble."

The voice was my husband's, and the statement that came next would forever change the course of my life.

"I was arrested... for soliciting a minor online."

The following week was a whirlwind of court dates, news vans and, eventually, a cross-country drive to start my life over in Las Vegas. The world I had previously known was gone. It was time for a rebirth.

The next few months were akin to a very long, very painful roller coaster ride. My parents promised I could live with them rent-free as long as I needed, provided that I went to therapy. What I had been through, they said, had the potential to destroy me, and they weren't about to let that happen.

I saw a therapist twice a week. We processed the experience. We delved into why I was attracted to this man in the first place. We discussed how to overcome trauma, and I read a few self-help books to round out my personal-development education. Okay, if I'm being honest, I read *every* self-help book.

But somewhere between my divorce papers being signed, my home being foreclosed on, and having to file for bankruptcy, the depression began to creep in. A degree in psychology did nothing to prepare me for what I was about to endure. Over the coming weeks, it became more difficult to get out of bed. I'd sleep later and later each day and live for the first thirty seconds of my "morning" when I'd open my eyes and not yet remember that my life as I knew it was over. Showering became a rare occurrence, and when it did happen, my tears would wash away the soap.

My rock bottom came that day on the cold tile floor. I wouldn't have called myself suicidal, but I would've welcomed an end. I didn't have the strength to stand up, and I truly didn't care if I ever did. Thankfully, my parents arrived home. My stepmom held out her hand to help me up and uttered the best advice I've ever been given: "Go help someone else."

I did. A lot of someones, in fact.

My Beagle/Lab mix, Akasha, had been my faithful friend for months. If there was anyone who deserved a break, it was her. We went to a local pet festival so she could sniff, snack, and dry out from me constantly crying into her fur. As she happily romped in the grass, smelling all the smells, a booth caught my attention. The sign read: Foreclosed Upon Pets. When I approached, the volunteers shared the group's story.

This was the height of the housing crisis, and real estate agents, bank personnel, and maintenance workers were entering foreclosed houses only to find that family pets had been left behind to fend for themselves. The organization was founded to rescue these animals, provide them with the care they needed, and find them new, stable forever homes.

My heart sank. Akasha had been my lifeline through everything. I couldn't imagine navigating these experiences without her. How could anyone leave behind their beloved pets?

With my stepmom's advice echoing in my head, I knew immediately what I needed to do.

"How can I help?" I blurted out with tears in my eyes.

"Money," the volunteers replied in unison.

I didn't have any of that. But I did have some untapped skills that could be used for this cause. With contact information in hand and a very tuckered-out pup in the back seat, I headed home to start planning. A few weeks later, I'd called on the few resources I had in town, worked hand in hand with the animal rescue, and filled my parents' garage from floor to ceiling with donated items. I held a yard sale that raised close to $2,000 for the organization.

That was just the beginning.

Over the next fourteen (and counting) years, I've raised money and awareness for animal-rescue groups. I've helped families stay together through the worst economic times our generation has ever seen. I've provided a voice for the voiceless, and I've helped save the lives of thousands of animals.

Want to know the cool thing?

For every life I've helped save, they saved me right back.

Animal rescue rescued me. I gained skills, made lifelong friends, and turned volunteerism into employment. Most importantly, it gave me something outside of myself to focus on.

Depression has a horrible way of isolating you when you need others more than ever. Depression whispers in your ear that there's no reason for you to be here — that the world would be a better place without you. Depression snuffs out the light at the end of the tunnel and leads you to believe that you'll never be able to help yourself out of the darkness.

Truthfully, you may not be able to help yourself. You can, however, help others. In the process, you may discover that when you help others, you'll actually help yourself.

It turns out that amazing things happen when you "go help someone else."

— Sheryl Green —

85

To Hug or Not to Hug

That's what people do who love you.
They put their arms around you and
love you when you're not so lovable.
~Deb Caletti

t was clear that my son had special needs when he was a newborn. The therapists who worked with my two little girls begged me to also get the baby evaluated for therapy. He didn't stop screaming for a second. Around the clock, I paced the floors with my howling bundle, and I wasn't sure how any of us would survive. To make matters worse, the baby refused to let my husband or anyone else hold him.

That crying baby grew into a wrecking ball of a toddler who craved movement and sensory input. Let him run free and wreak havoc on the world, and he'd be happy. But if we ever forced him to sit down for a moment, he kicked and screamed. He broke more valuables and hurt more people than any other child I'd ever met.

When we were walking, he'd kick dogs and hit elderly people who were unfortunate enough to cross paths with us. Once, he locked himself in a room in the pediatrician's office, and they had to call a locksmith to get him out. He pulled the fire alarm in a hospital and called the police from a hotel room. He was three years old when he removed the air conditioner from the bedroom window.

To further aggravate matters, Dovid was unable to speak until he was three and a half. He couldn't express his needs or wants, which was very frustrating for both of us. I simply didn't know what to do with my nonverbal tornado.

Then I heard advice that completely altered the way I dealt with Dovid. A parenting expert said that when a child deserves a hug the least, that's when he needs it the most.

Of course, it was true. As difficult as life was for me, my son had it pretty bad too. Since his body gave him uncontrollable urges and his mouth refused to speak, he was not a happy child.

When he was out of control, I tried to remember that he needed a hug. I would sit down and embrace him. As my arms wrapped around his precious body and he rested his head on my shoulder, I could feel the healing that was taking place inside us as we relaxed and remembered that we loved each other.

He acted like a caged animal, but the hugs reminded me that he was a little person in distress. I needed to help him, not just punish him. I needed to aid his growth, not knock him down further.

Time passed, and Dovid grew. He learned to talk eventually, but speaking still did not come easily for him. He was afraid to speak to strangers, teachers or peers. His processing was slow. He was jealous of his siblings, so he hurt them a lot. He got angry often, threw tantrums and broke things.

We made a book with pictures of calming techniques. When he was angry, I would show him the book, and he would choose how he wanted to calm down. He had several options in the book, but he always chose the same page. Whenever he was angry, he chose to come to me for a hug. And, in my arms, we healed together.

— Chana Rubinstein —

86

Elizabeth Versus Elizabeth

*Treat everyone with politeness and kindness, not
because they are nice, but because you are.*
~Roy T. Bennett, The Light in the Heart

"Do you want to race to the corner?" my cousin would ask me. I would always firmly shake my head from side to side with a definite no. I did not have a competitive bone in my body. Getting to the corner first, playing on a team, or watching sports of any kind did not interest me. I never wanted the shiny trophy to put on my dresser—until I met "the other Elizabeth."

Throughout my childhood, I loved to read, played school every day *after* school, and practiced my penmanship. I knew I wanted to be a teacher, and when I started my education classes at my small local college, it was the first time I longed to be the best. This feeling was heightened when my professor announced that one student would be receiving an Excellence in Education Award at our graduation ceremony. This student would be identified as not only having an excellent academic record but possessing the necessary characteristics to be an outstanding member of his or her chosen field. I pictured myself at the podium receiving the award, and suddenly I was a competitive person!

The following semester, I worked harder than ever. I was private about my lesson plans, stayed up late perfecting my term papers. I even upgraded my wardrobe to dress the part of the perfect teacher. I had risen to the top of my class except for one pesky student—"the other Elizabeth." It was as if I could feel her gaining on me each time she received an A on a paper or demonstrated an amazing lesson that made our classmates take notes. If only Elizabeth would make one mistake, then victory would be mine.

The next week, an oral presentation was assigned by our most discriminating professor. *This could be my big moment to shine,* I thought excitedly. I asked my good friend John if he would be my pretend audience member and help critique my work. After I finished presenting to him, I blurted out that my best hope was that "the other Elizabeth" would get stage fright and mess up her speech. He looked at me in surprise and disappointment. Feeling uncomfortable, I reminded him how competitively he played in sports, how he always wanted to win. "Well," he said slowly, "there is a real difference. I never hope that someone else will fail so that I can do better. I only hope that I do my best. The only competition I am in is with myself."

Suddenly, I felt the whole semester flash before me. I had stopped sharing my ideas with my classmates, and it made the entire process less enjoyable. I saw everyone as a threat instead of a friend. I had forgone the joy of bonding with my classmates, all in the hopes of experiencing one glory-filled moment — the moment when I would "win." I had especially made "the other Elizabeth" out to be my nemesis when all she was doing was her best. With a renewed spirit, I returned to school with an open heart.

The next day, as my classmates and I were getting ready to stand up in front of our professors, I noticed that Elizabeth was missing. Concerned, I slipped into the education office just as the administrative assistant hung up the phone and revealed that Elizabeth's father had passed away unexpectedly. I saw her dab the tears from her eyes as she added that he was a caretaker for her mother, who was dying of cancer. "Elizabeth has managed so many things this year," she sighed. "She helps care for her mother each evening and now this." I felt my heart sink, and I regretfully thought of all the ways I could have been a help to Elizabeth if I had not been blinded by the desire to win.

I went back into the hall where my classmates were ready to give their presentations. I shared the news about Elizabeth's father and what she had been struggling with at home. I wanted to help Elizabeth reach her goals, finish the semester and graduate on time. Each of my fellow classmates agreed. In the coming weeks, while she was home caring for her mother, we kept Elizabeth filled in on all our assignments. We brought dinner along with study materials to her house, gave her our notes and offered encouragement whenever we could. She was able to maintain her ambitious standards at school, and when "the other Elizabeth" received the Excellence in Education Award, no one cheered louder than I did.

If real competition is competing with myself, as my friend John had said, then I won, too. I was a better version of myself. And do you know what happened to my friend John who gave me that sage advice? I married him!

—Elizabeth Rose Reardon Farella—

87

One Final Lesson

*Character defines an individual, and honoring
commitments helps to define your character.*
~Gary Ryan Blair

itting on the cold, wooden floor of my room, tears streamed
down my face as I read through the pages in my hands. The
crying that racked my body was so loud that my roommate
knocked on my door in concern.

With tears blurring my eyes, I attempted to explain what had
upset me so greatly, but all I could gasp out were the same words on
repeat. "I didn't call. I didn't call."

My roommate sat down next to me. "Who didn't you call?"

"My gramma," I replied with tear stains streaking my cheeks.

She remained perplexed, as my gramma had passed away a couple
of weeks earlier.

In explanation, I handed her the calendar I was still clutching,
the one where my gramma had meticulously written the happenings
of each day. From the weather to the friends she played cards with to
the people she spoke with on the phone — every day, she had recorded
what occurred.

There, in my gramma's distinct scrawl, was the evidence. Evidence
that I had let her down.

July 5th — "No word from Laura." I didn't call when I'd promised to.

August 31st — "Laura isn't coming." I hadn't been there when I
said I would.

I had failed to show up for someone who had always shown up for me.

In that final year of my gramma's life in the upper peninsula of Michigan, I was living a very different life in Chicago—one where there was always a tomorrow, one in which my focus was on getting through the work day so I could spend time with friends. It was a life in which my desires always came first.

I relegated the one person who had been there for my literal first steps, and all my other momentous life steps along the way, to the back burner.

I'd told myself I would call when I had time. I would make the drive to visit when my schedule cleared up. I selfishly thought there would be more days ahead.

Until there weren't.

I was supposed to visit a few weeks before my gramma was diagnosed with cancer, but I didn't go.

The worst part is that I don't even know why. Perhaps I had a date or unexpected tickets to a concert, or I just wanted one last weekend at the beach with my friends before the cool weather rolled in. None of it mattered. I chose wrong.

My gramma was left waiting.

I was able to see her before she passed, but rather than her lively, chatty self, she was a shell of herself, knowing she was nearing the end.

Spending time by her bedside, I tried to fit in as much of the missed time as I could, but it was like trying to hold water in cupped palms. It slowly leaked away, no matter how hard I tried to hold on.

After she passed, the family pitched in to clean out her apartment. I opened her freezer and staring back at me was my favorite flavor of ice cream—black cherry with chocolate chips—waiting for a visit that never came.

Shame, guilt, sadness and self-loathing sat hard on my heart, and I could do absolutely nothing to assuage it. I couldn't pick up the phone and say how sorry I was. I couldn't get in the car for an impromptu visit. I would never have the opportunity to make it right.

As we'd packed up her belongings, I'd kept a few items to take home with me. Amongst the possessions was her calendar. While I didn't know what it contained, I took it because it was filled with her familiar handwriting, her words and thoughts.

When I returned home, I finally sat down and read what her days consisted of. It was filled with so much life. She had a plethora of people who cared about her, checked in on her and spent time with her. I wished I had been a bigger part of it.

As my roommate listened to my lamentations, she recited the rote words, "Your grandma loved you, and she knew that you loved her, too."

While I knew it was true, it still did nothing to lessen the pain I felt.

As the days and weeks passed, and I returned to the familiar groove of life, I became aware of the number of times that people canceled plans, didn't follow through on their word, or simply forgot about commitments they had made.

One night, as I was reflecting on my newfound awareness, I revisited the calendar. As I held it in my hands, I started crying again. Then, unexpectedly, I began to laugh.

It finally connected.

My gramma was still teaching and guiding me just as she had in life. I felt her presence surround me, and a warmth spread through me. Despite the fact that she would never again be by my side physically, she will always be a part of me, reside in my heart and be reflected in my actions.

Since that day over a decade ago, I have been diligent about keeping my word to my husband, son, friends, colleagues and myself.

I've realized that one of the biggest gifts we can give ourselves and others is being the person who is there when we say we will be. It's the building of a foundation of trust for those with whom we are establishing relationships. It's maintaining the bonds of trust for those with whom we are close. It's knowing that we won't give up on ourselves when life gets difficult.

While it may have taken me years to learn this valuable lesson, I have the rest of my life to put it into action.

My gramma was the rock in my life. She held my hand when I

was a little girl, lent an ear to my teenage woes, and gave me advice as an adult.

It's only fitting that she give me one final lesson from Heaven.

—Laura Niebauer Palmer—

88

A New World

*To care for those who once cared for us
is one of the highest honors.*
~Tia Walker, The Inspired Caregiver

I was exhausted after the Zoom call. I didn't know how my sister, Elaine, managed as our mom's primary caregiver. This call was especially troublesome. Elaine warned us beforehand that Mom was not doing well. That was an understatement. Mom was irritated, restless, and throwing tantrums like a three-year-old. She didn't recognize my younger sister or me. We tried to be positive and cheerful, but she wasn't having any of it. She even shouted, "Leave me alone!"

This was not the mother I'd known my entire life. My mom was always upbeat and optimistic. When she moved into her assisted-living facility five years earlier, she was made an ambassador for the community because of her outgoing personality. Dementia was robbing my mother of more than her memories.

This day, her condition was aggravated by an undiagnosed urinary tract infection (UTI). As we learned more about her dementia and the impact of things like UTIs, we knew to look for the signs of trouble — like the belligerent irritability that was so unlike her. We learned that Mom's personality would return to her "new normal" after she was treated for a UTI.

After that Zoom call, I sat in my recliner, feeling defeated. Out of the corner of my eye, I saw my copy of *Chicken Soup for the Soul: Navigating Eldercare & Dementia* on the table next to me. I'd submitted a story about my grandmother that took place more than thirty years ago, and it was chosen for publication. I reached for the book, looking for comfort, advice, and hope.

When the book was first released, I'd read through the stories and related to many of them. This time when I opened the book, it was different. I was experiencing dementia in my family like I never had before. I didn't realize then how much I'd been sheltered from the day-to-day challenges of my grandmother's Alzheimer's. It was sad watching my grandmother fade away, but it has been a whole different level of heartbreaking with my mother.

So many of the stories spoke to me. While the situations weren't identical to mine, I wanted to reach through the pages and hug the authors. I could feel the weight of emotions and better understood their experiences now that I was in the middle of a dementia whirlwind. Two stories in particular have stayed with me. Amy Newmark's "Determined, Distraught, and Demented" and London Alexander's "Ray of Light."

While I'm concerned about my mom, both authors were dealing with men — a father and a father figure — but the stories were relatable. They each shared a glimpse of the struggle to adjust to a loved one whose mind was slipping away.

I laughed out loud as Amy Newmark spoke of unplugging phones in her story. Oh, how I relate. My mom has a smartphone and loves to FaceTime people on her call list. She is especially chatty between the hours of 2:00 and 4:00 in the morning. Her family and friends have learned to put their phones on "do not disturb" during the overnight hours. My sister has also removed some friends from Mom's contact list to spare them the nocturnal calls, just as Amy had to do.

Amy also told how she learned to change the topic of conversation when her father was perseverating on one topic. Mom fixates on songs and stories, not always in a good way. I've tried Amy's method to divert the conversation to a new topic, and it sometimes works. Occasionally, Mom's obsession with the story stuck on repeat in her mind is too strong, and our conversation feels like I'm going in circles on a roundabout, desperately trying to exit.

Like Amy, my siblings and I have shared texts about our conversations with Mom. The sad is balanced out by the funny. And there have been plenty of funny moments — we just had to learn to savor them.

One sentence in Amy's story resonated with me. She wrote, "I entered my father's new reality." That is profound. Instead of trying to draw him back into her world, she accepted his. I paused there and reread that sentence several times. Accepting that this is Mom's new normal is not the easiest thing to come to terms with, but it will eventually make the journey smoother if we all roll with her in *her* world rather than try to drag her back to *ours*.

In "Ray of Light," London Alexander's father figure has spilled out nuggets of wisdom over the course of London's childhood, punctuating his stories with, "It is what it is," to make his point. When London returned to his hometown years later to care for Dad, he found a frail shadow of the man he once knew.

London talked about those "rays of light" in the midst of dementia — when you see a glimpse of the person you remember. I understand the emotion of grieving the loss of a person in bits and pieces long before their soul departs. London had shouldered the burden of caring for Dad in his final years and shared his sorrow at what was happening to his beloved father figure. Dad, in one last ray of light, told him, "It is what it is." As London summed up his feelings, he said, "I squeezed his hand, finally understanding. He was saying there was no point in dwelling on things. Sometimes, we just had to accept reality instead of trying to change it. In those moments, we needed to make the best of what we had."

Tears rolled down my face reading story after story. I know Mom will continue to have good days and bad days, but I treasure my memories of her — even the ones we are making now in her final years. I am comforted to know that our experience with Mom's dementia is one shared by so many who have taken this journey. I am thankful for such wonderful, relatable stories that show compassion, caring, endurance, and advice.

I closed the book thinking; *I've entered my mom's new reality. It is what it is.*

— Donna Anderson —

89

Assertive vs. Aggressive

Respect is a two-way street. If you want
to get it, you've got to give it.
~R.G. Risch

With ears perked, I leaned forward. Mom was telling Dad about an incident that happened at work. Always professional, she handled these incidents with a firm hand and, other times, with humor. But, every time, I learned something by simply listening. I grew as an employee and person from the stories my mother would tell.

Mother had started her career on the bottom rung of the ladder. She attended college at night while raising five children. This determined woman retired almost twenty-five years later as Vice President of Medical and Legal Services.

Facing my first job as a manager, I was eager to listen and learn from her stories. Moving into the kitchen, I topped off Mom's tea and joined the conversation. As she spoke, her beautifully manicured fingernails tapped the side of her cup, the only outward sign of the stress that today's incident had wrought on her psyche.

I had just started as Assistant Manager of Computer Operations at my company so I was eager to learn from my mother. In fact, later that week I had to address my own issue at work.

"We have a problem that I'd like to address today," I told my new boss. "Kim leaves the department for a few hours each day. I asked her about it, and she said that you approved her spending time helping the data-entry department."

"I did approve it. She's the fastest key pounder in the building. Occasionally, she helps them out when they fall behind."

"Unfortunately, the data-entry manager is pulling her daily," I said, "and Kim is falling behind in her work. I plan to remind everyone involved that she's only available once her work is complete."

"That's fine." Mr. Cannon sunk his face back into his coffee mug.

Back at Kim's office, I tapped on her door. "Before you leave for the day," I said, "we need to straighten out something. Beginning tomorrow, you are not to go to the data-entry department until all your work is finished."

"But I have to go. Mr. Cannon told me to help them out. And, besides, I like doing data entry."

"I hear you're very good at it and a big help to that department," I said. Kim flushed with pride.

"The problem is, you're not keeping up with your own work. We have deadlines to meet here as well. Once you've finished your duties, you may go and help them. I also want you to let me know when you are leaving our department."

"But what if the data-entry manager comes to get me? What am I supposed to say?"

"I'll speak to Mrs. Robertson before I leave for the day," I said. Kim wasn't happy with me. *It's tough at the top,* I thought as I left her pouting and went to meet with Mrs. Robertson.

"Hello, Mrs. Robertson. My name is Mary, and I'm the new computer-operations supervisor. Do you have a moment?"

"I heard Dan hired himself an assistant. What can I do for you?"

"I've come to speak with you about Kim."

"She's wonderful," gushed Mrs. Robertson. "I don't know how we'd keep up without her help."

"I'm happy to hear she's appreciated. However, we have a bit of a problem." Mrs. Robertson stopped smiling.

"Kim has fallen behind in her work because she spends so much time in your department. Therefore, Kim may come to your department only if and when she's completed her required tasks in our department."

"But we need her! You're new here. Maybe you're not aware that she's been helping us for the past year."

"I'm sorry you're struggling, but she has deadlines that are being missed. That means checks don't get processed for our clients, resulting in fines to the company. That's her priority. I've instructed Kim to check in with me before leaving her office."

"You can't come marching in here telling me we can't use her. What am I supposed to do?" Without waiting for an answer, she ranted, "We'll just see about this! I'll be speaking to Mr. Cannon first thing tomorrow."

"You can do that, but know that he and I have discussed this," I said. Mrs. Robertson threw open her door and waved me out. I'd been dismissed.

The clicking of my three-inch heels on the marble floor echoed in my ears. Rattled that it hadn't gone as smoothly as the incidents Mom had described, I felt disrespected. This was my first uncomfortable interaction with a member of the management team. However, I am my mother's daughter. I pulled back my shoulders, grabbed my purse, and locked the computer-room doors. It was time for a cup of tea and a talk with Mom.

"I am so proud of you," Mom said. "You stood your ground. But…"

"Uh-oh. What did I do wrong?"

"Did you use that same tone of voice with Mrs. Robertson as you used just now?"

I nodded.

"You sounded aggressive."

My face flushed. I guess I expected Mom to say that I did things right. That I was justified.

"Honey, there's a big difference between being aggressive and being assertive. Being aggressive comes across as confrontational. Being assertive implies forceful confidence."

My brows furrowed. "What should I have said?"

"This woman has been getting help from your employee for a long time. She's become dependent on her."

I sighed as my polished fingernails tapped on the side of my cup. Mom laid her hands over mine. "Did you give her options?"

"Is it my job to give her options?"

"If you want to leave her speechless, it is. Be assertive. For example, when she said, 'What am I supposed to do?' You can respond by saying, 'I sympathize with you on the issues of deadlines. We deal with them, too. To help you, I've made a list of local temporary agencies that hire out data-entry operators.'"

"I should actually make her a list?"

"Yes. Most likely, she won't want to take the money out of her operating budget to pay someone. But you've given her a viable option and a good answer to her question. Calmly explain again that you are not saying Kim can't work for her. What you are saying is that Kim must complete the work required of her in Operations before she performs data entry. Tell Mrs. Robertson that Kim may be available for only one hour some days. Other days, she may be available for more. It depends on Kim's workload on any given day." I nodded.

"This way, you've made it clear that Kim is not at her beck and call. You've given her a reasonable solution with the temporary agency, and you're willing to compromise. Trust me, she'll wait for Kim."

The next day, I met with Mrs. Robertson, with the list in my hand and a smile on my face. She and I grew to develop a mutual respect.

Learning to be assertive and not aggressive has served me well in all aspects of my professional career. It works beautifully when applied to our personal lives as well!

— Mary J. Staller —

90

Always Be Nice to the Receptionist

Kindness is not just about being nice;
it's about recognizing another human
being who deserves care and respect.
~Colin Powell

Back in the mid-1990s, freelance journalism took a big hit, and I was forced to look at my options. I was at a crossroad in my career and debated whether I should go back to school or seriously think about changing my profession.

The local college was offering a free, three-month Career Development Program valued at more than $5,000. The goal was to get you to thoroughly investigate three different career options before deciding which direction you were going to take. The program consisted of eight weeks of classes followed by four weeks of work experience in your chosen field.

The classes covered a range of topics, such as developing computer skills, refining resumes and cover letters, practicing and critiquing job interviews, learning good research techniques, networking, and participating in a variety of activities to build confidence. There would be regular guest speakers, including some who had previously completed the program and were there to offer advice and encouragement.

The Career Development Program was extremely popular, and the deadline was looming, so I filled out the application forms and raced them down to the college myself. When I got there, I stood in line behind a woman who was impatiently waiting for the receptionist to finish her phone call. When she hung up, she turned to the woman and said, "Good afternoon…"

But before she could say anything else, the woman thrust her application at the receptionist and said, "Here, I'm in a hurry. Just make sure the department head gets this application right away."

The receptionist smiled and said, "Don't worry. I'll make sure it gets to the right place."

"You'd better," said the woman, rushing off toward the exit.

I cringed as I witnessed the rude behavior. It had been obvious that the receptionist was helping someone on the phone, not taking a personal call. She had been professional, polite, and, even when faced with an irate customer, continued to remain calm.

I was up next. "Good afternoon," she greeted me. "How may I help you?"

I smiled and said, "Hi. I just wanted to tell you how sorry I am that you had to deal with such rude behavior. But you handled the situation very well."

The woman smiled and said, "Thank you. But I'm not really the receptionist. When things get busy, I like to send her for a break so I can handle the phones and potential students. It's always interesting to see how people behave when they're feeling stressed. By the way, I'm Rowena, head of the Career Development Program, and I make the final decision about who we accept into the program."

She explained that the program always attracted many good applicants, so it was often difficult to make the selections since only twenty-five students were accepted for each course. "But not when somebody is rude," she said. "Then, the decision is easy." With that, she dropped the woman's application onto the shredding pile.

She saw the surprised look on my face and chuckled. "I'll take yours and give it a thorough review. I'm sure you'll be hearing from us soon. We get a lot of applications, and I read through all of them — unless I don't want to. This helps me know who should be admitted to the program. If you're rude, I don't care who you are or what you have to offer; I don't want you in my program."

And, with that, she thanked me for coming and smiled at the next person walking up with their application.

Thankfully, I did get accepted and really enjoyed it. For my three career options, I researched everything involved in becoming a teacher, a 911 operator, and a communications specialist. I also met some wonderful people and learned a lot. A month after completing the program, I accepted a great job as a writer for an entertainment magazine.

To this day, I still try to be nice to every receptionist. I'm pretty sure I would anyway, but in this case, I actually saw how it paid off.

—Lori Kempf Bosko—

Chapter
11

Take Care of Yourself

91

Yes or No

*Half of the troubles of this life can be traced to saying
yes too quickly and not saying no soon enough.*
~Josh Billings

She was at it again. A relative I'll call Shirley was making her demands. A born people-pleaser, I'd deferred to her instructions for holidays, birthdays and other special occasions way longer than I should have. Her status as a senior member of the family only seemed to complicate the situation, as I felt that I should respect my elders.

It all started out innocently enough. First, Shirley extended holiday invitations to her home. It didn't matter that I already had long-standing plans. I was to cancel them and honor her wishes. If she preferred lunch over dinner, and the occasion took place on a workday, she harangued me into leaving work early.

Then, after my husband and I bought our own home, Shirley picked up her game a notch. She gave me a detailed menu and guest list of who I was to entertain around my own dinner table, including her and her extended brood. Never mind that I worked eight hours a day while Shirley was retired. If she said so, it had to be.

One particular Christmas Eve was the straw that broke the camel's back. My mother had recently passed away, and my husband and I agreed that the best way to handle the day was to have a quiet evening with only Dad and my brother. As the holiday loomed closer, I breathed a sigh of relief that Shirley had not gotten in the middle of my plans. Then, the phone rang. It was Shirley.

"I'm going to be alone Christmas Eve, and I want you two to come over."

I took a deep breath. "We've already planned to spend the evening with my father and brother," I explained. I thought quickly. "But you're welcome to join us."

Shirley would have none of it. She wanted us at her home — or else. Needless to say, I changed my plans.

Christmas Eve morning, I phoned Shirley to ask what time we were expected at her home. "Nah," she answered. "I don't feel like cooking a big meal just for you two. Just stay home tonight."

I was so angry that it's a miracle the phone didn't burst into flames. Shirley had gone way too far this time.

That afternoon, I baked a cake and two dozen of my brother's favorite Christmas cookies. Afterward, I pulled out whatever groceries I had in my pantry and put together an impromptu dinner that I brought to my very delighted dad at his house. Over coffee and cake, we discussed what had happened regarding Shirl's invitation — or dis-invitation, as it were.

Now, my father was a very wise man — wise in the way that only someone who had survived the Depression, served on both fronts in WWII, raised a family and was caregiver for an ailing partner could be. He looked at me squarely. "You know," he said, "there are two answers: yes or no. They're both good answers. You pick which answer you give."

I had fallen under Shirley's spell to such a degree that the fact that I had a choice in my response never even occurred to me. My dad's words were an awakening for me. How many other times and in how many other circumstances had I said yes because I didn't feel that I had a choice — because I felt that yes was the only acceptable answer. I had forgotten that no is a good answer, too.

From that point on, I started to say no to Shirley whenever the situation warranted. Oh, she was quite resistant at first, but I learned to stand my ground with her — and others as well. And my old enemy, resentment, soon went on a permanent holiday. It's quite wonderful to have a choice. Thanks, Dad, for pointing that out.

— Monica A. Andermann —

92

Never Look Back

Caring for myself is not self-indulgence;
it is self-preservation.
~Audre Lorde

"Go live your life and never look back." That was the advice Father Marc gave me the day I walked into church and told him, "Father, I'm calling it off."

My wedding was one month away, and things weren't going well. When you're planning a wedding, you expect family members to disagree about everything from the guest list to the color of the bridesmaids' dresses. There's bound to be drama, but my family had taken it to a whole new level.

Father Marc invited me to sit down. "Tell me what's going on now."

"Dad isn't speaking to me, and B.J. is giving me a hard time."

At the heart of the matter was my dad's fear of being left with my younger sister, B.J.

"What's going to happen to your sister when you're gone?" he had asked me.

B.J. and I were both adults living at home with our widowed dad. Mom had died two years earlier after a series of strokes. I worked in a bank, but at the age of twenty-four, B.J. was unemployed and still in college, exploring one path after another. Dad paid most of her bills. I offered transportation, extra money for incidentals, and moral support.

Dad and B.J. depended on me, but not in a healthy way. It was partly my own fault. As a natural-born people pleaser, I never wanted to cause trouble. Most of the time, I went along with whatever my family asked of me, putting aside my plans for a college education and a life on my own. I didn't have the courage to stand up for myself.

The current situation had escalated to the point that I felt the only option left was to cancel the wedding. My last conversation with Dad before going to see Father Marc was short but definitely not sweet.

"Don't expect me to pay for anything!" Dad told me.

My fiancé and I agreed that we could handle the wedding expenses ourselves. My older sister and brother-in-law, who had a catering business on the side, offered to provide the meal for our reception as their wedding gift to us. I put my gown, flowers and other accessories in layaway and paid for them in installments. My cousins and my best friend hosted the bridal shower.

Father Marc listened to all of this with his head down, not offering comments. He hadn't been in the parish long before he figured out how dysfunctional our family was. Not your ordinary clergyman, he had come to his vocation later in life. As an ex-military man and a widower with grown children, he brought with him a depth of understanding about marriage and family life lacking in most Catholic priests. Because of his compassion, I had gone to him often to ask for advice. Here I was again, pouring my heart out.

I finished by saying, "I don't think my dad and sister can function without me. Father, I think the best thing to do would be to cancel the wedding."

The military man in him must have kicked in at that point because his expression changed from understanding pastor to commanding officer. He shifted his gaze from the floor to me and, in his most authoritative voice, said, "Now, you listen to me. You've done all you can here. God brought you and your fiancé together. Talk to your family about this. Be firm. It's time for you to move on. Go live your life and never look back!"

That threw me. I had expected him to agree with my decision, but he was telling me to do the exact opposite. How could I do what he asked without creating more problems? How could I talk to people who weren't speaking to me? How could I be firm after a lifetime of giving in to the wishes of other people? On the other hand, how could I give up the man I was in love with and with whom I wanted to spend the rest of my life? I took it to prayer.

Not long after that meeting, fed up with all the drama, I confronted my dad.

"It doesn't matter what you do. I'm getting married. You might as well get used to the idea."

After that conversation, there was a noticeable shift in the atmosphere. He started speaking to me again, albeit curtly. I had a similar talk with my sister, who broke down and admitted she didn't know how she could live without me.

"You'll be fine," I told her. "You're stronger than you think."

The wedding wasn't quite a disaster, but it came close. We weren't sure that Dad would show up, so my brother-in-law sat in the back of the church wearing his catering clothes, apron and all, ready to escort me down the aisle. As it turned out, Dad did show up, and he did walk me down the aisle. But he wasn't happy about it.

Father Marc gave us a beautiful wedding Mass. College friends provided gorgeous music and took our photographs. My best friend from high school gave us the wedding cake. We had no music at the reception because my sister "forgot" to bring her stereo system. On the other hand, we had the best food thanks to my brother-in-law and his catering staff. Forty-one years later, people still talk about that meal.

After a period of adjustment, Dad and B.J. learned how to live without me. They did better than I even thought they would.

So did I. Over the years, my newfound courage served me well. Whenever I had a decision to make that threatened the status quo, I remembered Father Marc's advice. I resisted the urge to be the people pleaser I had been taught to be, and I tried to be true to myself. Because of Father Marc, I have lived my life with a loving husband and three beautiful, talented, hard-working daughters. And I have never looked back.

— Elizabeth A. Dreier —

93

Attraversiamo

I survived because the fire inside me burned
brighter than the fire around me.
~Author Unknown

ttraversiamo. With this last printed word, meaning "let's cross over" in Italian, I close the book and stare through tears at the wood-paneled wall before me. Sitting alone on a Friday night in my small, newly acquired two-bedroom mobile home, my thoughts are focused on the book I have just read.

Eat Pray Love by Elizabeth Gilbert was just a random bookstore purchase, like so many before, but this one changes everything.

I am thirty years old, and my second marriage has just ended.

My children from my first marriage — two adorable, bubbly redheads who are the only lights in my life — are at their dad's for the weekend. I have no distractions, no bedtime baths or tuck-ins to take my mind off the nagging lessons that *Eat Pray Love* has instilled into my brain.

I've messed up. This thought bursts forth before all others and refuses to be ignored. I look down at the closed book on my lap, and those three words are all I see.

I've messed up.

In *Eat Pray Love*, Elizabeth Gilbert documents leaving her life to travel for a full year. Could I do that? Could I travel the world in search of the "me" that got lost in those last two marriages? Would a plate of Italian spaghetti or an Indonesian medicine man fix everything for me like it did for Liz?

Of course not. I'm a mother. A broke, divorced mother. I can't leave.
So, what then?

Prior to my second marriage, I was what some would call a fireball. A fiery, spirited gal with red hair, nothing could get me down. Even my first failed marriage, painful though it was, did nothing to stop my headstrong determination. I was still the same, just a little broken-hearted and slightly off course. But with a little time and forgiveness, both my kids' dad and I would see the split for what it was: necessary. We would soon learn to co-parent and eventually even call each other friends. I was going to be okay.

And then I met my second husband.

I wonder what drew me to him. Although my feisty personality gave off the aura of independence, the truth was that I wanted someone to take care of me. I didn't want to be worrying about bills and packing school lunches alone. I wanted a partner. Then, suddenly, there he was.

Hindsight is always 20/20 as they say. In retrospect, I see the red flags I overlooked then. A controller can easily be disguised as a caregiver. He wanted to do things for me. For a tired, overworked single mom, this was a welcome turn of events. Little by little, he began to take care of it all, making decisions for me to help clear my heavy load.

Then came the other changes: what clothes I wore, how I kept my hair, what friends I could keep. Others seemed to notice what was happening, but not me. It just felt so good to be loved. To be noticed.

This couldn't go on forever, though. One morning as I sat in my doctor's office trying out yet another depression medication, my doctor said something I would never forget. She pulled her chair right over to me, sat down and looked me straight in the eyes. "Melissa," she said, "I do not have a medication that is going to fix your marriage."

Fix my marriage?

Armed with that old redheaded stubbornness, I marched out of that doctor's office with the certainty that she was a quack. If she wouldn't give me a different medicine, I'd find another doctor who would. Something was wrong. It was chemical, I was sure of it. My life was great.

But later that night, lying in bed beside my snoring husband, the doctor's words kept running through my mind. I needed to talk to someone. But who? The only friends I had now were my husband's friends. I used to have friends from work, but my husband had convinced me to take a job in a smaller office where there weren't so many annoying office functions and parties to attend. I cut contact with all of them at his suggestion — moving on was easier if you just forgot.

Maybe one of my old theatre friends? I once loved community theatre so much. It had been a huge part of my life…. Where had it gone? Ah, yes. My husband didn't like the time that it consumed. My place was at home with him and the kids, not out doing God knows what with God knows who. It was time to grow up and be a wife and mother. Isn't that what he had said? So, no, the theatre friends were out. I hadn't talked to them in so long that I couldn't call them up now in the middle of the night.

I had some friends from a women's church group that my husband allowed me to go to on Monday nights. Maybe I could call one of them? No, I couldn't. He told me that talking about my problems in that group was only asking for trouble. He made it clear to me that our business needed to remain private and was not to be shared with a bunch of busybodies who wanted nothing more than to spread the news throughout the church.

So, who could I call?

Mom.

I snuck out of bed and walked into the living room. I pulled out my cellphone and, just as I had her number keyed in, my husband walked into the room. Of course, making a phone call in the middle of the night could only mean one thing: I was cheating on him. I attempted to show him the number I was dialing and tried to prove that it was only my mother, but he wouldn't listen.

I had to be stopped from making that call.

I packed my bags the next day.

Now here I am, only a few short weeks later, closing the last page of *Eat Pray Love* and sobbing.

Elizabeth Gilbert's words fill my mind.

"If you're brave enough to leave behind everything familiar and comforting — which can be anything from your house to your bitter old resentments — and set forth on a truth-seeking journey… then the Truth will not be withheld from you."

Where is my Truth, Liz? Where is it?

"If you're brave enough…" Is that what I was? Was I brave to leave my husband?

Just like that, I received my answer. Somewhere deep inside me, a fiery redheaded, community-theatre actress screamed, "YES!"

Yes. This is it. This is why this book has gotten to me. Today is the start of my journey. It may look like a little rented, singlewide mobile home, but to this lonely, lost sojourner, it is the first step toward the journey of freedom.

Attraversiamo.

I head to the telephone to call my mom.

— Melissa Edmondson —

94

Through His Eyes

When admiring other people's gardens,
don't forget to tend to your own flowers.
~Sanober Khan

"Dad, will you write a short letter for me?" I peered at my dad sitting at his kitchen table.

"What kind of letter?" he asked.

Dad's love for me was huge, but getting involved in something like this wasn't really his style. It was a big ask. "Just a few short sentences about what you think I need to work on, what you'd want to tell me."

"When do you need it?"

"Next week would be fine." I walked over and gave him a hug.

My counselor had suggested the exercise as part of my sessions. I'd been in therapy for a few months, working on feeling better about myself as a member of Al-Anon. My then husband had joined Alcoholics Anonymous. In order to work on our marriage, I sought out counseling to dig deep into my feelings of being a bottomless giver.

Maybe it all started when I was young. At ten years old, I chose to help my mom, riddled with rheumatoid arthritis, and became a little mother to my new baby brother. A need was there, and I filled it, rushing home after school, forsaking friends and events.

Later, as a young wife, I did all I could to make my husband and kids happy.

"Can we go to the drive-in movies tonight, please, Mom and Dad, please?" Two rambunctious boys with pleading eyes looked up at us.

"Sure, let's do it." I brought out the big green Tupperware bowl and began to pop the popcorn. "Do you guys want to salt it and shake it?"

"Me, me!" they both shouted.

"Okay, put it in the back seat until we leave."

Happy kids were the glue that held my marriage together. We took them on camping trips where they built huge bonfires, waterskied behind our small boat, and fished in nearby creeks. I drew the line on putting worms on the hooks or cleaning the smelly fish, but we all had fun.

Karate classes were a great outlet for the boys, who were a year apart in age. They looked cute in their white shirt and pants with colored sashes around their waist as they practiced their kicks. When the boys were in school, I did the room-mother events, baked cookies or cupcakes, and volunteered when needed for classroom outings.

Even though it was scary when my husband drank too much, he did go to work to provide for us. His job was outside, though, and during the winter months when it rained or snowed, he was often home for days without a paycheck. I humbly accepted state assistance. We needed to feed the boys, and there were only so many times the local grocery store would accept a check. It would take at least five days for a check to clear the bank, and though that worked for a while, I couldn't keep doing it. I came home from the assistance center with a cardboard box filled with bread, powdered milk and big blocks of cheese. Sometimes, grilled-cheese sandwiches and a glass of milk were all we had.

Eventually, I got a night job where I was gone for just a few hours. I was still available for the boys when they came home from school and still did the room-mother duties. As the boys grew, I encouraged them to work hard, save their allowance money, and do jobs around the neighborhood if they wanted to buy something we couldn't afford. I didn't buy new clothes, shoes, or much at all for myself, only necessities. I like to think those tough times made us stronger.

The boys grew, and my husband still drank excessively. Finally, I joined Al-Anon and asked him to quit. To my surprise, he did, but that didn't alleviate all the problems in our marriage, so I began the sessions with a counselor.

And that's where Dad came in. The counselor wanted me to look at myself through the eyes of a family member. The letter was meant to deliver ideas or suggestions on what I might need to work on. I didn't expect what Dad wrote.

"She needs to think of herself more," said the familiar handwriting on the letter. "She puts others before herself too often."

Dad's comments were not something I took lightly. A man of few words, I listened intently whenever he spoke. This letter spoke volumes, and I cried when I read it.

I'd been thinking of others and putting their needs before my own my whole life. I didn't really know how to live any differently. My motto was that it was better to give than to receive.

Those tears I cried were cleansing, and the counselor didn't stop my emotions. Then she gently responded, "Giving to others is a very good thing. But so is giving to yourself."

"But that's selfish," I replied, wiping my eyes and blowing my nose.

"Not selfish," she said. "Self-caring."

She went on to let me know that giving all of me to others could eventually lead to burnout or even resentment. She asked me to start with little things and to build from there.

I sat down and read a book one night after dinner. It was only for a half-hour, but it felt good. I bought a new purse — on sale — but still it counted as doing something for me. Small efforts led to bigger ones, and my self-caring and self-confidence grew.

Dad's eyes twinkled many months later when I hugged him tight.

"What's that for?" he said.

"For your love," I whispered in his ear. "Thank you for loving me and for having the courage to tell me what I needed to hear."

Dad hugged me back tight and said, "Always. And anytime."

— B.J. Taylor —

95

Winds of Change

*Every one of us needs to show how much we care for
each other and, in the process, care for ourselves.*
~Princess Diana

I tossed another graded paper onto the growing stack and, blinking away heavy fatigue, gazed out at the brick courtyard from my office window. Spindly vines that just months ago were green and supple now hung on for dear life as the blustery November winds bore down. A successful first term in my new position as a nursing instructor was ending. A magical holiday season shared with our four little boys neared. But, instead of reveling in the excitement, I sat alone waging a private battle against the winds of change.

Was it really just six months ago that I had received that most unexpected call? Breathless, I'd hung up the phone and squealed my delight as the twins, bottles dangling from their mouths and eyes as round as beach balls, watched in awe as their mother pranced.

"Guess what?" I chirped as my husband came home for what he thought would be a quiet lunch. But, by then, all four boys had joined in the dance. "The school of nursing has offered me a permanent position!"

Surprise gave way to relief. "That's wonderful news!"

"And it's not just any job."

Erik's eyes brightened.

"I'll be teaching nursing while providing healthcare to infants, children and teens. Not only that, but it's part-time. I'll be working twenty hours a week with summers and holidays off."

I'd finally landed my dream job. After years of juggling graduate studies, temporary jobs, childcare, and the ever-changing needs of our growing family, the work-life balance that had eluded us was finally within reach. Or so I thought.

I swiveled the chair around and got back to work grading papers. I'd been carrying a knot in my stomach for months now. "It's just nerves," I reasoned. "It'll pass." But I knew better.

"Do you have to go, Mommy?" Sam had asked early one morning. He padded down the stairs in his footed sleeper and followed me to the door.

"I'll be home when you wake up from your nap," I reassured him, although I could never be sure. I watched Erik and Sam, hand in hand, fade from view in the rearview mirror and, like a compass guiding my way, the knot that'd taken up residence in my stomach inched closer to my heart.

There was no denying it: The heartache of leaving my children was tearing me apart. When I was at work, I was thinking of the boys. When I was home, I was thinking about work. My children needed me. Erik deserved more of me. My students relied on me. My clients depended on me. Meetings were scheduled on my days off. Childcare was a constant worry.

There wasn't enough of me to go around. Something had to give.

Erik was settling the boys down for the night when I bustled into the house and kicked off my snow-caked shoes. An emergency at the clinic coupled with a snowstorm had delayed my return by hours.

"Mommy's home," they all squealed as I sat down in the living room. The boys shuffled toward me in their flannel PJs, dragging their blankets behind them. They looked like a small herd of cuddly, long-tailed creatures.

I gathered their warm bodies around me and inhaled their sweet smell. Then I said goodnight and tucked them into bed, trusting my love would envelop them while they slept.

"I'm lucky I made it through before they closed the pass," I told Erik later between bites of meatloaf. "The road was a sheet of ice."

The lines on his face softened, but his eyes were somber. "I just wanted you home safe."

We looked at each other. My dream job was turning out to be anything but. I was miserable. And, though he didn't say it, Erik knew it, too.

"This just isn't working, is it?" I finally admitted.

Erik shrugged. "This is your career, your choice. Whatever you decide, we'll make it work."

His words crashed over me. I had worked years, surrounded by caring, devoted colleagues at the pinnacle of their careers, to reach this goal. But my career aspirations were frozen in time. They were a reflection of who I once was and not who I'd become. Our four little boys had changed me.

The wind howled outside my office window as I recalled the conversation I'd had days earlier with the department chair. I'd submitted my resignation — in the middle of the academic year, no less. There was no going back now. After that meeting, I buried my face in my arms and wept.

Releasing old dreams to make room for new ones hurts. I couldn't shake the nagging feeling that I was taking the easy way out or, worse, that I'd failed.

As I reached for the very last term paper I'd ever grade, I heard a gentle tap-tap-tap on the office window.

I looked up to find my colleague standing in the doorway. Tall and slender, her graying blond hair gathered into a French knot, she could've graced the cover of *Vogue*.

She started talking before I could invite her in. "I just learned that you resigned," she said, her voice a whisper.

My stomach flipped. So, the word had gotten out. I took a deep breath and braced myself for a torrent of criticism.

She leaned in, pulling the door tight against her.

"I wish…" Her voice cracked. "I wish I had resigned my position when my four were young."

The room grew quiet. For a split second, our eyes met. Tears welled in the corner of her eyes, each one worth a thousand words.

She wasn't here to belittle me or question my decision. In spite of her pain, she was here to support and encourage me.

My distress gave way to calm.

Before I could thank her, she was gone.

With four little boys waiting, I switched off the lights and closed the office door, eager to head home to the life I chose.

—Mary T. Post—

96

Wise Granny

Few things help an individual more than to place
responsibility upon him, and to let
him know that you trust him.
~Booker T. Washington

Last April, my youngest son got married. At the bridal shower, they had those cute cards for advice for the married couple. I grabbed mine and began to fill it out with the best advice I got from my own wedding, which was from my precious grandmother. She adored my son, so I thought it was the perfect thing to share with him and his new bride. I wrote on the card: "Don't ever start something that you don't want to continue for the rest of your life."

My aunt was sitting next to me filling out her card. I asked her what piece of advice she was giving them. She said, "Granny used to say," and we finished the sentence out loud together.

When I got married, Granny did not want me to do things for my husband that he was capable of doing himself. She used dirty underwear as an example. I can still hear her saying, "Now Amy, if he puts his dirty underwear on the floor, you just leave them there." I remember asking why. Her answer was serious. "If you pick them up the first time, you will be picking up those dirty drawers forever. Don't ever start something that you don't want to continue for the rest of your life."

At the shower that day, my aunt told a similar version of her mother giving her the same piece of advice. We laughed because my grandmother must have thought this was incredibly important if she gave this advice to all the young married women. We also laughed at the fact that both of us had written the same thing on our cards.

And when I pause and think about this piece of advice, it is true. How many times in life do we start doing something for someone that we think is helpful, and, in the end, it becomes hurtful to them and us? This happens because we think that helping them clean up the mess they made is what they need. But in reality it creates an expectation that someone else will clean up their messes.

I used this advice when raising my sons, too. I needed to let them take responsibility for their own things. If I constantly came in and did the chore, homework, project, or whatever for them, was I teaching them to be responsible or was I enabling them? Sometimes, we have to remember that our greatest lessons in life come from our failures and mistakes. If we are not allowing children to make these, how can they grow into responsible citizens?

As a teacher, many times I see parents who have picked up their child's dirty underwear and now cannot stop because it has become the expectation. Children, husbands, friends, or family — no matter who is in your life — need to be responsible for their own actions.

Grandma had notebooks full of advice that we found once she passed away. They contained stories, poems and thoughts that she had collected over the years — true treasures for my family. Never did I think that I could learn a life lesson from a theoretical pair of dirty underwear: "Don't ever start something that you don't want to continue for the rest of your life."

— Amy Mewborn —

97

I Whispered, "Yes..."

Sister. She is your mirror, shining back
at you with a world of possibilities.
~Barbara Alpert

"Leave him," my little sister ordered, "or you can never call Mom or me again. Your husband is determined to destroy you and the baby! Leave him and find yourself!" she screamed.

"Oh, my God, help me!" I cried. My head was throbbing, my body tired, my arms bruised, my spirit lost. This was the fourth time in four years that I had called my mom and sister to come and help me. Each time, I left him for a short while but always returned, convinced that I was the one who could open his heart.

Early in our marriage, he spoke similar words, ordering me to leave him. He threatened to destroy me because it was his nature to destroy anything good that came into his life. I had also read distressed words from his deceased first wife in a little collection of handwritten notes that he conveniently left for me to find. I knew what she would write because I was living the same life as she had!

He had left me alone a few hours earlier. I had no car keys and no way to leave. He left me empty and cold like our house, which I referred to as the "mausoleum." All my attempts to make our house a home had been crushed by him. He had a secure profession and made a generous salary, but he controlled the money and me. Everything had its place in this structure, and if one thing was out of place, I suffered.

I never knew what to say to please him. I danced around my words and walked on eggshells, not knowing what would make him crack and cause another episode of terror for me.

It's a living nightmare to lie next to a man you vowed to love and yet be so afraid of him that you can never close your eyes for fear of his next actions. There were nights when he would physically pull me out of bed, demand his ways of pleasing him, and then belittle me for not making him happy and comparing me to other women he had in his life.

He was a master at playing games, too. Every now and then, he would do something kind and extraordinary. Yet, for each kind gesture, there would be several horrific ordeals I would endure as payback.

And then, there was my guilt. Leaving him would prove that I was a failure at marriage. I would be the first in my family to be divorced. Our family that celebrated silver and gold anniversaries with spouses they loved and respected.

The reality of being a single mother frightened me as well. How would I support our child, only four months old? I had a musical career that involved traveling and touring, which I would not be able to pursue with a little one. I had no other career options.

Leaving him meant returning to my mother's home. She was a widow without much money, providing care for my sister who was partially disabled. Returning home with a baby would surely put a burden on them. Yet, there was my darling little sister, standing in front of me, anxious for me to make a decision. She had pulled the safety net out from under me with her words of tough love but was desperately trying to rescue me. Yet, she made it clear, both she and my mom would no longer be there to pick up my broken pieces if I stayed. This was my defining moment. Either I stay or leave.

My sister again demanded an answer. "Yes or no?" she shouted, bringing me back to reality. After a long pause and a deep breath, I whispered, "Yes." It was a simple, quiet yes that could hardly be heard but changed the direction of my life and my daughter's forever.

We had no time to waste. My sister moved quickly with her arrangements to move me out. She became a warrior who had a plan in place. In the early morning hours, I escaped. I left my house key under the doormat and climbed into an old rental truck with my precious daughter in my arms, my cat in a carrier, and a few personal items. When we pulled up in front of my mother's home, she was waiting with loving arms and the words, "You're home. You're safe now!"

I spent nine years raising my daughter under that loving roof before moving us into our own place. Over the years, there were many challenges, threats and court appearances from my ex-husband, but each one made me stronger. I chose new directions in life that brought me balance, security, happiness and peace. I pursued a steady career in the corporate world while embracing new venues to keep my artistic spirit alive through writing and entertaining children. My daughter was miraculously protected by the courts from her father, who died never knowing her. All grown up, she is a beautiful, strong, loving young woman who received twenty-one scholarships to college and is pursuing an artistic career that takes her to sites around the world.

My little sister is no longer with us, but remains forever in my heart for her unwavering ultimatum that made me create a new happily ever after for my daughter and myself.

— Lainie Belcastro —

98

Not Chopped Liver

*When you refuse to settle for less than the best... the
best tends to track you down.*
~Mandy Hale, The Single Woman

y parents had dragged me to a bar mitzvah in San Francisco.
The kid was the son of a family friend, and I was not given a
choice about attending. As a sophisticate of seventeen, I had
no interest whatsoever in being there. When the ceremony
ended, I separated myself from my parents as soon as I could, dodg-
ing past the bejeweled and well-coiffed women, balding and middle-
aged men, and packs of thirteen-year-olds who jockeyed for position
in front of the mounds of chopped liver and towering platters of
cookies. I piled a few items on my plate and headed toward the far
reaches of the room so I could sit alone and wallow in my adolescent
angst.

An elderly lady, balancing a cane and a plate of goodies, had the
same idea and sought a chair next to mine. Now I was stuck talking
to a total stranger who was older than God. I hoped she wouldn't
bother me.

But, no, she struck up a conversation, beginning with all the usual
questions about school and my interests. There is never a good answer
to the "How's school?" question when you are a teenager. Whatever I
said seemed to satisfy her, so I turned my attention to my plate, trying
to decide whether to eat the little bagel first or start with the lemon bar.

I stuffed the lemon bar in my mouth and braced myself for the next inevitable question from the old busybody. "Do you have a boy-friend?" she asked.

Oh, boy. Did I ever. And he was part of my misery. For some reason, I opened up to her about this guy who either made me swoon with desire or infuriated me, with not much middle ground. I told her about the movie dates where he would buy his ticket and then wait, avoiding eye contact, while I fished around in my purse for money to buy my own. I told her about the way he would pull up in his car and sit there in the street with the engine running and wait for me to come out. I told her about the other girls I knew he was seeing behind my back. I told her that he could be very romantic, but that he usually needed a couple of drinks first. I told her that he was tender and sweet in private but totally ignored me in public, especially around his friends. I told her how he called me a million times while I was babysitting once, and the kids must have told their mother because she never asked me to babysit again. I felt bad about that. I told her that he made me laugh — when he wasn't making me cry.

And I also told her that there was this other guy, a friend. He was a good listener, laughed at my jokes, and had good manners. He and I went to a movie together, just as friends, I pointed out, and he came to the door when he picked me up and paid for my ticket even though he didn't have to. And he didn't mind when I cried through the whole thing, including the credits.

And then I talked about my boyfriend's eyes, hair and life story. I tried to explain what was so irresistible about him, leaving out the part about how I loved the way he kissed but that he wouldn't hold my hand. I didn't talk to her about things we did in the dark. She wouldn't have understood anything about it. She probably never felt that way herself or was too old to remember if she had.

"He wrote poetry for me," I explained. I was helpless to resist him when he was around. He was romantic, poetic, Irish, exuberant, and quick with quips and snappy rejoinders.

"Sounds like he's got the gift of gab," she said, like it wasn't such a great thing.

After listening as I chattered some more about the boy I thought

I loved, she held up her hand, leaned over and looked right into my eyes. Her mouth was tight, and her lips formed a thin line.

"You should never take a back seat to anyone," she said. "You don't let people treat you that way. Not a boy, not anyone." Her crooked index finger pointed at me. "You know what I mean?" she asked.

"I think so," I said. My family wasn't too big on fostering self-esteem. I had never thought about how I might deserve to be treated.

She leaned back in her chair and took a thoughtful bite of her food. "That other boy, the one who took you to the movie, he sounds like a better bet. Stick with him."

I broke up with my boyfriend soon after my conversation with the wise old woman. The breakup was painful and dramatic.

As for me... I did stick with that other boy. We've been married for almost fifty years.

— Risa Nye —

99

Fast Wisdom

Don't settle for something that's not great.
Don't feel like having a relationship that
is not serving your needs is more important
than having a relationship with yourself.
~Michael Franti

The best advice I ever received came riding in on a loud motor-cycle — unsolicited and unexpected but always welcome. Cousin Frank was like that, dropping by in the right place at the right time. These coincidences sometimes made it seem like he and the universe were conspiring in a mysterious sort of way.

Two decades later, the day is still a vivid memory. My mother, siblings and I rode along the highway in our amethyst Jeep. Suddenly, out of nowhere, a loud motorcycle sped by, passing us safely but still in a way that made everyone take note.

A few miles later, we turned off toward a rest stop. The lot was nearly empty aside from one car and a motorcycle. The same?

As we stretched our legs and moved toward the facilities, a familiar voice said, "Heya, Shorty."

The tall, dark-haired man wore a black leather vest with patches from the local motor club, matching chaps, and a broad smile. To some, he might seem an intimidating figure, but I knew better. Cousin Frank was never anything but light, laughter, and magic tricks. Frank knew the best words to use for Hangman and how to make a quarter disappear into thin air. He was protective in a fatherly kind of way but never dangerous.

After laughing at the coincidence of stopping at the same rest area at the same moment, it was determined that we were all headed north. That being the case, Cousin Frank asked if any of us wanted to join him on the bike for the next portion of the ride. I quickly volunteered.

After donning a helmet, we set off, with the fresh air and scenery soon whipping by. It was far more exciting than riding inside the Jeep on such a perfect summer day.

When we'd gotten a bit too far ahead, Frank stopped beside the river, allowing my mom and siblings the opportunity to catch up. As we watched the water rushing and the sky taking on soft colors as the sun began to set, Frank started to talk.

"I was glad to hear you broke it off with Rob. I'm sorry to say that, but he wasn't good for you. You don't need that kind of trouble in your life."

"I know," I said, nodding in defeat. Breaking it off with my first serious boyfriend hadn't been easy, but I knew in my heart it was the right move. I should have done it much sooner.

"Don't be in a hurry to find someone else either," Frank continued. "You are young. Don't settle for less than you deserve. Wait for the right one." His words were muffled slightly through the thickness of my helmet but clear enough to resonate for years to come.

"I'm not in a big hurry. I'm going away to college next month anyway."

"Good. I know it's not my place to butt in," Cousin Frank admitted, "but that is my unsolicited advice. I wish someone had told me that when I was younger."

"It's wise advice. I appreciate it."

"Good. Now look, there's your mom," he said, nodding toward the mirror that reflected the road behind us.

I spotted a blur of amethyst approaching from around the corner.

"Want to get her wound up a little?" he asked with a slight gleam in his eye.

I shrugged and then nodded hesitantly, curiosity getting the best of me.

Cousin Frank chuckled. "Good. Now, when I say go, put your arms up at your sides like this." He modeled, raising his arms to shoulder height.

I nodded, and away we went. Before long, Frank gave the signal, and I put my arms up, feeling the freedom of no longer holding on. Closing my eyes just briefly, it almost felt like I was flying.

"Fun, isn't it?" Frank asked as we slowed down, approaching town.

"I love it," I said, putting my arms back down regretfully.

"Your mom is probably losing it," he laughed. "But I wouldn't let you do anything if it wasn't safe."

Before long, we were parked beside the Jeep, and I was taking off my helmet, trying to smooth my hair back into place. As I hugged Cousin Frank goodbye, he whispered in my ear, "Remember what I said. No settling unless they're worth it."

Still a teen, it was rare in those days to be addressed like an adult — more than just a kid but still needing guidance.

I'm not sure if I heard the advice loud enough at the time, but I am hearing him now. Wait until it is right. Never settle for less than you deserve. It's okay to be single. He dropped his wisdom and then rode off into the setting sun like some kind of Harley-riding hero.

That advice has become the standard I use to assess my personal relationships. When I consider how certain connections help or hinder my wellness and my goals — whether they are adding or subtracting happiness and comfort — I find myself better equipped to make good choices.

As I turn a page on the last chapter of my life, I am definitely striving to follow that advice this time, and it is serving me well. It's okay to be single and take care of yourself until you meet the person who is ready to grow with you.

Not only is it okay, but it's exhilarating once you get the hang of it. It's a lot like riding on the back of a motorcycle with your arms outstretched — a bit like flying.

That particular day, my mom may have lectured me about holding on when riding, but the real magic trick is knowing the right moment to let go.

— Charlotte Louise Nystrom —

100

Simplify!

When you're clear about your purpose and your priorities,
you can painlessly discard whatever does not support these,
whether it's clutter in your cabinets or commitments
on your calendar.
~Victoria Moran, Lit from Within

Sometimes, good advice takes time to sink in. I recall when I first read Thoreau's *Walden*, I was captivated by his call to simplify our lives. "Simplicity! Simplicity! Simplicity!" he said. Nevertheless, I ignored his advice for forty years. During this time, I cluttered my life with possessions. But, one morning, an incident occurred that laid bare the wisdom of Thoreau's advice and changed my life for the better.

It is January 13, 2008, a bright Sunday morning at my home in Shoreview, Minnesota. My challenge is to remove twelve inches of snow from my driveway before the NFL playoff game begins. It is not going well. In fact, I am on the verge of declaring war on my snow blower. Three times, I have tried to blow out my driveway. Three times, my snowblower runs just long enough to plug the auger with snow and stall. Each time, I wheel the machine back into the garage, unplug it, and tinker with the carburetor.

Twenty minutes to game time. The house door to the garage swings open.

"When are you going to be done?" asks Carolyn, my wife. "I need my car to go to the store."

"Before game time," I say. The calmness in my voice belies the war clouds that are building.

One last try. I square off my snowblower in front of a drift as my neighbor's snowblower sends a glorious arc of snow cascading down onto his lawn. He smiles and waves as he heads for his garage, no doubt to get ready for opening kickoff.

I push the start button. My blower starts but idles roughly. I ease the throttle forward and engage the auger. I slip the shifting lever into gear. The instant the auger bites into the drift, the machine sputters and dies. That's it! War! I abandon the blower in mid-drift and grab a shovel. While my adrenaline is flowing, I clear a path through the driveway wide enough for Carolyn's car to back out. In fifteen minutes, I am done. Game time!

After the game, I retrieve the unsuspecting snowblower from the drift and push it into the garage where I disassemble it piece by piece. As I drop the engine, auger, handle, and wheels into a large trash can, I feel a rush of freedom. No more trips to the gas station, and no more oil changes, breakdowns, tune-ups, or storage. I have a Thoreauvian epiphany: I didn't own this snowblower; it owned me.

I share my insight with Carolyn, who is less excited than me but supportive. Whenever it snows heavily, we skip working out at the gym and shovel the driveway together instead. The task never takes more than thirty minutes and is followed by a celebratory cup of hot chocolate. A new tradition is born.

I vow to follow Thoreau's advice to simplify life by ridding myself of unnecessary possessions. The timing is perfect since we plan to relocate to Saratoga, New York in the spring. Having recently become empty nesters with one daughter in college and the other working, we could significantly reduce the amount of furniture we own. I check the inventory from our last move and find our belongings totaled over 15,000 pounds. Two people should not require seven and a half tons to live!

I read articles and books on how to declutter. I develop a system for sorting through my possessions to decide what to keep, sell, donate, or discard. I encourage Carolyn to join me in my effort. Our five large boxes of Christmas decorations become two. Our two bookcases teeming with tattered volumes become one. We cull duplicate or unused kitchen utensils and appliances. I sort through items in the garage and decide I don't need ten screwdrivers, three hammers, and an assortment of dried-up cans of paint. We adopt a rule that requires us to dispense with an old item when purchasing a new one.

When we pack for our spring move, we reduce our clutter further as we are forced to examine everything we own. To pack or not to pack is the question. The total weight of our packed belongings drops to 10,000 pounds, a 33 percent reduction. Progress. Four years later, we move to an apartment and reduce the weight of our possessions to 5,000 pounds. By the time we retire, we have brought the weight down to a manageable 2,800 pounds. We move ourselves to a retirement community with a small rental truck, saving thousands of dollars.

In retirement, we sell one car and replace it with a maintenance-free electric scooter. That's all I need to get to the pickleball courts, two hilly miles away. We continue to enjoy the benefits of owning no more than we need. The less we own, the less we have to take care of, and the more time we have to pursue activities that bring us joy: biking, hiking, pickleball, kayaking, reading, and traveling. After forty years of ignoring Thoreau's advice to simplify, we finally take it. And we are glad we did.

— D.E. Brigham —

It's Okay to Say No

Real freedom is saying "no" without giving a reason.
~Amit Kalantri, Wealth of Words

For some reason, I have always had a hard time saying no. This is especially true when the person doing the asking is someone I admire or am emotionally close to, or when the cause they're supporting is near and dear to my heart. And, after eighty-three years, I've had a lot of time to cultivate friendships and identify noble causes.

I have always been a frequent target for "good cause" leadership responsibilities, but the issue became overwhelming when I retired from teaching in 2001. Requests arrived via telephone, e-mail, messenger, postal service, and the surefire clincher—an in-person visit that invariably lasted until I broke down and said, "I'll do it."

A few of the requests were frivolous (Would you watch my dog while my husband and I take an Alaskan cruise?), but most involved people or pertained to issues near and dear to my heart.

Would I consider assuming the presidency—for the second time—of the philanthropic educational organization I belong to? Could I chair the upcoming church dinner? How about being on the calling committee for the hospital's spring luncheon? Would I teach the nature-writing segment at the annual Buchanan County fifth graders' field-day excursion? Would I please be the recorder for the P.E.O. Sisterhood (for the twelfth consecutive year) because I am a published writer and therefore taking and typing up minutes should be no problem? Could

I spare one day a month to work in the hospital gift shop? How did I feel about helping out with hospice? And the list went on.

Yes, I am in high demand—not because I am more capable than others but because I live in a small community of 6,000 where everybody knows everyone and their dog by name. And because I had never given myself permission to say no.

In retrospect, I think I must have gotten some satisfaction from being needed. If that were not the case, I might have addressed the situation sooner than I did. But I left off my thinking cap, kept on my blinders, and continued saying yes when what I really wanted to do was whisper, "Maybe another time," or scream, "No!" I was frustrated in my never-say-no rut, but I didn't know how to get out.

And then, in 2021, I read Tyann Rouw's "Fifty and Fabulous" story in *Chicken Soup for the Soul: Making "Me Time."* Tyann's issue that led to her lifestyle change was much different from mine, but there were commonalities.

Neither Tyann's nor my concerns fell into the "here today, gone tomorrow" category. Both of our issues had been alive and well and more or less undisturbed for a very long time. Each of us had half-heartedly attempted to institute change, and we had both failed. But that's where the similarities ended.

According to Tyann's story, she did something about her concern. She reached out to others who had experienced and ultimately solved a problem similar to hers. She investigated their recommendations, altered their suggestions to suit her circumstances, and then went to work. And, hallelujah, she was successful. (Sidebar: As I was writing this story in August 2022, I reached out to Tyann to see if the lifestyle transformation she described in her story was still holding. She assured me it is.)

Tyann's story was a motivator and, to some extent, a guidepost for change. I began scouring the Internet and reading all the advice I could find pertaining to people like me who couldn't say no.

I learned that many people agree to things—even things they would prefer not to do—simply to avoid the considerable discomfort of saying no. One psychologist says that because we are social creatures, wanting to be part of the herd, we also want to preserve our relationships. Consequently, we might blurt out yes because we don't want to be seen as difficult.

Several writers talked about not wanting to disappoint a good friend or hurt someone's feelings. And, according to one behavior analyst, some of us say yes because we sincerely want to help but forget that our ability to accommodate others isn't a bottomless well.

I related to all of those explanations, but they weren't shining any light as to how I could improve my situation. And then, a few hours into my research, I found it: "Learning to Say NO Without Explaining Yourself."

I am sorry the article's author was not identified because she deserves recognition. Her three no-nonsense suggestions, accompanied by detailed instructions for implementation, became my roadmap for change.

She said: Have the courtesy to listen, establish your priorities, and be fast and firm with your response.

I read and reread her words, and then I went to work. My lifestyle transformation is currently a work in progress. I have not found the courage to abandon any of my previously made long-term commitments, but I have boldly (albeit kindly) turned down several new requests.

What did I learn from this experience? I learned that I can be a good person with a kind heart and still say no. I no longer make excuses or over-explain myself. I simply decline with a smile and move on.

Tyann's story illustrated the fact that it's never too late to change how we live. Age, time, and responsibilities don't have to hinder our desire to live in a manner that makes us feel happy and fulfilled. We have but one life to live, and it's worth making it a great one.

— Jacquie McTaggart —

Meet Our Contributors

Devora Adams is first and foremost mother to five beautiful girls and wife to the most incredible husband. In her side job as writer and life coach, she has published several books and coached many women toward a more balanced, fulfilling lifestyle. This is her fifth story published in the *Chicken Soup for the Soul* series.

Monica A. Andermann lives and writes on Long Island where she shares a home with her husband Bill and their tabby Samson. Her work has been included in such publications as *Woman's World*, *Guideposts* and *Sasee* as well as many other titles in the *Chicken Soup for the Soul* series.

Donna Anderson is a wife, mom of three boys, and grandmother to four boys. She lives in Texas with her husband and two senior dogs. Aside from writing, she enjoys genealogy, antiquing, and photography. She also volunteers for the local museum as a researcher and exhibit curator.

Elizabeth A. Atwater lives in a small Southern town with her husband Joe. She discovered the joy of reading in first grade and that naturally seemed to evolve into a joy of writing. Writing brings Elizabeth so much pleasure that she cannot imagine ever stopping. She sold her first story to a romance magazine when she was seventeen years old.

Sarah Barnum is an award-winning freelance editor. When she's not writing her own narrative nonfiction or working with words, Sarah enjoys dabbling in design and exploring new trails with her Appaloosa horse. She lives in Virginia with her husband and children. Learn more about TrailBlaze Editorial at www.trail-blazes.com.

Carolyn Barrett is a lifelong New Jersey resident who enjoys her job as an ultrasound technologist. With four children grown and now a granddaughter to brighten her days, she has many stories to tell from a lifetime of memories. Carolyn most enjoys reading, writing, and flower gardening. Read her blog at www.lifeisnteasy.com.

Lainie Belcastro is blessed to have her ninth story published in the *Chicken Soup for the Soul* series! She is a published poet and author writing for children, women, life and her heart. Lainie and her daughter Nika are the creators of Mrs. Terra Cotta Pots, an eccentric storyteller for children. Learn more at www.lainiebelcastro.com.

Tamara Bell is honored to be featured for the fifth time in the *Chicken Soup for the Soul* series. Her work has also appeared in *Angels on Earth*, *All Creatures*, and *Good Old Days* magazine. She enjoys traveling with her family and working part-time at a local antique shop. Her writing career has been a lifelong dream come true.

Laura Jane Bender is a retired U.S. Navy chaplain who served in Iraq, Cuba, aboard the USS New York and with USMC Wounded Warriors. She enjoys writing, genealogy, and volunteering. She and her husband Ken Anderson, a retired police officer and reservist, live in rural Michigan with three beloved ducks. E-mail her at laura.bender@yahoo.com.

Sophie Bolich is a Milwaukee-based bilingual journalist. The twenty-four-year-old received her Bachelor of Arts in Journalism and her Master's degree in Spanish Literature. She loves to stay busy writing poetry, playing piano and running marathons.

Lori Kempf Bosko is a Canadian writer who lives in Sherwood Park, Alberta with her rescue pup Lucky. She has a journalism background and enjoys writing, travelling, photography, and spending time with family and friends.

D.E. Brigham lives and writes in Tellico Village in eastern Texas. He enjoys pickleball, kayaking, hiking, bicycling, gardening, and traveling. E-mail him at davidbrigham@gmail.com.

Cate Bronson is an accountant turned award-winning author whose narrative nonfiction reflects her devotion to family and animal welfare. Cate lives in Florida with her husband and rescued racing dogs. She enjoys time reading and writing in the sunshine while giant hounds lounge by her side.

Thomas Brooks received his M.Ed. from Ashland University and is a retired communications technician and technical educator. He is married to a high school science and math teacher and has two adult children. He enjoys carving, making and flying kites, fixing things, and writing when time allows.

Jill Burns lives in the mountains of West Virginia with her wonderful family. She's a retired piano teacher and performer. She enjoys writing, music, gardening, nature, and spending time with her grandchildren.

Kay L. Campbell has worked in education marketing and publishing for more than twenty-five years. An avid mystery reader, she also enjoys social art, golf and gardening. Since her new favorite pastime is pickleball, she may often be found playing at her local outdoor courts in southern Connecticut.

Jim Cathcart is the author of twenty-three books, a member of the Speaker Hall of Fame and Sales & Marketing Hall of Fame, past president of the National Speakers Association and a full-time mentor who trains experts to become leading authorities. He dreamed of doing what Earl Nightingale did in "Helping People Grow" and did it.

International speaker **Kitty Chappell** has authored three nonfiction books; *Soaring Above the Ashes on the Wings of Forgiveness, Friendship: When It's Easy and When It's Not,* and *Good MewsInspurrational* stories for cat lovers. Kitty volunteers for her local police department. Learn more at www.kittychappell.com.

Jan Comfort is a retired librarian, originally from West Virginia. Currently she is living in Sunset Beach, NC with two spoiled cats.

Gwen Cooper received her B.A. in English and Secondary Education in 2007 and completed the University of Denver Publishing Institute in 2009. In her spare time, she enjoys traveling, gardening, and spending time exploring the outdoors with her husband and Bloodhounds. Follow her on Twitter @Gwen_Cooper10.

RoChelle Crow is a Registered Dietitian with a desire to see people steward their bodies well. She has a love for missions, adoption, and mentoring youth. She has lived in Africa, but currently she is living in Texas with her husband and two daughters. She is thankful for every experience that God has allowed her.

Elton A. Dean is an Associate Faculty Lead and Computer Information Systems instructor at Post University. He retired from the Massachusetts Army National Guard in 2016 and lives in North Carolina with his wife and son.

Elizabeth A. Dreier received her Bachelor of Arts with honors from Ohio University in 1984. She is a retired reading teacher who enjoys gardening and spending time with her husband and grandchildren. Currently, Elizabeth writes a humor column for *Mahoning Matters*.

Melissa Edmondson is thrilled to appear for the tenth time in the *Chicken Soup for the Soul* series. She is a mother of four wonderful adult children and the lucky wife to her gentle husband, Richard. She loves to write (and wishes she had more time to do it!) and is honored to have her work recognized again.

Elizabeth Rose Reardon Farella received her Bachelor of Arts, with honors, from Molloy College and a Master of Science from Adelphi University in Literacy Development. She is currently a first-grade teacher, avid reader and writer and loves to travel to new destinations with her husband and children. E-mail her at jeeec@aol.com.

Glenda Ferguson is very grateful for her friend's advice and the Lilly Teacher Creativity Fellowship she received twenty-plus years ago. Glenda graduated from College of the Ozarks and Indiana University. She writes devotions and volunteers for Indiana Landmarks. Glenda and her husband Tim live in southern Indiana.

Ander Fernán is a student from Latin America. Since a young age, he has been interested in the arts, writing stories and poems, playing different musical instruments, and has immersed himself in the visual arts. He plans to pursue a career in design.

Carole Brody Fleet is a multi-award-winning author, media contributor and seven-time contributor to the *Chicken Soup for the Soul* series. An expert in grief and life-adversity recovery, Ms. Fleet has made over 1,300 radio appearances and has appeared on numerous television programs, as well as in worldwide print and web media.

Kathleen Gerard is an award-winning writer. She is the author of the novels *The Thing Is*, *In Transit* and *Cold Comfort*. Learn more at www.kathleengerard.blogspot.com.

Robyn Gerland is the author of *All These Long Years Later, Hand-Me-Downs,* and *Change — The Face of Time,* all of which are available in libraries across Canada. She has been a columnist for several magazines and newspapers and taught creative writing classes for both Conestoga College and Vancouver Island University.

Sheryl Green is the author of five books, including *Surviving to Thriving, Do Good to Do Better,* and *Intentional Decision Making.* She also ghostwrites and coaches others to write their own books. She lives in Las Vegas, NV with the most amazing man in the world, two adorable fuzzy faces, Bodhi and Buddy, and 150 houseplants.

Jill Guerin holds a B.A. in Psychology from LaSalle University and an M.S. from Fordham University. She has worked as a mother, teacher, mental health manager and more. She recently published her first children's book. She and her husband live in Florida and are the proud parents of three sons. Learn more at www.jillguerin.com.

Lila W. Guzman is the author of middle-grade and young adult novels. *Lorenzo's Secret Mission* (Arte Publico Press) tells the story of Spain's contribution to the American Revolution. E-mail her at lorenzo1776@ yahoo.com for information about author visits.

A freelance writer and former piano teacher, **Wendy Hobday Haugh's** short stories, articles, and poetry have appeared in dozens of national and regional publications. Wendy lives with one wonderful husband, two frisky felines, and dozens of white-tailed deer in the foothills of upstate New York.

Samantha Hawkins is a Christian, a daughter, and a sister. Her writing has appeared in many print and online publications, including *Madame Noire, The Atlanta Journal-Constitution,* and *The Journal of Emergency Dispatch.* She is also the author of the children's picture book, *My Mommy Marches,* published by Lantana Publishing.

Darlene Carpenter Herring received her Bachelor of Arts in Education and Master's from the University of Texas. She has two daughters and loves sharing her passion for reading and writing with her three grandchildren. She is a retired English teacher and enjoys traveling with her husband.

Janice Preston Horton writes and gardens on a farmstead in upstate New York. She holds a Master's in professional writing from Chatham University with work published in *Piecework*, *Touchstone*, *Kaleidoscope* and others. Her memoir *Signs of Respect* is about raising a deaf son. E-mail her at jphorton4@gmail.com.

Darrell Horwitz is always evolving and looking for new adventures to tackle. Nothing is impossible if he puts his mind to it. He's been a writer, sports radio host, podcaster and lived his dream life. His most important goal is still helping young people to not let fear keep them from achieving their dreams.

David Hull is a retired teacher living in upstate New York. Besides writing, he also enjoys reading and watching too many reruns of *Star Trek*. E-mail him at Davidhull59@aol.com

Daryle Elizabeth Hunt has a Bachelor of Arts from University of Toronto. She has a son and daughter along with two young grandchildren. Daryle enjoys traveling, tennis, golf and swimming. She recently rescued a dog who is being very spoiled and is currently pursuing her passion for writing.

When **Jeanette Hurt** isn't shopping for beans, she's usually developing recipes and writing about beverages. Her latest books are *The Unofficial ALDI Cookbook*, *Wisconsin Cocktails* and *Dehydrating*. She loves hiking in the Wisconsin woods with her family. Follow her on Twitter @byJeanetteHurt.

Monty Joynes, a UVA graduate, is the author of twenty-two books that include five novels, two making-of-the-movie books, and two biographies. He is a national award-winning author for his military combat fiction, and he is the librettist for an oratorio that premiered in France in 2019. He lives in Boone, NC.

Kiesa Kay, poet and playwright, creates works that reinforce resilience. She grew up in Gardner Lake, KS. Nowadays, Kiesa writes and plays fiddle at her cabin in the Blue Ridge Mountains.

Jennifer Kennedy is a freelance writer passionate about advocating for rescue dogs. Her profile of Miranda Lambert and her shelter support foundation, MuttNation, was the cover story for *Pet Lifestyles Magazine*. She lives in suburban Philadelphia with her husband, sons and magnificent mutts. Follow her on twitter @Jenkennedy2.

Voiceover actor **Jody Lebel** writes romantic suspense novels and short stories that have sold to *Woman's World*, the *Chicken Soup for the Soul* series, and others. She was raised in charming New England, was an only child who had an only child (claiming she didn't breed well in captivity), and now lives with her two cats in South Florida.

Brenda Leppington lives in Saskatchewan, Canada and retired from a career in health information management. Brenda enjoys writing, travelling and enjoying the freedom that comes with retirement. She is a previous contributor to the *Chicken Soup for the Soul* series.

Don Locke worked as a fine artist in Laguna Beach in the 1970s. He was in charge of graphics for *The Tonight Show with Johnny Carson* and *Jay Leno* for thirty-three years. He enjoys writing movies and has had two novels published. He spends his time writing songs and oil painting, but what he enjoys most is making his grandson laugh.

Barbara LoMonaco is the Senior Editor for the *Chicken Soup for the Soul* series and has had stories published in many titles. She graduated from USC and has a teaching credential. She lives in Southern California where she is surrounded by boys: her husband, her three grown sons and her two grandsons. Thankfully, her three lovely daughters-in-law have diluted the mix somewhat, but the boys are still in the majority.

James C. Magruder writes reflective essays and contemporary Christian fiction. He is author of *The Glimpse*, an inspirational novel. His work has been published in *Writer's Digest*, eleven *Chicken Soup for the Soul* books, as well as *HomeLife*. He blogs about maximizing life by reducing the speed you live it, at Jamescmagruder.com.

In 2021, **Keith Manos** was honored as the national wrestling Sportswriter of the Year by *Wrestling USA* magazine. He is also a 2009 Inductee into the Ohio Wrestling Coaches Association Hall of Fame. His books can be found at www.keithmanos.com.

Cherry March is a graduate of the University of Pennsylvania. She has one son and works as a pediatrician in Phoenix, AZ. She enjoys food, music, travel and literature.

Adrienne Matthews received her Bachelor of Science from Bowling Green State University and Master of Social Work from Indiana University.

She is retired alongside husband Greg and is proud mom to Eric. Adrienne enjoys traveling, entertaining and sharing her stories of how God, family and friends have impacted her life.

Zirrina Maxwell is a U.S. veteran who is currently pursuing her Bachelor of Arts in English and Creative Writing. When she's not writing, she can be found playing video games and spending time with her loved ones. Her goal is to pursue a career in the video game industry as a narrative designer.

Laura McKenzie is a retired kindergarten teacher living in Abilene, TX with her husband Doug. She enjoys seeing the country with their travel trailer and visiting her children and grandchildren along the way. Laura loves to read, write, and take long walks in the countryside.

Phyllis McKinley lives in South Central Florida in a home with books in every room. She is the author of four poetry books and one children's book. Her nonfiction has been published in several *Florida Writers Collections* as well as the *Chicken Soup for the Soul* series. She enjoys making delicious soups for her husband.

Courtney McKinney-Whitaker lives in Pennsylvania with her family. An award-winning author of historical fiction, she recently founded The Hourglass House, a website dedicated to helping make history accessible and relevant to real life. Learn more at hourglasshouse.com.

Jacquie McTaggart lives in Independence, IA with Willow, a feisty two-year-old Shih Tzu. Jacquie retired from teaching in 2001 and embarked on two new careers: public speaking and writing. She has spoken at literacy conferences, authored books, contributed stories to anthologies, and been published in numerous magazines.

Amy Mewborn is a four-time contributor to the *Chicken Soup for the Soul* series. She is a 1992 graduate of East Carolina University and teaches English in eastern North Carolina. Writing is her favorite pastime — especially when she is blogging or posting at thepecanseeker. com. Besides writing, she enjoys reading, gardening and time with her family and friends.

Jennifer Priest Mitchell, an Ohio native, lives in Arizona and writes essays, poetry, and fiction. She is a Daughter of the American Revolution and pursues genealogy and historical recipes. She holds a

B.A. from Capital University and an M.A. from Arizona State University. Jennifer enjoys hiking and traveling with her family.

Charlie Morrow is a wellness coach living in Massachusetts with her husband and dogs. She enjoys helping others on their own wellness journeys.

Risa Nye is the author of *There Was a Fire Here: A Memoir* (She Writes Press). She is co-editor of *Writing on Empty: The Upside, Downside, and Everything in Between When Children Leave the Nest*. Her articles and essays have appeared in numerous publications and anthologies, including several in the *Chicken Soup for the Soul* series.

Charlotte Louise Nystrom is a creative writer and poet from the rocky coast of Maine. When she isn't working on her novel, Charlotte enjoys quiet pastimes such as painting, yoga, hiking mountains, camping with her son, drinking too much coffee, and discovering new music.

Barbara Espinosa Occhino is a copywriter for her marketing agency. She is a singer, takes dance classes, and volunteers as a student entrepreneurship mentor. She enjoys traveling with her husband, two daughters, and granddaughters. Born in Cuba, her writing is inspired by the people and places that have colored her life.

Maureen R. O'Donnell writes literary and Christian fiction and articles. She has worked as a newspaper reporter and won a state journalism award. The pandemic has kept her home more than she wants, and she looks forward to spending more time soon with her amazing children and grandchildren.

Chelsea Ohlemiller is a writer best known for her brand "Happiness, Hope & Harsh Realities" a blog and social media platform that honors grief. She's a sappy romantic, passionate Alabama Crimson Tide alumni and fan, and person who wears her heart on her sleeve. She lives in Indiana with her husband and three children.

Marie T. Palecek loves discovering profound insights in simple, everyday things. She shares these nuggets in her transformational devotional book, *Listen for His Voice*. Marie lives in Minnesota and enjoys all four seasons outdoors with her family and dogs. Learn more at www.marietpalecek.com.

Laura Niebauer Palmer received her degree in English from

DePaul University and lives in Austin, TX with her husband and son. She finds inspiration in everyday experiences, especially in the wild world of parenting. This is her third story in the *Chicken Soup for the Soul* series and she is working on her first children's book.

Nancy Emmick Panko is a retired pediatric RN turned writer. A frequent contributor to the *Chicken Soup for the Soul* series, she has authored three award-winning books: *Guiding Missal*, *Sheltering Angels*, and *Blueberry Moose*. Nancy and her husband love being on the water of Lake Gaston, NC with their family. Learn more at www.nancypanko.com.

Ree Pashley is a mom (through adoption, marriage, and birth) to eight amazing kids. She is a freelance writer living in Tanzania, East Africa. Her son, featured in this story, is now a thriving four-year-old who loves bubbles, playing in dirt and climbing anything potentially dangerous.

Jon Peirce is an essayist, social historian, actor and playwright living in Gatineau, Quebec. He's currently working on a book on work hours and a play about Canadian residential schools. This will be Jon's fifth story published in the *Chicken Soup for the Soul* series.

Ava Pennington is a writer, speaker, and Bible teacher. She writes for nationally circulated magazines and is published in thirty-plus anthologies, including twenty-seven *Chicken Soup for the Soul* books. She authored *Reflections on the Names of God: 180 Devotions to Know God More Fully*, endorsed by Kay Arthur. Learn more at AvaPennington.com.

Connie K. Pombo is an inspirational speaker, freelance writer and frequent contributor to the *Chicken Soup for the Soul* series. When not speaking or writing, she enjoys combing the beaches of Florida and spending time with her four grandchildren. Learn more at conniepombo.com.

Wendy Portfors turned to writing after retirement. She has published two books, been published in several anthologies, and is a previous contributing author to the *Chicken Soup for the Soul* series. Wendy is a member of the Writers Guild of Alberta. She is married and enjoys golf and traveling.

Mary T. Post resides in rural Oregon with her husband, Erik, of thirty-four years. She enjoys writing about family, faith, and life married to a Lutheran pastor and is working on two book-length projects. When not writing, Mary enjoys hiking, gardening, baking, and spending time with her four adult sons and their growing families.

Connie Kaseweter Pullen lives in rural Sandy, OR near her five children and several grandchildren. She earned a B.A. degree, with honors, at the University of Portland in 2006, with a double major in psychology and sociology. Connie enjoys writing, photography and exploring nature. E-mail her at MyGrandmaPullen@aol.com.

Jamie A. Richardson is a freelance writer and editor who lives in Northeast Texas. Her passion is connecting people with worthwhile nonprofit projects around the globe through her work with Legacy Voyages. Learn more at jamiearichardson.com or e-mail her at wondervoyage.com.

Eve S. Rossmiller has a bachelor's in mass communications, a bronze medal in storytelling and thirty-plus years of experience. After madcap adventures in Central America and Europe, she and her husband are building their forever home in northern Idaho, where she hauls wood, bakes bread, and wins *Scrabble* matches.

Chana Rubinstein has written four novels and her work has been published in several magazines. When she's not writing, her six children keep her busy.

Patricia Ruhaak was born and raised in Colorado. She has a degree specializing in psychology. She has a son, daughter, and husband Michael. Her family continues to reside in Colorado and Patricia currently works in healthcare administration. Patricia enjoys traveling, reading, writing, and spending time with family.

Emily Rusch is a wellness advocate, health coach and fitness instructor. She received her BSA in Health Science from Brenau University. The mother of three boys, Emily believes a life full of learning, laughter and movement is the happiest kind of life. She lives with her family in Türkiye.

Stephen Rusiniak is from Wayne, NJ and was a police detective specializing in juvenile/family matters. Today he shares his thoughts through his writings, including stories in several titles in the *Chicken*

Soup for the Soul series. Contact via Facebook, Twitter @StephenRusiniak or learn more at stephenrusiniak.com.

Ashleigh Russell received her bachelor's degree in law from Derby University in 2017. She currently works to help improve access to the police service for those in the deaf community and lives with her partner in Rotherham. Ashleigh loves to travel and plans to continue writing in the future.

Jesica Ryzynski is a writer from Ontario, Canada and the mother of four children. She writes about the challenges of parenting children of all ages at the same time, as well as mental illness and autism. She loves coffee and spending time in the woods surrounded by nature.

Linda Sabourin lives in western Arkansas. She is an Ebay seller, specializing in vintage items found at local estate auctions. She enjoys writing and enjoys it even more when one of her stories makes it into a *Chicken Soup for the Soul* book!

D.J. Sartell is a freelance author and content creator who lives in Roseville, a suburb of Sacramento, CA.

Claudia Irene Scott is a freelance travel writer, feature newspaper columnist and national women's magazines contributor. A retired educator and a native New Englander, she now lives in Jacksonville, FL with her husband Barry of fifty years. They enjoy bike riding and old movies. E-mail her at cipscott@comcast.net.

Judith Shapiro is a writer who spends half the year on the opposite coast, confused about which way is north and marveling at the sun that sets over the ocean instead of rising. When the novel she's writing looks the other way, she secretly writes anything else. Learn more at PeaceInEveryLeaf.com.

Billie Holladay Skelley received her bachelor's and master's degrees from the University of Wisconsin-Madison. A retired clinical nurse specialist, she is the mother of four and grandmother of two. Billie enjoys writing, and her work crosses several genres. She spends her non-writing time reading, gardening, and traveling.

Kelly A. Smith is a four-time contributor to the *Chicken Soup for the Soul* series. She is a writer and educator living with her husband, three sons, and three dogs in Missouri. In her career as a high school

English teacher, she hopes to inspire the next generation of writers.

Mary Staller is a member of the Florida Writers Association and co-founder of a critique group. Published in short stories, she is currently working on a novel. A volunteer judge of writing contests, Mary advocates for writers helping writers. For fun she grabs her ukulele and heads to the beach. Learn more at marystaller.com.

Gary Stein co-founded an NYSE-member investment-banking firm. He was a strategy advisor to Lionsgate, Miramar and Seventh Generation and built a thirty-time Emmy-winning kids TV business. Gary is proud to be a mentor to several outstanding young women. He is an eight-time contributor to the *Chicken Soup for the Soul* series. E-mail him at gm.stein@verizon.net.

B.J. Taylor values immensely the relationship she had with her father. That letter changed her entire life for the better. She's an award-winning author whose work has appeared in *Guideposts*, many *Chicken Soup for the Soul* books, and numerous magazines and newspapers. Learn more at bjtaylor.com.

Writing stories for the *Chicken Soup for the Soul* series is how **Susan Traugh** plays. Writing curricula for teens with disabilities is her life's work. *Daily Living Skills* helps teens learn to adult; *The Edge of Brilliance* addresses the heroism of kids with mental illness. She lives in Oregon with her husband and grown kids. Learn more at susantraugh.com.

Rosanne Trost is a retired registered nurse. She received a master's degree from the University of Texas, and lives in Houston, TX. After retirement, she realized her passion for creative writing. Her work has appeared in a variety of print and online journals, including *Chicken Soup for the Soul: Inspiration for Nurses*, *Amsterdam Quarterly*, *Commuter Lit* and *Nerve Cowboy*.

MaryBeth Wallace wanted to be a teacher before she had even started school. She has taught middle and high school students, home-schooled her own children, and taught just about every age group at Sunday school. She enjoys reading, writing, crafting, watching movies and spending time with her family.

Stephanie Schiano Wallace is a youth minister in Lexington, KY. She shares her home with her beloved husband, two children, and ten rescue pets. She is an avid scooter rider and loves nature. This is her second story published in the *Chicken Soup for the Soul* series.

Debbie Jones Warren grew up in Nigeria where her parents were missionaries. She lives in California, with her husband Chris, her biggest encourager. They have three wonderful young-adult children and an amazing daughter-in-law. Debbie collects china and hosts teas for friends and neighbors. Learn more at debbiejoneswarren.com.

David M. Williamson is a husband and father of four, serving the U.S. Air Force as a contractor on Okinawa, Japan after twenty-four years of active-duty service. He has served for several years as a vocalist, pianist, and worship director for various churches. Dave writes fantasy, short stories, worship music, and song parodies.

Marvin Yanke is a licensed therapist and life coach. This is his third story published in the *Chicken Soup for the Soul* series. He feels blessed that his Chicken Soup for the Soul stories may be inspiring others to live more fulfilling lives. E-mail him at MarvinYanke@gmail.com.

Meet Amy Newmark

Amy Newmark is the bestselling author, editor-in-chief, and publisher of the *Chicken Soup for the Soul* book series. Since 2008, she has published 189 new books, most of them national bestsellers in the U.S. and Canada, more than doubling the number of Chicken Soup for the Soul titles in print today. She is also the author of *Simply Happy*, a crash course in Chicken Soup for the Soul advice and wisdom that is filled with easy-to-implement, practical tips for enjoying a better life.

Amy is credited with revitalizing the Chicken Soup for the Soul brand, which has been a publishing industry phenomenon since the first book came out in 1993. By compiling inspirational and aspirational true stories curated from ordinary people who have had extraordinary experiences, Amy has kept the thirty-year-old Chicken Soup for the Soul brand fresh and relevant.

Amy graduated *magna cum laude* from Harvard University where she majored in Portuguese and minored in French. She then embarked on a three-decade career as a Wall Street analyst, a hedge fund manager, and a corporate executive in the technology field. She is a Chartered Financial Analyst.

Her return to literary pursuits was inevitable, as her honors thesis in college involved traveling throughout Brazil's impoverished northeast region, collecting stories from regular people. She is delighted to have come full circle in her writing career — from collecting stories "from the people" in Brazil as a twenty-year-old to, three decades later, collecting stories "from the people" for Chicken Soup for the Soul.

When Amy and her husband Bill, the CEO of Chicken Soup for the Soul, are not working, they are visiting their four grown children and their spouses, and their five grandchildren.

Follow Amy on Twitter @amynewmark. Listen to her free podcast — Chicken Soup for the Soul with Amy Newmark — on Apple, Google, or by using your favorite podcast app on your phone.

Thank You

We owe huge thanks to all our contributors and fans. We received thousands of submissions for this popular topic, and we spent months reading all of them. Crescent LoMonaco, Susan Heim, and D'ette Corona read all of them and narrowed down the selection for Associate Publisher D'ette Corona and Publisher and Editor-in-Chief Amy Newmark. Susan Heim did the first round of editing, and then D'ette chose the perfect quotations to put at the beginning of each story and Amy edited the stories and shaped the final manuscript.

As we finished our work, D'ette continued to be Amy's right-hand woman in working with all our wonderful writers. Barbara LoMonaco, Kristiana Pastir and Elaine Kimbler jumped in to proof, proof, proof. And yes, there will always be typos anyway, so please feel free to let us know about them at webmaster@chickensoupforthesoul.com, and we will correct them in future printings.

The whole publishing team deserves a hand, including our Vice President of Marketing Maureen Peltier, our Vice President of Production Victor Cataldo, and our graphic designer Daniel Zaccari, who turned our manuscript into this beautiful, entertaining book.

Sharing Happiness, Inspiration, and Hope

Real people sharing real stories, every day, all over the world. In 2007, *USA Today* named *Chicken Soup for the Soul* one of the five most memorable books in the last quarter-century. With over 110 million books sold to date in the U.S. and Canada alone, more than 300 titles in print, and translations into nearly fifty languages, "chicken soup for the soul®" is one of the world's best-known phrases.

Today, thirty years after we first began sharing happiness, inspiration and hope through our books, we continue to delight our readers with new titles, but have also evolved beyond the bookshelves with super premium pet food, television shows, a podcast, video journalism from aplus.com, licensed products, and free movies and TV shows on our Crackle, Redbox, Popcornflix and Chicken Soup for the Soul streaming apps. We are busy "changing your life one story at a time®." Thanks for reading!

Share with Us

We all have had Chicken Soup for the Soul moments in our lives. If you would like to share your story or poem with millions of people around the world, go to chickensoup. com and click on Submit Your Story. You may be able to help another reader and become a published author at the same time. Some of our past contributors have launched writing and speaking careers from the publication of their stories in our books!

We only accept story submissions via our website. They are no longer accepted via mail or fax. Visit our website, www.chickensoup. com, and click on Submit Your Story for our writing guidelines and a list of topics we are working on.

To contact us regarding other matters, please send us an email through webmaster@chickensoupforthesoul.com, or write us at:

Chicken Soup for the Soul
P.O. Box 700
Cos Cob, CT 06807-0700

One more note from your friends at Chicken Soup for the Soul: Occasionally, we receive an unsolicited book manuscript from one of our readers, and we would like to respectfully inform you that we do not accept unsolicited manuscripts, and we must discard the ones that appear.

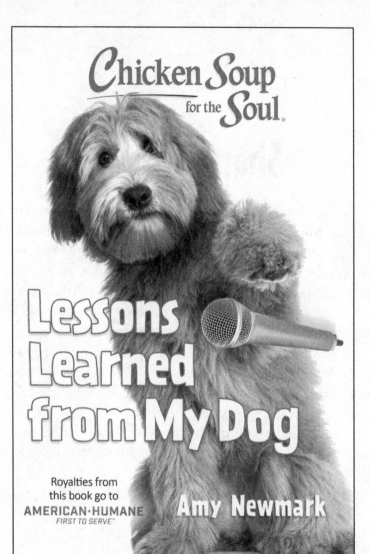

Paperback: 978-1-61159-098-2

eBook: 978-1-61159-335-8

More advice and lessons learned

Chicken Soup for the Soul

Lessons Learned from My Cat

Amy Newmark

Royalties from this book go to
AMERICAN·HUMANE
FIRST TO SERVE

Paperback: 978-1-61159-099-9
eBook: 978-1-61159-336-5

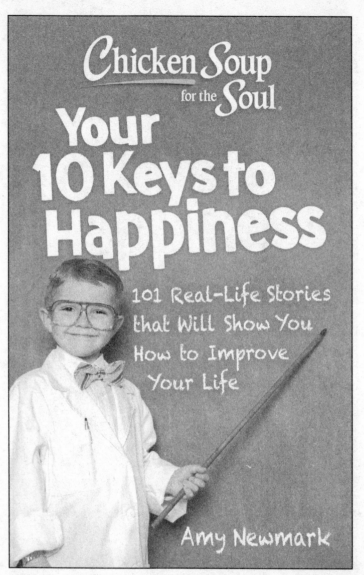

Chicken Soup for the Soul
for the Soul.
Your 10 Keys to Happiness

101 Real-Life Stories
that Will Show You
How to Improve
Your Life

Amy Newmark

Paperback: 978-1-61159-091-3
eBook: 978-1-61159-330-3

More great tips and advice

The Best Advice I Ever Heard

101 Stories of Epiphanies and Wise Words

Amy Newmark

Paperback: 978-1-61159-984-8
eBook: 978-1-61159-284-9

For living a happy, purposeful, joyful life

Changing your world one story at a time®
www.chickensoup.com